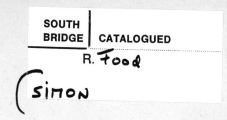

FOOD

FOOD

by
ANDRÉ SIMON

President of The Wine and Food Society

The Pleasures
of Life Series

LONDON
BURKE PUBLISHING COMPANY LTD

First Published
1949

PRINTED IN GREAT BRITAIN
BY W & J. MACKAY & CO., LTD., CHATHAM

FOR BURKE PUBLISHING COMPANY LTD.,
180 FLEET STREET, LONDON, E.C.4.

CONTENTS

CONTENTS

6

ILLUSTRATIONS

COLOUR PLATES

BLACK AND WHITE PLATES

I

LET'S EAT

FOOD IS life: to live we must eat; it is a law which all must obey, a rule which has no exceptions.

Food is fuel: it supplies the power and the materials which the body needs and must have. But food can and should also be fun: it has in its gift some of the joy that makes life worth living.

Food is one of the pleasures of life, as well as one of life's prime necessities, and Food is the one and only pleasure of life which all may enjoy, the youngest and oldest among us, any day and every day.

There are, most unfortunately, millions of men, women and children who have been robbed by the greed and folly of other men of the joy that is good food: they live on the verge of starvation, eating what and when they can, to cheat hunger, and for them food is fuel, not fun.

There are also many people who have the means and the chance to enjoy their meals, but they refuse to do so or—maybe they know not how to set about it. Those who are proud to tell us that they do not live to eat, but eat to live are beyond all help. They accept their daily food with as much feeling and gratitude as the tank of their car shows when being refilled. Their own dog is more gracious: he wags his tail when he gets a bone. Such very superior people are really very stupid. Since they must eat and drink every day, and as a rule at least twice a day, they surely would show greater intelligence if they were to take greater interest in such an inescapable necessity. Is it not more sensible to make a hobby of our meals instead of letting them become a boring duty? It costs no more in cash and whatever the extra time, labour and imagination may be called for, they are amply repaid by the happier disposition that waits upon a better digestion, a joy that no money can buy.

It is, after all, very much the same with dress: the woman who takes no interest in what she wears may consider herself a very superior person, but nobody else will: she is simply silly: lack of interest is the surest sign of lack of intelligence, and clothes are not meant merely to cover the body any more than food is meant to fill the stomach: the job has to be done with taste to be well done. There is this difference, however, that lapses from good taste have far more serious consequences internally than externally. A silly hat or a badly fitting dress will merely make a woman look silly or dowdy; bad food or badly cooked food will make her ill or irritable and unhappy. Looks do matter very much, of course, but when it comes to our food, the food which has not only got to keep us going, but some of which will also become part of us, 'quality' matters far more than looks. By quality we mean goodness, the sum total of whatever there is in food to appeal to all senses, chiefly sight, smell and taste, as well as being the more highly suitable to do the work that food is meant to do, that is to repair tissues, keep up the heat of the blood, and supply the necessary energy for every one of all the wonderful bits and pieces of our inner works each to do their assigned task in the best possible manner.

Taste is a matter of personal choice; but quality is a matter of fact. The two may be difficult to dissociate when it comes to classic and modernist painting or music, but it is fairly easy where food is concerned. Of course, there are

fashions in food and in the preparation of food, and these
vary from time to time and from land to land, but there is
none the less the constant factor of digestion which does
not allow anybody to eat bad fish or the wrong mushrooms with impunity. We can be talked into understanding and even into praising cubism, pointillism, and other
such 'isms' on canvas or in marble: we are merely asked to
look at such curious-looking pictures or sculpture, not to
eat them. But food is not given us to be looked at: we must
eat it; whether we happen to like it very much or not at all
makes quite a difference; there is no question that it is the
food that we like best that will do us most good. But what
of its quality? This is far more important. Bad quality in
food is a real menace, and it is no use our imagining that
nobody could be so stupid as to eat bad food: one has only
to remember how often one reads of school children being
seriously ill after 'enjoying' some bad ice-cream; or how
often one hears of people being taken ill, some even unto
death, after a meal which all 'enjoyed'. Thus taste is not
altogether a sure and safe guide: more particularly taste
wholly untrained, and, even worse, taste wilfully ignored
by the people for whom food is fuel and not fun, people
who 'eat what is put before them to eat', and pride themselves on 'not being particular'.

The main object of education is to teach the young to
love the good and to hate the bad, which they cannot do
until they be taught to tell good from bad, and also better
and best from the merely good. Whether it be behaviour
or speech, reading or writing, work or sport, food or dress,
differences between good and bad are much more obvious
than differences between that which is better and best;
and yet those sometimes very slight differences make all
the difference. The whole of our civilization has been
built upon the recognition of the importance of such small

differences, whether it be a matter of colour, shape, sound, smell or taste. It is true that mediocrity still proves acceptable to the majority, but it is no less true that there are many more people today than ever before who are aware of the desirability of higher education and the better training of all their senses, not excluding the senses of smell and taste. Far too long have those two senses been ignored as if their training implied a surrender to greed and self-indulgence. Every one of our senses has been given to us for use and not to be abused any more than to be ignored altogether. And unless our senses of smell and taste be properly trained and attuned, what chance have we got to choose and demand the right food, that is food that has been well bought, well cooked, well served, the sort of food that will call forth gastric juices in plenty, all ready to tackle their business with gusto, to deal with the fat and the tough, the lean and the rough, the moment they reach the lower regions? Such food will be more quickly and more satisfactorily digested than twice the quantity of the same materials poorly prepared, unappetizingly presented and dull to eat. For we must never forget that as there is no heat in a lump of coal until it is burning brightly, there is no goodness in food until it is properly digested.

There is nothing more important than food, nothing more rewarding. This is why in all times and among all nations, a feast, that is an occasion to eat more and better food in company, has always been considered the best way to celebrate a victory, a birth, a wedding or an anniversary, or to welcome one's friends and honour a distinguished guest.

FOOD IS FUEL

The great discovery of recent years, the greatest discovery chemists have yet made, is that our food, whether vegetable or animal, is a veritable storehouse of drugs *which we must constantly have to live:* we live bedrugged lives; the pain we suffer is caused by them; they are at the root of our pleasures and our dreams. Food seen in such a light takes on meanings hitherto unperceived. It is at once clear that we must pay utmost attention in making our choice. The aesthetic appeal that is made by well cooked food should be but the lure to proper choice and treatment.

Most of our food isn't food in the ordinary sense but just fuel. We are heat engines, as much dependent upon combustible material being fed into our stomachs as any steam engine is upon coal being shovelled into the firebox below the boiler; as the motor car is upon the injection of petrol into the engine cylinders. All alike, ourselves, steam engine and internal combustion engine, use a vast amount of air to burn the fuel that is consumed. The quantity of heat produced depends entirely upon the quantity of fuel burnt and its special heat value. Fat has a much higher fuel value than starch; we tend to eat more of it in cold weather.

We are built more upon the lines of a modern central heating system, only the place of the stove is taken by a pump (the heart) and there is no tank, apart from the stomach, except for waste water. The pipes (arteries and veins) are full of hot liquid (the blood) which is kept in constant circulation by the pump. Air is blown into the circulating liquid by bellows (the lungs). The food in solution, specially introduced from the stomach, as it is digested, is carried everywhere and either burnt or used as building material, wherever it is wanted, being burnt locally, particularly in the muscles. In fact, combustion goes on over the whole system. The hot water stream—the blood—carries both air and fuel and serves also to bring away the waste, dropping some of it into the waste water tank, some going to the bellows to be expired as gas.

Man is not one machine—*he is a big factory, with a great variety of small machines working in co-operation,* each doing appointed work—the heart, the lungs, the liver, the kidneys and a variety of glands, the brain with a marvellous telegraphic system of nerves acting as the head centre of control. Each organ is not merely a special machine but has its special factory, in which one or more special secretions are formed: these are definite chemical substances, often of great potency as drugs. One of the simplest, a product of the sympathetic nervous system, adrenaline, has an extraordinary influence in constricting the blood vessels, being active in most minute proportions: the circulation of the blood is largely controlled by variations in the amount that is produced and sent into circulation. Even the emotions may affect its production: anger, for example, as shown by a sudden rushing of the blood to the face.

One of the best known of these body-made drugs is insulin, now successfully used as a palliative of diabetes. The main fault in diabetes is inability to burn up sugar completely: in what way insulin makes it possible for sugar (eaten as such or as starch in bread and potatoes) to be burnt up we do not know. The great fact before us is that, however much we may stoke the fire with starch, we cannot burn it usefully in the absence of the special drug insulin made in the pancreas.

In addition to these *endogenous* (within-made) drugs, we have to recognize the need of a great variety of *exogenous* (outside-made) accessory agents, in part derived from the soil, in part made within the plant: hence our demand for vegetable food. First come a number of minerals, potash, lime, iron, iodine, phosphate, common salt and probably not a few more. Then come the organic, accessory food factors, of which the number seems ever on the increase. A few years ago these mysterious agents merely bore alphabetic signs. *A* promoted growth; *B* was associated with certain nervous symptoms; *C* was the cure for scurvy; *D* made bones. Now we know them as definite crystalline substances. *A* is derived from carotene, the colouring matter of the carrot, present together with chlorophyll (the green colouring matter) in all green vegetable growth; also in milk and therefore in butter. Hence the value of green vegetable food. *C* is particularly abundant in lemon and orange fruits. The story is too long to be told now.

One great fact that stands out in connection with all the minute components of our food is that, little as man may want of each of them, to produce a complete effect, the *mens sana in corpore sano*, they must be used together and in proper balance. To use one or other of them separately, as purchased manufactured drugs, will be most dangerous, only permissible in special extreme cases, under advice, because of the impossibility of prejudging the dose, especially of striking the right balance. We are necessarily wedded to Nature and committed to her care, through usage throughout time. Our great task, in the future, is to produce, cook and use *natural foodstuffs* to the complete satisfaction of Nature's demands.

(Professor Henry E. Armstrong, F.S.A.)

FOOD IS FUN

I like eating, and I like to cook, especially if I can make something very delicious without taking too long about it. I am not an expert cook; there are lots of gaps in my knowledge of cooking and half the time I don't know why I do this or that. I am lucky rather than skilful so that the things I make almost always turn out well. Even my own special dishes hardly ever taste the same twice running owing to an incurable tendency to experiment with strange spices and herbs. My sole *à la Luia* never has quite the same sauce and my *Crêpes Suzette* are always being tried with a new liqueur. But although I say it, the result is good and I have attained that happy position of having my food praised to my face and, what is perhaps more rare, behind my back. The knowledge I have, has been obtained in many ways. Bear with me, kind reader, while I tell you a few of its sources:

We are always told that forbidden fruit is the sweetest, and I certainly proved it in my case, as, for some reason only known to my mother, the kitchen in my childhood's days was a forbidden domain and much of my time and ingenuity was taken up avoiding the keen vigilance of my nurse or my governess. Sometimes I managed to escape to that enchanted realm which was ruled over by fat, motherly Mrs. Gill: she adored the 'children' and from her able hands came those delectable little jellies decorated with cherries, or a wobbly blanc-mange covered with 'hundreds and thousands'.

Mr. Gill, the butler, was a willing ally, though no more loyal servant to my parents could have been found; but he sympathized with my desire to see how things were made and so, unknown to my mother, for ten years of my young life I was seeing, when I could, cooking at its best, absorbing the ideas of what constituted a big dinner party.

I can see dear 'Gilly' to this day clearing her aspic jelly with countless eggshells and letting it drip through a jelly bag hung between two chairs—a process I always found intriguing. How easy life has been made by having aspic jelly out of a packet, although it never tastes the same as that made with care and patience in old-fashioned kitchens.

My childhood days were full of interesting experiences. There were hunting expeditions with my beloved father on the High Karoo in South Africa where our meals were cooked by Kaffir 'boys' on an open fire, and where I first tasted the joys of a sheep roasted whole, in after life to be met again as 'Barbecue' in Mexico and as 'Pachamanca' in Peru. During these expeditions we lived on all kinds of game, but the sight of a small 'springbok' (deer) bleeding its life away on very white snow, although I had been congratulated by my father on having made a good shot (he had kindly left it for me), made me realize I could never kill any living thing again.

I shall never forget my disgust at seeing large fat caterpillars roasted on little sticks and eaten with great relish by white-teethed Kaffirs. But my father very wisely reasoned with me as to their merit and cleanliness, and in Mexico I was one of the few foreigners who really enjoyed eating the fried maguey caterpillar.

Then there were fishing expeditions, and I saw fish cooked by Malays, nice clean olive-skinned men and great cooks. I must also mention holidays spent on African farms where I saw Boer women making preserves and jams unequalled anywhere. Subconsciously I must have absorbed all these forms of cooking and now, when I make a dish and put in odd ingredients that give it a subtle flavour, I am asked 'Where did that recipe come from?' and I don't know myself; it is accumulated knowledge used with much luck.

My cooking faculty has stood me in good stead. In the Great War, as a young bride, very anxious not to fail with the proverbial burnt chop, I was lucky enough to engage an old French woman as cook. We often thought she was a spy, as it seemed such amazing luck to have fallen to a young inexperienced bride.

'Marie' used to get wonderful titbits from her French and Italian friends in Soho and taught me how to make very good and tasty meals out of very little. To her I owe my very vivid remembrance of Armistice Day. She had kept a bottle of excellent French wine in her bedroom to be drunk on this eventful day and asked me to share it with her—so at eleven o'clock on that welcome morning of 11th November, when bells were pealing and sirens hooting, she and I, with tears of joy streaming down our faces, in my very pretty London drawing-room, solemnly drank a toast together to the memory of our fallen loved ones and to the glory of England and France. Never was there a closer *Entente Cordiale* than between us two women that morning. Alas, how different the picture is today.

I think the greatest satisfaction I have had in knowing how to cook was soon after we were appointed to the Embassy in Madrid. I was giving my first big dinner party, including the Minister of Foreign Affairs and three Ambassadors. The flowers were perfect and I had thought out a really good menu. At six o'clock, for some unknown reason, my cook suddenly developed 'Andalusian blues', a form of melancholy caused by home sickness for her native village. Wailing songs were wafted up to me from the kitchen and as I had not been long in Spain, I first took it to be some form of incantation in honour of the coming feast. To my horror, however, the butler then arrived to inform me that Carmen was having hysterics and she had to be put to bed with vine leaves on her brow. I 'turned to' with a determined courage but a sinking heart and certainly had to live up to my family motto which, translated, means 'Strong under difficulties.'

At nine-thirty I was dressed, ready to receive my guests—dinner was served—and as each course was passed successfully, the gratitude in a pair of eyes lifted to mine across the table will never be forgotten. Imagine how full my cup of happiness was when a very charming ambassador, famous for his dinners, said: 'Well, Mrs. Forbes, we now know where all Madrid will want to come and dine—I must congratulate you on a first-class chef; that duck was a dream'.

When I studied singing in Paris I had the privilege of being the pupil of Jean de Reszke, not only the greatest singing-teacher of his day, but also, perhaps, one of the greatest cooks. His knowledge of caviar was as world-famous as his 'B flat', and in the *salle à manger*, in his beautiful Paris home, there were always three little tubs of these precious eggs set in massive silver receptacles surrounded by ice.

The little theatre where we had our lessons was connected to the dining-room by a glass corridor. Here 'Jean' would go hurrying along after a particularly trying lesson to snatch a spoonful of his extra-special pale grey caviar, which would soothe him as nothing else and make him ready to face a nervous Aïda or breathless Parsifal. On very rare occasions when I managed to satisfy *Le Maître*, I was taken along this almost sacred passage and given a spoonful myself. *Voilà Petite Juta*, he would say with an enchanting smile, 'Your Tosca has certainly earned you the food of the gods today'.

And while on the subject of caviar, I must relate the shattering story of the able seaman in the Royal Navy, after a visit to a Russian port where the British Fleet had been tremendously fêted even to the extent of caviar and champagne for the lower decks. As they left port, the commanding officer asked the lieutenant the real opinion of the men as to the lavish entertainment they had received. 'Well, sir, they were delighted with it all, their only adverse comment being that the black jam tasted fishy.'

But it was whilst studying during vacation, all through which he very kindly gave me a lesson every day, that I learnt from de Reszke to appreciate the capacity of a Polish-cum-Russian appetite. Those of my readers who have ever had the privilege of seeing Lucien Guitry in the role of *Le Grand Duc* will remember his Russian breakfast consisting of thirty-five separate dishes of *hors d'oeuvre*, through which he solemnly ate every night on the stage. I have never seen appetites to equal those of Edward and Jean de Reszke, and, Edward would laughingly say, that before singing any big role, he always consumed half an ox. Jean was the better cook, perhaps because he was the greatest artist, and his Polish concoctions were culinary *chefs-d'oeuvre*. Alas, I never got the chance of staying with him in Poland and partaking of bear's heart as cooked by him, the excellence of which, he assured me, was only surpassed by his interpretation of his role of Lohengrin.

One morning, Melba, who never thought it necessary to knock at any doors or wait to be announced, rushed into the theatre and flung her arms around Jean saying: 'Jean *chéri*—my voice is quite awful this morning—give me some exercises—and then some lunch with your divine Polish cabbage'. How I disliked Melba stealing my lesson, though I did have the joy of hearing her go through, phrase by phrase, the difficult aria from Othello, which opera she was singing that night.

I don't know why it is, but nearly all singers think they are great salad mixers. They are almost as jealous about their special 'dressing' as about their box-office drawing capacity. Caruso used to have his salad oil especially bottled for him and I have seen him in white apron and chef's cap mixing a *mayonnaise* as if his livelihood depended upon its success.

Chaliapine was another zealous salad mixer, but he would insist on putting caraway seeds into an otherwise perfect salad.

(*Dinner is Served*, by Luia Forbes)

STILL LIFE

Whither the light, and whence? for only glancing
Does it contrive to reach the bread; advancing
It teases the broad knife, continues, flatters
The sultry sides of oranges, the platters,
And a jug's earthen belly; then it wells
To a faint modulation, silver shells
Of Zeeland oysters, fades again to leave
One single hyacinth no time to grieve;
And rousing one great glow, we watch it pass
Towards its death, as, traversing the glass,
It vanishes; that thin green cave of wine
That turns old Hollands to a topaz-mine.

(Lord Derwent)

FOOD IN THE OLD TESTAMENT

One of the earliest recorded impromptu meals is reported in the Book of Genesis (xviii), as follows:

6. Abraham made haste into the tent to Sara, and said to her: Make haste, temper together three measures of flour, and make cakes upon the Hearth.

7. And he himself ran to the herd, and took from thence a calf, very tender and good, and gave it to a young man, who made haste and boiled it.

8. He took also butter and milk, and the calf which he had boiled, and set before them; but he stood by them under the tree.

Moses had given to the Hebrews strict and detailed instructions regarding the beasts, fishes and birds which they were permitted to eat, and those which they must leave alone, in Leviticus (xi):

3. Whatsoever has the hoof divided, and cheweth the cud among the beasts you shall eat.

4. But whatsoever cheweth indeed the cud, and hath a hoof but divideth it not, as the camels and others, that you shall not eat, but shall reckon it among the unclean.

5. The cherogrillus which cheweth the cud, but divideth not the hoof, is unclean.

6. The hare also: for that too cheweth the cud, but divideth not the hoof.

7. And the swine, which, though it divideth the hoof, cheweth not the cud.

8. The flesh of these you shall not eat, nor shall you touch their carcasses, because they are unclean to you.

9. These are the things that breed in the waters, and which it is lawful to eat. All that has fins, and scales as well in the sea, and in the rivers, and the pools, you shall eat.

10. But whatsoever hath not fins and scales, of those things that move and live in the waters, shall be an abomination unto you.

Then follows a long list of various birds, most of them very difficult or impossible to identify among the birds that we know today, some of them lawful and others not lawful to eat. And shortly before his death, Moses, repeating and confirming many of the instructions which he had previously given to his people, referred again to the foods which were 'clean' and permitted, and those which were 'unclean' and forbidden. (Deuteronomy, xiv.)

3. Eat not the things that are unclean.

4. These are the beasts that you shall eat, the ox and the sheep and the goat.

5. The hart and the roe, the buffle, the chamois, the pygarg, the wild goat, the camelopardalus.

6. Every beast that divideth the hoof in two parts, and cheweth the cud, you shall eat.

7. But of them that chew the cud, but divide not the hoof, you shall not eat, such as the camel, the hare, and the cherogril: because they chew the cud, but divide not the hoof, they shall be unclean to you.

8. The swine also, because it divideth the hoof, but cheweth not the cud shall be unclean; their flesh you shall not eat, and their carcasses you shall not touch.

We gain some knowledge of the magnificence of Solomon's court, and we can form some idea of his princely hospitality from III Kings (iv):

22. And the provision of Solomon for each day was thirty measures of fine flour, and three score measures of meal;

23. Ten fat oxen, and twenty out of the pastures, and a hundred rams; besides venison of harts, roes and buffaloes, and fatted fowls.

FOOD IN ANCIENT GREECE AND ROME

Homer enjoined a simple mode of living to princes and
people alike, but there was no austerity in what he deemed
simplicity:

> 'The tables in fair order spread,
> They heap the glittering canisters with bread,
> Viands of simple kinds allure the taste,
> Of wholesome sort, a plentiful repast.
>
> (Odyss, iv. 54)[1]

When catering for heroes, Homer spares them cheese-
cakes and boiled lettuce: there is always roast meat for
them, and nearly always beef. Thus Agamemnon feasted
Ajax, after a single combat with Hector, with a rumpsteak:

> 'A rump of beef they set before the king'.
>
> (Iliad, xxiv. 262)

And when it was a case of entertaining honoured guests,
counsels of moderation were forgotten and hospitality was
unstinted. Thus when Menelaus welcomes Telemachus:

> 'The table groan'd beneath a chine of beef,
> With which the hungry heroes quell'd their grief.'
>
> (Odyss, iv. 65)

This is why Eubulus, in the jesting vein of Greek comic
poets, wrote:

> 'I pray you, where in Homer is the chief
> Who e'er eat fish, or anything but beef?
> And, though so much of liberty they boasted,
> Their meat was never anything but roasted.'
>
> (Athenaeus, i. 46)

Of course, those were leisurely days and banquets sometimes lasted more days than ours last hours:

[1] All Homeric translations are from Pope's *Homer*.

'There Lycis's monarch paid him honours due,
Nine days he feasted, and nine bulls he slew'.

(*Iliad*, vi. 174)

Such prolonged feasting may have been exceptional, but there is ample evidence that the Greeks loved banquets, on the principle that:

'Dear friends should never long abstain from feasts,
For e'en the memory of them is delightful'.

(*Athenaeus*, v. 2)

After the fabulous times of Homeric heroes, the Greeks, then as even now incorrigible individualists, appear to have approached the problems of the table in entirely different ways, the Spartiates all for the most rigid austerity, the Boetians for sheer gluttony, and the Athenians steering the middle course of gastronomy.

The Spartiates were not allowed more than one dish at each meal, that dish a mess and day after day the same; stewed pork or donkey's flesh with beans and lots of garlic. Water was their only drink. The Boetians, on the contrary, had the reputation of being the worst gluttons in Greece:

'We are courageous men to toil and eat,
And to endure sharp pain; the Attic race
Is quick and eloquent, and they eat little,
But the Boetians eat enormously'.

The Athenians certainly had a more intelligent appreciation of both wine and food: they realized that meals, among civilized people, should be occasions for relaxation quite as much as restoration. They ate sparingly in the morning but spent long hours at table in the evening, eating and drinking with gusto and discrimination, and entertaining each other with music, verse, mimicry, or merely lively conversation. Thus Pyrrho the Elean, gently reproaches his host for too costly a feast:

'I will for the future not come to you if you receive me in this manner; that I may avoid being grieved by seeing you go to a great expense for which there is no necessity, and that you, too, may not come to distress by being overwhelmed by such expenses; for it is much better for us to delight one another by our mutual companionship and conversation, than by the great variety of dishes which we set before one another, of which our servants consume the greater part'.

(Athenaeus, x. 14)

According to Philodemus, an author of the first century B.C., who also owes it to Athenaeus that we know his name, what we call a Dutch treat is by no means a novelty:

Artemidorus gave us a Cabbage, Aristarchus caviare, Philodemus a small liver and Appolophares two pounds of Pork, and there were three pounds left over from yesterday. Go and buy us an egg and garlands and sandals and scent. I wish them to be here at four o'clock sharp.

.   .   .   .

In Greece, as in Rome, the greater part of the events of life occasioned the joyous meeting of relations and friends. At the birth of a child a banquet was given in his honour; he was named on the tenth day, and the ceremony terminated with a banquet, in which they offered the guests Cherso cheese, cabbage boiled in oil, pigeons, thrushes, fish, and brimming cups of excellent wine. The teething repast took place when the child had attained his seventh month, and the weaning supper when he began to eat.

(Alexis Soyer. *The Pantropheon*, 1853. p. 357)

The Romans were greater eaters than the Greeks, but not such great talkers. They also loved feasts and banquets, large quantities of food and wine, rare, exotic and costly fare which was sought more for the sake of ostentation than of its gastronomic excellence. It was not always thus: it might even be said that the greatness of Rome was built on porridge and austerity. It took the Romans two hundred years to conquer all the different tribes who peopled the Italian Peninsula, and their historians tell us that during the whole of that time the staple food of the Romans was barley and hard wheat boiled to a paste; they also drank milk and made some kind of cheese, but they did not make anything resembling bread before the sixth century of the foundation of Rome. Such austerity came to an end when the Roman legions conquered more and ever more of the much less warlike and less frugal peoples of the near east. Conquering heroes did not bring home merely rich booty in the guise of gold and precious stones, silver and rich silks, but pheasants and peacocks, peaches and cherries, and many more birds, fruits, vegetables, and other foodstuffs, which greatly stimulated the taste of the elite of Roman society for the pleasures of the table. At different times some of the tribunes individually and the Senate collectively issued orders or made laws devised to place a check upon the rapidly growing gastronomical extravagance of the rich Romans. According to the Fannian law nobody might entertain to a meal more than three guests, besides members of the household; except on market-days, when five guests were permitted; and there were not more than three market-days in each month. The same law made it an offence for anyone to spend more than two drachms and a half on provisions, or to serve at any one meal more than one hen, with the ridiculous proviso that it was not to be fattened. Obviously such needlessly excessive interference defeated its own object, and it is not surprising to learn that so unreasonable legislation was mostly unheeded.

Lucullus is generally credited with the introduction of extravagance and ostentation in the way of living of the richer Romans. He appears to have been most abstemious as a young man, and he was certainly a remarkably successful general who defeated two of the more powerful potentates of his time, Mithridates, king of Pontus, and Tigranes, king of Armenia. He brought back from Pontus the cherry tree, which has been with us ever since, and he also brought back immense wealth: but the rest of his life was spent in wasting it on high living. His couriers were combing incessantly the farthest parts of the then known world in search of rare and fine fare, oysters from Colchester, flamingoes from the Nile, peacocks from Persia, and many other dainties which Roman cooks did their best to prepare in the most remarkable manner to please their masters.

The example set by Lucullus was soon followed and dining became in Rome a specialized and ruinous form of art, dinner being a costly and lengthy performance in three acts or courses. The first consisted generally of all kinds of tasty but comparatively light dishes, such as small fritters of sheep's brains, little liver sausages just grilled and served piping hot; poppy seeds in honey; dressed snails, Lucrine oysters, slices of goose liver and of salted sturgeon; asparagus, lettuce and radishes, in season; eggs, real ones and imitation eggs made of dough and with a 'surprise' inside, such as a rare fruit or a boned fig-pecker.

This first 'service' was followed by a more substantial one when the guests were given the choice of all kinds of fish, flesh and fowl, as well as fruits and vegetables, many of these victuals being presented in some novel and more or less fanciful fashion. At a dinner, in 63 B.C., when Mucius Lentulus Niger entertained Julius Caesar, there were ten preliminary dishes and ten 'main' ones to follow. The third or last course was the time for sweetmeats, fruits, cakes and such like; also for music, recitations, exhibition dances and fights. Unlike the quick-witted Greeks, who were able to entertain each other by anecdotes, reminiscences, tales, grave or gay, the Romans had to be entertained by paid singers, dancers or clowns, somewhat on the lines of the 'Cabarets' of modern times.

In due justice to the Roman people, may we be permitted to say that proverbial excesses were exceedingly rare occurrences. The follies and the vices of a Nero, a boy Heliogabalus, a Pollio, a Vitellius and a few other notorious wasters are spread sporadically over a period of at least eight hundred years. Between these cases of gastronomic insanity lie well-nigh a thousand years of everyday grind and drudgery of the Roman people. The bulk was miserably fed as compared with modern standards of living. Only a few patricians could afford 'high living'. Since a prosperous bourgeoisie (usually the economic and gastronomic background of any nation) was practically unknown in Rome, where the so-called middle classes were in reality poor, shiftless and floating freedmen, it is evident that the bulk of the population because of the empire's unsettled economic conditions, its extensive system of slavery (precluding all successful practice of trades by freemen), the continuous military operations, the haphazard financial system, was forced to live niggardly. The contrast between the middle classes and the upper classes seemed very cruel. This condition may account for the many outcries against the 'extravagances' of the few privileged ones who could afford decent food, and for the exaggerated stories about their table found in the literature of the time. . . .

Apicius used practically all the cooking utensils in use today. He only lacked gas, electricity and artificial refrigeration, modern achievements while useful in the kitchen and indispensable in wholesale production and for labour saving, that have no bearing on purely gastronomical problems. There is only one difference between the cooking utensils of yore and the modern products: the old ones are hand-made, more individualistic, more beautiful, more artistic than our machine-made varieties.

(Joseph Vehling. *Apicius: Cookery and Dining in Imperial Rome*)

A FOURTEENTH CENTURY GAME PIE RECIPE

'Put me in the middle of the pie three young partridges
large and fat;
But take good care and fail not to have six fine quail to
put by their side.
After that you must take a dozen sky-larks, which
round the quail you must place;
And then you must take some thrushes, and such little
birds as you can to garnish the pie.
Further you must provide yourself with a little bacon,
which must not be in the least rank,
And dice it in little pieces which you'll sprinkle into the
pie.
If you want it to be in quite good form, put in some sour
grapes and a little salt .   .   .
Eggs you should use in making the paste, and flour of
pure wheat for a hard paste.
Use no spices and no cheese.
Put in the pie in the oven at the proper heat,
The bottom of the oven quite free from ashes.
When the pie shall be baked enough.
Isn't that a dish to feast on!'
(Paul Lacroix. *Manners, Customs, and Dress during the
Middle Ages and during the Renaissance period.* London.

c. 1878)

RABELAIS

*How Pantagruel and his company were weary in
eating still salt Meats: and how Carpalin went a
hunting to have some Venison.*

Thus as they talked and chatted together, Carpalin
said, 'And by the belly of St. Quenet, shall we never
eat any Venison? this salt meat makes me horribly dry,
I will go fetch you a quarter of one of those horses
which we have burnt, it is well roasted already: as he

was rising up to go about it, he perceived under the
side of a wood a fair great roe-buck, which was come
out of its Fort (as I conceive) at the sight of Panurge's
fire: him did he pursue and run after with as much
vigour and swiftnesse, as it had been a bolt out of a
Crossbowe, and caught him in a moment; and whilest
he was in his course, he with his hands took in the
aire foure great bustards, seven bitterns, six and twenty
gray partridges, two and thirty red legged ones, sixteen pheasants, nine wood-cocks, nineteen herons, two
and thirty coushots and ring-doves; and with his feet
killed ten or twelve hares and rabbets which were then
at relief, and pretty big withal, eighteen rayles in a
knot together, with fifteen young wilde boares, two
little Bevers, and three great foxes: so striking the kid
with his fauchion athwart the head he killed him, and
bearing him on his back, he in his return took up his
hares, rayls, and young wild boares, and as far off as
he could be heard, cried out, and said, Panurge, my
friend, vineger, vineger.'

(Rabelais)

DYETARY OF HELTHE

'Fair woman, could your soul but view
　　The intimate relation
'Twixt food and fate, there'd be a new,
　　And higher dispensation.

Could you but see for "destiny"
　　A synonym in dinners,
And what the kitchen's alchemy
　　Can make of mortal sinners,
You'd leave odd fads, and learn to bake
　　A loaf, and cook a "tater";
To roast a joint, or broil a steak,
　　Than which no art is greater!

"Man cannot live by bread alone,"
　　'Tis well and wisely spoken;
But make that bad, he'll die unknown,
　　And give the world no token

Of high ambitious potencies,
  Or genius' slumbering fires,
Inbred in him through galaxies
  Of grand illustrious sires!

Then all ye dames, and maidens fair,
  Who burn with high ambition,
Who crave to nobly do your share
  To better man's condition,
You'd give us, could your soul but view
  The intimate relation
'Twixt food and fate,—ere long—a new
  And higher dispensation.'
(From *Dyetary of Helthe*, by Dr. Andrew Boorde, 1536)

IN IMITATION OF HORACE

'Of wheaten walls erect your paste,
Let the round mass extend its breast:
Next slice your apples picked so fresh;
Let the fat sheep supply its flesh;
Then, add an onion's pungent juice—
A sprinkling—be not too profuse!
Well mixt these nice ingredients, sure,
May gratify an epicure.'

'Long while, for ages unimproved we stood,
And Apply Pye was still but homely food,
When God-like Edgar of the Saxon Line,
Polite of Taste, and Studious to refine,
In the Dessert Perfumery Quinces cast,
And perfected with Cream, the rich repast.
Hence we proceed the outward parts to trim,
With crinkum cranks adorn the polished brim,
And each fresh Pye the pleased spectator greets
With Virgin Fancies, and with New Conceits.'

· · · · · · ·

'Our fathers most admired their sauces sweet,
And often ask'd for sugar with their meat:

They butter'd currants on crude veal bestow'd,
  And Rumps of Beef with Virgin Honey strew'd.'

.   .   .   .

'The things we eat by various Juice controul,
The Narrowness or Largeness of our Soul.
Onions will make ev'n Heirs or Widows weep,
The tender Lettice brings on softer sleep.
Eat Beef or Pye-crust if you'd serous be:
Your Shell-fish raises Venus from the Sea:
For Nature that inclines to Ill or Good,
Still nourishes our Passions by our Food.

.   .   .   .

A Widow has cold Pye, Nurse gives you cake.
From gen'rous Merchants Ham and Sturgeon take.
The Farmer has brown Bread as fresh as Day,
And Butter fragrant as the Dew of May.
Cornwal Squab-Pye, and Devon White-Pot brings,
And Leister Beans and Bacon, Food of Kings!'

(*The Art of Cookery in imitation of Horace's Art of
Poetry*, London, c. 1708. pp. 71–75)

THE COMPLEAT CITY AND COUNTRY COOK

Our Island is blest with an uncommon Plenty and
Variety of most, nay, I may venture to say all the sub-
stantial Necessaries of life; the produce of both the
Land and Sea, whether Flesh, Fowl, or Fish, and also
Fruits, edible Roots, Plants and Herbs, the Product of
our Fields, Meadows, Orchards, and Garden, in such
Plenty that scarce any of our neighbouring Nations can
boast the like; for Flesh, as Beef, Mutton, Veal, Lamb,
Pork, Bacon, etc. what Market in Europe, nay in the
World, can shew the like as *Leadenhall?* which is but
one of the many that supply the single City of London,
and they not much inferior, even to the Surprize of
Foreigners; and as for Fowls we have no scarcity, either
tame or wild; as for Fish, the Seas that surround Great
Britain, and the innumerable Rivers that water the
Inland Parts, sufficiently supply us with that: Witness

Billingsgate, Fishstreet-Hill, and many Fishmongers in all our Markets, and intersper'd thro' the City, that scarce a Capital Street is without: As for Fruits, Herbs, edible Roots and Flowers, Stocks Markets, *Covent Garden*, and many others, are sufficient Demonstrations of our Superabundance: so that it may justly be said of Great Britain as of the Land of Canaan, that it is a Land flowing with Milk and Honey.

(Charles Carter. *The Compleat City and Country Cook.*
London. 1732. Preface. pp. vi and vii.)

ENGLISH CHEESE

When our grandfathers exclaimed 'That's the cheese', meaning 'That's the right stuff', those of them who had lived in India were aware that curded milk was not meant. They knew that the allusion was to the Hindustani word *chiz*, meaning 'a thing'. But most people who used the ejaculation took it literally, believing that good dairy cheese was a standard of honest value. They were right. Cheese, as cheese, cannot be faked. One make of cheese may be passed off for another, such as Canadian for Cheddar, Australasian for Cheshire, Danish for Roquefort, and so on; but fundamental cheese, despite any naughty misnamings, is cheese, just as 'eggs is eggs'. It is true that there are many *ersatz* attempts at cheese. There is the so-called vegetable cheese, made from that admirable soya-bean which Europeans will soon know better than they know it now. There is 'margarine cheese', as well as 'filled cheese', which has been largely made up with animal fats other than milk and cream. But no *ersatz* can deceive a sound palate for more than a fraction of a second. Cheese is cheese.

The British Isles are odd, from the caseic standpoint. Look at Ireland. She greets the traveller's eyes as an Emerald Isle by virtue of her green pastures, and is a land flowing with milk, if not with honey; yet her people eat very little cheese themselves and make

B

hardly any for export. It was not always so. Diggers in Irish soil have often brought to light tiny kegs of 'bog butter' which the growing peat has preserved from decay during many hundreds of years. Intrepid antiquaries who have tasted this bog butter tell us that it was not so much a butter as a kind of cheese. Ireland has had so many leaders and reformers that one hesitates to cry for more; yet there is certainly room for some patriot to come forward with the slogan: 'Make and eat Irish cheese'.

England, despite long-continued agricultural depression and ruthless competition, has gone on bravely making and enjoying a wide variety of first-class cheeses. Although her once famous Banbury is no longer manufactured, her Stilton, which nobody had heard of in Banbury's heyday, has climbed to a higher than Banbury's place, while we still have our Cheddar and Cheshire, our Leicestershire and Lancashire, our Gloucester and Wiltshire, our Wensleydale and Dorset. But he who would taste all the fine cheeses of England needs to be a man of iron will, endowed with that doggedness which has made our island race what it is. He must be afraid of nor waiter nor waitress, of nor shopman nor housekeeper. Like good wine, good cheese must be insisted upon. It must be sought for and fought for; and sometimes the searches will be vain and the fights will end in defeats.

On a market-day I once went to an ancient hostelry in the good town of Leicester. It was an inn with a delightful name, eloquent of good cheer; but, instead of the traditional and succulent old 'ordinary', the management served what they described as a four-course luncheon on pseudo-French lines. At the end of my meal I begged to be excused from eating two tinned apricots and a spoonful of custard; and I asked that I might be served with Leicestershire cheese. The waitress was not content to reply that she hadn't any. She affirmed that there is no such thing as Leicestershire cheese. The house could offer Cheddar, Camembert, Roquefort, Gorgonzola, and also some infantile

wedges of new-style Gruyère, made without holes and
without rind, and wrapped up in silver paper. When
I ventured to persist that Leicestershire cheese does
exist and that the best of it is equal to a good Cheshire,
the waitress was annoyed and simply brought me a tray
on which the foreign products were reposing. A young
farmer came to my help. He himself was consuming
one of the unmanly little wedges of Gruyère; but he
spoke up handsomely and told the waitress that Leicestershire cheese is first-rate cheese, and that a first-rate
Leicester restaurant ought never to be without it. All
the same, I didn't get it.

Last summer I was in Cardiff, a city with public
buildings which would do credit to a great metropolis.
Having taken advice as to the best eating-place, I
found myself in a beautifully fitted restaurant where,
as at Leicester, the service was performed by waitresses
and not by waiters. A truly excellent and inexpensive
luncheon wound up with a local dainty in the shape of
a small bilberry (or blaeberry, or whortleberry, or
whinberry) pudding which had been steamed in a
basin not much bigger than a teacup. A bright hope
flashed up within me. Within two leagues of maritime
and industrial Cardiff stands the ancient burgh of
Caerphilly, with the ruins of a castle as big as Royal
Windsor's; and Caerphilly has long been renowned
for a very pale cheese, made in cakes not much thicker
than the much more modern Italian Bel Paese. It oc-
curred to me that in a restaurant so laudably regional
as to serve bilberry (or blaeberry, or whortleberry, or
whinberry) puddings made from local fruit, I might
expect to find the local cheese. My Hebe, during a
long and audible conversation with a sententious client
at the next table, had revealed herself as an intelligent
young woman; but when I asked for Caerphilly cheese
she laughed. She could bring me Cheddar, Camembert,
Roquefort, Gorgonzola, and also little wedges of
Gruyère wrapped up in silver paper; but not Caerphilly. Remembering that she might be a new arrival in
Cardiff from London or Penzance or Southend-on-Sea,

I inquired if she had ever heard of Caerphilly. The damsel replied that she 'ought to have', seeing that her father was born there; but when I said: 'Surely you know that there is Caerphilly cheese', she answered saucily that she 'expected there was plenty of cheese in the Caerphilly shops the same as everywhere else'. Thus it dawned upon me that Caerphilly was without honour in its own country, and that this bright young person had never heard of one of the chief glories of her father's native place. I told her that I would be lunching the next day at the same table and that I should look forward to Caerphilly cheese. The morrow came, but not the cheese. Instead, a manager was brought to me who admitted the propinquity of Caerphilly, as well as Caerphilly's connection with cheese, but added somewhat reproachfully that nobody ever asked for it and that the last time he bought any most of it went bad.

I have chronicled two defeats and have left myself little room in which to speak of victories. But an inch or two will suffice to mention a spot where the search for English cheese never goes unrewarded. In the heart of Manchester there is an old street in which some of the buildings are as quaint as the gabled and timbered fronts in old Chester. It is in the very heart of the city, near the Exchange, and it commands a view of Manchester's broad-beamed Cathedral. This short street is a kind of market in which one can buy many regional delicacies, such as Cumberland sausages in coils and Bury black puddings in little bunches, as well as freshly-potted shrimps from Southport. But I am speaking of cheese. On the right-hand side, looking towards the Cathedral, there is a long shop, so narrow that the back wall is not much more than 8 ft. or so from the front door. Therein can be found nearly all the illustrious English cheeses. There is new Stilton, curd-white. There is Cheshire cheese, old and new, from prize dairies. Leicestershire cheese has not been there on the days of my visits, but I have always found Glo'ster and Wensleydale and Cheddar in various stages of maturity, though generally young. Naturally, Lancashire cheese is prominent in the stock. The humble Dorset, which has to be eaten with the right kind of rough bread to be thoroughly enjoyed, is lacking; but I have never been into that poky shop without finding my call worth while. Perhaps the most remarkable fact concerning it is that the buyer or taster who selects the stock has a regional palate, with the result that his choice of Cheshire and Cheddar, and the other cheeses, is not quite the choice which a great London cheese-merchant would make.

(Ernest Oldmeadow)

GOOD FARE AND GOOD LOOKS

A series of exact and rigorous observations has proved that a succulent, delicate and well-ordered diet long delays the outward and visible signs of old age.

It lends new brilliance to the eyes, new bloom to the skin, and new strength to the muscles; and as it is certain, physiologically, that depression is the cause of wrinkles, those dread foes of beauty, so it is no less true to say that, other things being equal, those who know how to eat are ten years younger than those to whom the science is a mystery.

Painters and sculptors have long been aware of this truth; they never represent a miser or an anchorite, or any being who makes a choice or duty of abstinence, but they give him the pallor of sickness, the wasted frame of poverty, and the wrinkles of decrepitude.

(Brillat-Savarin. *The Physiology of Taste*. Meditation xi. 58)

RICE

How nice
Is Rice!
How gentle, and how very free from vice
Are those whose fodder is mainly Rice!

Rice! Rice!
Succulent Rice!
Really it doesn't want thinking of twice:
The gambler would quickly abandon his dice,
The criminal classes be quiet as mice,
If carefully fed upon nothing but Rice.
Yes; Rice! Rice!
Beautiful Rice!
All the wrong in the world would be right in a trice
If everyone fed upon nothing but Rice.

POTS AND PANS

It is a great mistake to believe that in order to cook well one must have a kitchen full of 'gadgets' and complete with what house agents call 'every modern improvement'. Modern improvements, where cuisine is concerned, are conducive to indifferent food: they tend to make cooking more difficult than it need be, and in some cases impossible. We must be conservative, since science has done nothing for cooking except spoil it.

In the same way that charcoals are better for grilling, and the spit for roasting, than anything invented since almost prehistoric days: copper, earthenware, and iron have not yet been surpassed by anything else. Which is a consolation; for it means that you can cook equally well in the cottage and in the mansion.

First of all, the size of the kitchen is supremely important: a large kitchen is a nuisance, not an advantage. Nothing is more tiring than having to walk to a distant sink or run round a table to get at something urgently wanted. The ideal kitchen is the one in which you can put your hand on anything practically without moving. So the stove, the sink, the cupboard, the dresser, the table, ought to be near each other—in which respect the small kitchen of an ordinary modern house is entirely satisfactory.

As for 'pots and pans', the collection is, on the whole,

a small one, and, incredible as it may seem, all the so-called complicated cooking, all these fine dishes, these elaborate sauces, can be prepared with very few utensils.

But they must be good ones; and I must say that the English cook is not always to blame if the special delicate dish—say, with a cream sauce—ordered by her mistress is not a success. The half-failure may be caused by the saucepan. It is much easier to make a good sauce in a copper saucepan than in anything else. It is thicker, it retains the heat, and its contents do not burn. There is a certain prejudice, as far as I can see, in this country against copper, partly on account of the price (this is the mistress's point of view), partly on account of the trouble it is supposed to give (this is the cook's point of view). In fact, copper saucepans are just as easy to keep clean as anything else, and all they want is re-tinning about twice a year, which is a question of pence. On the other hand, you may have to pay fifteen or eighteen shillings for one copper saucepan, but it will last for ever, while the others do not.

So, four saucepans of different sizes, two frying-pans made of ordinary iron (one smaller, kept for omelettes and never washed), a cocotte or casserole (either cast iron or earthenware), one whip, two strainers (one with holes, the other with fine mesh), a couple of bowls, and really sharp knives (indispensable), are about all that is required besides the usual tins, wooden spoons, and the deep frying affair with the wire basket.

For those who have only very elementary cooking conveniences and no space even for our little collection of utensils, an extremely useful implement is a thing called *fait-tout*.

It is a deep pan made of cast iron, enamelled or not, and can be used on any fire or stove for many purposes, the great point being that the thick iron retains the heat very well and will not 'catch' unless really ill-treated.

You can use it for making soup or ragouts, for cooking vegetables or for deep frying; and as the heavy lid closes well it is most valuable for braising and all sorts of slow cooking dishes with a short sauce. You can also use it most successfully for roasting; in fact, you will obtain by roasting in it crispness which it is difficult to obtain in an oven. In this case the meat must be cooked, with butter at the bottom of the *fait-tout* (basted, and turned occasionally), without the lid, so that the pan really acts, radiating heat, as do the sides of an oven. It is, incidentally, the nearest approach to roasting on a spit in front of a fire which modern conditions can provide.

Grilling, so much neglected in private houses, can also be done perfectly, even without a grill. The principle of grilling is to cook the meat in such a way that it retains its richness, its flavour, its essential qualities. Therefore you bring it suddenly in contact with heat, you 'seize' it and close it so that nothing escapes. This you do on both sides of the meat: a good 'grillade' is slightly charred and fairly red inside.

The other method is not generally known and would be very useful to people with a week-end cottage or a bungalow, where they cook on oil. All that is required is an ordinary iron pan like an omelette pan. Have it very clean, very dry, and very hot. Dry your piece of meat in a cloth and simply put it in the pan dry. It will start grilling in the metal as well as if it were on a grill, browning nicely. Shake it occasionally. Do one side, then the other, a few minutes each side, according to your taste and the thickness of the meat.

Season afterwards only, put the meat in a hot dish, and spread over a few pieces of butter *maître d'hôtel*. You can grill in the same way by putting your meat straight on the hot top on an ordinary coal range.

A great many people object to cooking because, as they say, it makes such a mess in the kitchen. After they have prepared a meal everything is dirty, and there is no room on the table, the sideboard, or the sink-board.

My answer, and my advice, to these people who are either careless or untidy is: wash up as you go along.

The professional cook, as well as the amateur, will profit by it. When the meal is prepared and ready to be served, the kitchen should be almost as clean and clear as before it was started.

It is easy enough. When you use a knife, wash it and use it again instead of taking another; and do not forget, if you have cut onion or fish, to wash the knife in cold water. Wash your hands at once, also in cold water, and you will find that not a trace of smell remains. But if you make the mistake of using hot water, it softens the skin, opens the pores, and you will be unable to get rid of the smell for days.

When a saucepan is finished with—quick, a small piece of soda and hot water—it is clean in a few seconds and ready for something else! So you avoid dirty saucepans, in which congealed fat complicates the cleaning, those discouraging piles of plates, those mountains of cutlery. Your few utensils, always ready, will be worth a large collection; your work will be simplified because systematic, and you can serenely sit down to the good meal you have prepared, and enjoy it.

(X. Marcel Boulestin)

One morning in the garden bed
The onion and the carrot said
Unto the parsley group:
'Oh, when shall we three meet again,
In thunder, lightning, hail, or rain?'
'Alas!' replied, in tones of pain
The parsley, '*in the soup.*'

The farmer's daughter hath soft brown hair,
    (Butter and eggs, and a pound of cheese.)
And I met with this ballad I can't say where,
    which wholly consisted of lines like these:
(Butter, and eggs, and a pound of cheese.)

(C. S. Calverley's *Fly Leaves*)

B*

II

DINNERS AND DINERS

DINNER IS the chief meal of the day; it is also, on most weekdays, the last meal of the day. In the 'good old days', when city streets were badly lit and as little safe as most country roads, the dinner hour was at four o'clock, when the day's work was done and one could look forward to the evening hours for relaxation and entertainment, talk or music, wine or games, after dinner. Gradually the dinner hour became later, as men saved more and more time and had less and less leisure: today dinner is mostly at seven o'clock, in New York, eight, in London, nine, in Paris, ten or later in Madrid. In pre-war England, the Sunday Dinner was in a class by itself. It was the chief meal of the day, usually beginning at two o'clock, always graced with a large joint, never less than two 'vegs.', a pudding or a tart, or both, cheese, and dessert: it lasted practically until it was tea time, with an interval for the Sunday nap. Under post-war austerity conditions, the English Sunday Dinner is but a shadow of its former self, but it is still the chief meal of the day.

Like all arts the art of dining has known many vicissitudes, and like all arts, the art of war excepted, it needs peaceful and prosperous times to attain any degree of perfection. Greed and ostentation are its two worst enemies. The art of dining is a matter of appreciation, the appreciation of what is good, better and best to eat and to drink; also a matter of flair and skill in the preparation, presentation, and above all the combination of different foods and drinks; it is a matter of a right understanding of values.

THE ART OF DINING

By way of illustration of what I have said, on the subject of choice plain dinners, I will give an account of one I once gave in the chambers of a friend of mine in the Temple, to a party of six, all of whom were accustomed to good living, and one of whom was bred at one of the most celebrated tables in London. The dinner consisted of the following dishes, served in succession, and with their respective adjuncts carefully attended to. First, spring soup from Birch's on Cornhill, which, to those who have never tasted it, I particularly recommend in the season, as being quite delicious; then a moderate-sized turbot, bought in the city, beautifully boiled, with first-rate lobster sauce, cucumber, and new potatoes; after that, ribs of beef from Leadenhall market, roasted to a turn, and smoking from the spit, with French beans and salad; then a very fine dressed crab; and lastly, some jelly. The owner of the chambers was connected with the city, and he undertook specially to order the different articles, which it would have been impossible to exceed in quality; and though the fish and beef were dressed by a Temple laundress, they could not have been better served, I suppose principally from the kitchen being close at hand, and her attention not being distracted; and here I must remark that the proximity of the kitchen was not the least annoyance to us in any way, or indeed perceptible, except in the excellence of the serving up. The beef deservedly met with the highest praise, and certainly I never saw even venison more enjoyed. The crab was considered particularly well introduced, was eaten with peculiar zest, and the simplicity of the jelly met with approval. The dessert, I think, consisted only of oranges and biscuits, followed by occasional introductions of anchovy toast. The wines were champagne, port, and claret. I have had much experience in the dinner way, both at large and at small parties, but I never saw such a vividness of conviviality,

either at or after dinner, which I attribute principally
to the real object of a dinner being the only one studied;
state, ornament, and superfluity being utterly excluded.
I hold this up as an example of the plain, easy style of
entertaining. There was nothing which anybody may
not have with the most moderate establishment and the
smallest house, perhaps not always in exactly the same
perfection as to quality of materials, but still sufficiently good, with a little trouble and judgment.

(30th September, 1835)

.   .   .   .

Whilst I was writing the above, a friend of mine
called to propose that we should dine together at the
Athenaeum, and he would send a brace of grouse he
had just received. We dined very satisfactorily, but
agreed that a perfect edition of our dinner would have
been as follows :—First, a dozen and a half of small
oysters, not pampered, but fresh from their native bed,
eaten simply, after the French fashion, with lemon
juice, to give an edge to the appetite. In about twenty
minutes, the time necessary for dressing them, three
fine flounders water-zoutchied, with brown bread-
and-butter—a dish which is better served at the
Athenaeum than anywhere I know. At a short interval
after the flounders, the grouse, not sent up together,
but one after the other, hot and hot, like mutton chops,
each accompanied by a plate of French beans. With
the flounders half a pint of sherry, and with the grouse
a bottle of genuine claret, which we get for three-and-
sixpence a bottle; after which, a cup each of strong
hot coffee. This is a style of dining, which made us
think of the gorgeous, encumbered style with pity and
contempt, and I give these particulars by way of study,
and as a step towards emancipation. After my desul-
tory manner I must mention an instance of barbaric
ornament I witnessed a short time since at a dinner
which, substantially, was excellent. I had to carve a
tongue, and found my operations somewhat impeded
by a couple of ranunculuses stuck into it, sculptured,

one in turnips, and the other in carrot. It was surrounded by a thin layer of spinach, studded with small stars, also cut in carrot. What have ranunculuses and stars to do with tongue and spinach? To my mind, if they had been on separate and neighbouring dishes, and unadorned, it would have been much more to the purpose.

(7th October, 1835. *The Original*, by Thomas Walker, M.A.)

A Table, richly spread, in regal mode
With dishes piled, and meats of noblest sort
And savoury beasts of chase or fowl of game
In pastry built, or from the spit, or boyl'd
Gris amber steam'd—
And at a stately sideboard by the wine
That fragrant smell diffus'd, in order stood
Tall stripling youths rich clad—
Such was the splendour. . . .

(Milton)

AN IDEAL DINNER

Forced by a whim of Fortune to decline
Dinners abroad, we stay at home and dine.
Forbid to dine in fact, we dine in fiction
And spurn the mere material restriction.
No need have we of such base, earthly matter
As glass and silver, cutlery and platter;
Where fancy lays the table we can dine
Off ghostly gold, sip our imagined wine
From cups of chrysolite, and poets shall be
Our caterers, ransacking every sea
And all the earth's five continents to afford
The feast that loads our metaphysic board.
We're not like Horace, most content with least:
Let Persian preparations fill the feast,
Stay us with oysters from the Lucrine shore,
Ligurian turtle and Illyrian boar,

Quails from Egyptian fields and, after these,
The golden apples of the Hesperides.
And of the wines, each vintage and each kind,
Grown, gathered, cellared by the brooding mind,
Shall answer bravely to the final test,
Each being a mere diversity of best.

(Martin Armstrong)

GROANING BOARDS

In Britain of old the man on the land—there were men
on the land long before there was a 'man in the street'—
fared very poorly but royal and princely feasts were extra-
vagantly lavish.

King Cassibellan, for one festival, slew 40,000
kyne and oxen; 100,000 sheep; 30,000 deer and other
wild beasts of the wood; besides poultry, wild fowl
and game, of sea and land, with other purveyance of
victuals; on which occasion were introduced many
disguisings, plays, minstrelsy, and sports.
(*A Collection of Ordinances and regulations for the
government of the Royal Household*. Printed in London
for the Society of Antiquaries, in 1790. p. xi)

Above 30,000 dishes were served, in 1243, at the Wedding Breakfast of Richard, Earl of Cornwall and Cincia,
daughter of Raimund, Earl of Provence. At the nuptials of
Alexander III, King of Scotland, and the Princess Margaret
of England, at York, in 1252, the Archbishop of York

made the king of England a present of sixty fat oxen;
which made only one article of provision for the mar-
riage-feast, and were all consumed at that entertainment.
(Mathew Paris. Edit. 1684. p. 53)

King Edward I, preparatory to his coronation feast,
in 1274, directed his precepts to the sheriffs of several
counties, to purchase and send up to London 278

bacon hogs, 450 porkers, 440 fat oxen, 430 sheep, 22,600 hens and capons, and 13 fat goats.

(Rymer's *Foedera*, II. 21)

The first 'austerity' measure appears to be, in England, the Ordinance of the ninth year of the reign of Edward II, declaring that :

> by the outrageous and excessive multitude of meats and dishes, which the great men of the kingdom used in their castles, and by persons of inferior rank imitating their example, beyond what their stations required, and their circumstances could afford, many great evils had come upon the kingdom, the health of the King's subjects had been injured, their property consumed, and they had been reduced to poverty; but the King being desirous to put a stop to such excesses, with the advice and consent of his Great Council, had ordained: That the great men of the kingdom should have only two courses of flesh meats served up to their tables; each course consisting only of two kinds of flesh meat; except Prelates, Earls, Barons, and the great men of the land, who might have an *entremest* of one kind of meat if they pleased. On fish days they should only have two courses of fish, each consisting of two kinds, with an *entremest*, of one kind of fish, if they thought fit. And those who should transgress this Ordinance should be severely punished.

(Ryley's *Placita Parliamentaria*, p. 552., from the Close Roll of 9 Edw. II. m. 26. dorso)

There is no evidence, as far as we know, that this Ordinance had the desired effect, nor that it was ever cancelled, but there is ample proof that the love for great feasts was in no way checked: on the contrary, it grew as never before, as we can realize from the accounts of dinners provided for the Lords of the Star Chamber by Henry VIII, Queen Elizabeth, James I, and Charles I, from 1519 to 1639. There were

never less than twelve nor more than twenty present at such
dinners, but it must be borne in mind that these few exalted
persons were waited on by a large retinue of officials, who
also had healthy appetites. It is the same today, and even
worse: thus the last time Mr. Molotov attended the Foreign
Ministers' Meeting in London, no less than seventy-four
'experts' came over with him to advise him how and when to
say 'No', and all of them had to be found hotel accommoda-
tion and full board.

When the Lords of the Star Chamber met, at Westminster, four times a year, they were not feasted but given a
plain dinner each day, meat on most days and fish on days of
abstinence, that is on Fridays and Saturdays, and, as they
dined at the sovereign's expense, accounts were kept of what
they did eat and drink, and the cost thereof. Such accounts
supply first hand evidence of the variety and cost of food in
the course of some one hundred and twenty years.

20 November, 1519

	£	s.	d.
BREAMS, three . . .		2	0
COD, one		1	8
EELS, two		2	0
GURNARDS, three . . .		5	0
HERRING for baking . .			6
LAMPREYS for stew . . .		1	0
LING, one		1	2
PIKES, two		6	8
PORPOISE, one . . .		6	8
WHITINGS, fourteen . .			10
EGGS, fifty at 1s. 6d. per 100 .			9
APPLES and WARDENS, 10d., ORANGES, 4d. . . .		1	2
BUTTER, 1s., SALT and SAUCE, 8d., HERBS, 4d . . .		2	0
BREAD, 1s. 6d., FLOUR, 1s. 2d. .		2	8
SPICES		4	0

	£	s.	d.
ALE, 2s., BEER, 9d.		2	9
TRENCHERS and CUPS, 6½d., BOAT HIRE, 1s. 1d., WASHING, 1s.		2	7½
COOK'S WAGES		2	4
	2	5	9½

24 January, 1520

	£	s.	d.
BEEF, a sirloin and a double rump		2	2
LAMB, one		2	0
MUTTON, two loins and a neck		1	6
VEAL, a breast and a leg		1	1
MARROWBONES and POTTAGE FLESH		1	8
CAPONS, three		6	0
CRANE, one		5	0
GOOSE, one			8
HENS, two		1	2
CONEYS, four			10
LARKS, three dozen		1	8
PARTRIDGES, three		2	0
PHEASANT, one		1	8
TEAL, five		1	0½
WOODCOCK, five		1	8
EGGS, 10d. for fifty. BACON, 8d.		1	6
APPLES, 1s. 2d., ORANGES, 3d.		1	5
BUTTER, 1s., SALT and SAUCE, 8d., HERBS, 4d.		2	0
SPICES		4	0
BREAD, 1s. 6d., FLOUR, 8d.		2	2
ALE, 2s., BEER, 9d., WHITE WINE, 3d.		3	0
CUPS and TRENCHERS, 7d., BOAT HIRE, 1s. 1d.		1	8
COOK'S WAGES		2	4
	2	8	2½

9 June, 1535

	£	s.	d.
BEEF for boiling, 2s. 4d., a rump, 10d.		3	2
MUTTON, two loins, 1s., two necks, 7d.		1	7
VEAL, two loins . . .		1	2
LAMB, one		1	8
MARROWBONES, 8d., BACON, 8d.		1	4
CAPONS, three . . .		6	4
CHICKENS, twelve to boil . .		3	4
GEESE, five		3	4
HERONS, four . . .		8	0
QUAILS, fourteen . . .		4	8
RABBITS, four for 1s. and six to roast, 1s. 6d. . . .		2	6
STRAWBERRIES for TARTS, 1s. and STRAWBERRIES to eat, 1s. .		2	0
CHERRIES, 1s., PEAS, 8d. . .		1	8
ONIONS and HERBS, 4d., SALT and SAUCE, 8d. . . .		1	0
EGGS, 1s. 2d., SPICES, 5s. .		6	2
BREAD, 2s., FLOUR, 1s. . .		3	0
ALE, 2s., BEER, 4d. . . .		2	4
CUPS and TRENCHERS, 7d., BOAT HIRE, 1s. 2d. . .		1	9
COOK'S WAGES . . .		2	4
	2	17	4

Wednesday, 16 October, 1605

	£	s.	d.
BREAD, 47s., BEER, 12s., ALE, 5s., FLOUR, 6s. . . .	3	10	0
OYSTERS		7	0
COLLARED BRAWN, three . .		15	0
BEEF, forty-nine stone at 1s. 8d. per stone	4	1	8
NEAT'S TONGUES, six . .		8	0

	£	s.	d.
PORK, two chines . . .		5	o
VEAL, seven joints . . .		17	6
MUTTON, eight joints . . .		16	o
SUET		4	o
MARROWBONES . . .		2	o
GEESE, five		16	8
CAPONS, seven	I	1	o
PULLETS, nine		15	o
RABBITS, twelve . . .		12	o
PHEASANT, one		13	8
HERONS, three		15	o
GODWITS, eight . . .	I	16	o
RUFFS, four		18	o
PARTRIDGES, seven . . .	I	4	o
HEATHCOCK, one		2	6
CHICKENS, eighteen . . .		12	o
HOUSE PIGEONS, twenty-four . .		16	o
LARKS, six dozen . . .		6	o
WOODCOCK, six		10	o
POUNDED BUTTER . . .		17	o
CREAM		2	8
EGGS		9	o
HERBS		3	o
APPLES and PEARS . . .		3	o
ORANGES and LEMONS . . .		4	o
BARBERRIES		1	o
ROSEWATER		1	o
BOAT HIRE		4	o
PORTAGE		3	8
	24	12	o

Friday, 15 February, 1638 (n.s. 1639)

	£	s.	d.
BREAD, 37s., BEER, 12., ALE, 5s.,			
FLOUR, 7s. 6d. . . .	3	1	6
COLCHESTER OYSTERS . .		7	6
OLD LING		16	o
GREEN FISH, five . . .		8	6
SALT SALMON . . .		13	o

	£	s.	d.
SALT EELS		8	6
PIKES, three great Pikes . .	2	0	0
PIKES, two small Pikes . .		8	0
CARPS, three great Carps . .	1	4	0
CARPS, six small Carps . .		12	0
BREAMS, three great Breams .	1	0	0
EELS, three great Eels . .		13	0
EELS, twelve small Eels . .		6	0
PERCHES		8	0
FLOUNDERS		8	6
SALMON, one calved Salmon .	2	15	0
SALMON, three chines . .		13	0
TROUTS, three great Trouts and two Salmon peals . .	1	6	8
SOLES, three pairs . . .		11	0
LOBSTERS, fifteen . . .		12	6
SMELTS		6	0
COCKLES		7	0
OYSTERS, one gallon great Oysters		10	0
BACON		2	6
ANCHOVIES		3	6
PICKLED OYSTERS . . .		2	6
CRAYFISH		5	6
MARROWBONES . . .		2	0
SUET to fry with . . .		3	4
LAMB, three sides of . .	1	0	0
VEAL, three joints . . .		15	6
MUTTON, two necks . .		5	6
CAPONS, three . . .		13	6
PULLETS, seven . . .	1	3	4
CHICKENS, nine crammed Chickens	1	0	0
TAME PIGEONS, seventeen .		18	0
BUTTER	1	5	0
EGGS		7	0
CREAM		3	6
HERBS		3	6
ORANGES and LEMONS . .		6	0
WARDENS		3	0

	£	s.	d.
Pippins and Pearmains . .		4	0
Quinces		6	8
Potatoes and other Roots .		3	6
Cheese		4	0
Salad Oil		2	0
Mustard and Onions . .		1	0
Rosewater and Barberries .		2	0
Portage and Boat Hire . .		7	6
	30	9	0

ELIZABETHAN DINING

In number of dishes and change of meat the nobility of
England, (whose cooks are for the most part musical
headed Frenchmen and strangers) do most exceed,
sith there is not day in manner that passeth over their
heads wherein they have not only beef, mutton, veal
and lamb, kid, pork, coney, capon, pig, or so many of
these as the season yieldeth, but also some portion of
the red and fallow deer, beside a great variety of fish
and wild fowl, and thereto sundry other delicates wherein the sweet hand of the seafaring Portugal is not
wanting; so that for a man to dine with them, and to
taste of every dish that standeth before him (which
few used to do, but each one feedeth upon the meat
him best liketh for the time, the beginning of every dish
notwithstanding being reserved unto the greatest per-
sonage that sitteth at the table, to whom it is drawn up
still by the waiters as order requireth, and from whom
it descendeth again even to the lower end, whereby
each one may taste thereof) is rather to yield to a con-
spiracy with a great deal of meate for the speedy sup-
pression of natural health than the use of a necessary
means to satisfy himself with a competent repast to
sustain his body withal. But as this large feeding is not
seen in their guests, no more is it in their own persons;
for, sith they have daily much resort to their own
tables, (and many times unlooked for) and thereto

retain great number of servants, it is very requisite for
them to be somewhat plentiful on this behalf.

(Holinshed's Chronicle. Ed. Furnivall. p. 88)

IFS . . .

If the soup had been as warm as the claret . . .
If the claret had been as old as the chicken . . .
If the chicken had been as fat as our host . . .
It would have been a splendid meal.

(Mr. Donald McCullough's after-dinner 'Grace')

THE HONOURS OF THE TABLE

'Eating quick or very slow at meals is
characteristic of the vulgar; the first
infers poverty, that you have not had a good
meal for some time; the last, if abroad,
that you dislike your entertainment; if
at home, that you are rude enough to set
before your friends, what you cannot eat
yourself. So again, eating your soup with
your nose in the plate is vulgar, it has the
appearance of being used to hard work, and having,
of course an unsteady hand. If it be
necessary then to avoid this, it is much more
so, that of smelling to the meat whilst on
the fork, before you put it in your mouth. I
have seen an ill-bred fellow do this, and have
been so angry, that I could have kicked him
from the table. If you dislike what you have,
leave it: but on no account, by smelling to,
or examining it, charge your friend with putting
unwholesome provisions before you.

'To be well received, you must always be
circumspect at table, where it is exceedingly
rude, to scratch any part of your body, to spit,
or blow your nose (if you can't avoid it, turn
your head,) to eat greedily, to lean your elbows

on the table, to sit too far from it, to pick your
teeth before the dishes are removed, or leave the
table before grace is said.'

(*The Honours of the Table*, by Trusler. 1791)

JAMES BOSWELL, GOURMET AND GOURMAND

James Boswell who is known to most of us as Dr.
Johnson's shadow and for his recording of the bulky
sage's wisdom and frailties—was in his own right no
untutored stooge. And a fact which has hitherto received remarkably scant biographical notice is that
Boswell had epicurean tastes, and quite a sensitive
palate; he was also blessed—or maybe cursed—with
an abundant gusto in, and a lively appreciation of,
hearty good living.

His ruling passions, indeed, were wine, women, and
literary notoriety. All his life was an experiment to him
—on his Continental travels, at home on his estate, in
the salons of literary London and Paris. He could stimulate his mornings with drams of whisky; and his even-
ings with claret, hock, and port—served unstintingly
after dinner.

In a letter to Sir David Dalrymple, Boswell once
wrote: 'I have much vivacity, which leads to dissipation
and folly.' The truth was, he was restless, eager for
change and novelty, bent on establishing himself; at
the same time, a social creature, ready to yield to
'convivial indulgence', as he called it; supported,
however reluctantly, by his dour, hard-headed, sharp-
tongued judge of a father—who even had wrangling,
hot arguments with Dr. Johnson, when the latter was
a guest. It was, felt Boswell, at any rate better to put
up with the thunderous ways of his father than to
buckle down—for life—to the reading of law at
Edinburgh, Glasgow, or Utrecht in Holland. His
father believed law would be Boswell's ultimate professional destination. James knew better. In the inter-
vals of waiting for Dr. Johnson to emerge—and

afterwards as well—he managed to display his 'avidity for delight' and to indulge quite frequently in highly refined living.

His Commonplace Book is full of references to food and drink, to estimates of vintages, to many a 'sober bit of supper' in continental inns, together with detailed descriptions of more elaborate, more formal dinners and banquets. His descriptions are virtually menus— eighteenth-century style. As was customary in eighteenth-century England—and Scotland—these menus are heavy, solidly reinforced with the staple roast beef, but still plentifully washed down with a variety of excellent wines.

Boswell dined out quite often with the notables of London society—with literary, political, and social lions. The names of guests attending many of these banquets are commonplaces in the history of English literature and English social life. But withal, Boswell had a homely streak, a rooted affection for the old Scottish dishes he knew from childhood. Thus at breakfast once with the Earl of Eglinton he noted with delight a proper Scottish menu—marmalade, honey, currant jelly, muffins—both toasted and buttered.

It was a strange faculty that Boswell possessed—to have a deep sincere interest in the literary life, in the better life, in a kind of political idealism—he was the champion of the oppressed Corsicans; and, on his return to England after visiting the island, was their spokesman in audience with Prime Minister Pitt; and at the same time to have a passion for the better foods, for the better wines; filling his diaries with detailed notes on breakfasts and dinners, tippling parties, culinary delights.

In Turin he invites Mr. Wilkie to a dinner, promising 'a feast of most excellent wine and choice conversation'. Later, there is a letter—this time in Latin— to the same recipient. There will be wine and joviality, he promises—*vinum et hilaritas erunt.*

At the Mansion House in London, on Easter Tuesday, 1775, there was a great dinner, among the 'elegant and orderly company'—as the press notices put it—being our Boswell. 'There was a profusion of wines and eatables, which were remarkably good in their kind.' Boswell, we may conjecture, certainly relished that.

The only meals he did not relish were those he had to attend on his visits to his father. To soften the ordeal, Boswell would consume enormous amounts of strong beer.

At Sir Alexander Dick's, in Edinburgh, there was a dinner and dance, with the emphasis on the former—'boiled beef and greens, a large turkey, some fine chickens, 250 fine asparagus (from Sir Alexander's hothouse), and a fine pig; wine from the farm (currant and gooseberry), Greek wine from the Consul at Leghorn, claret, port and punch, and a fine Parmesan cheese, also from Leghorn. Of course, Boswell—under such conditions—stayed on, without missing London's joys.

Even in incidental letters, memoranda, and notes of various kinds, Boswell's mind seems to dwell on metaphors and allusions drawn from the gustatory fields. He writes: 'My journal is ready; it is in the larder, only to be sent to the kitchen, or perhaps trussed and larded a little.'

When he saw his *Life of Dr. Johnson* in proof, he indulged so well in port that the proof sheets still show the signs—in some cases the same phrase or correction being written four times.

From his student days on Boswell was a heavy wine tippler—punch too had its quick effect on him, notably during his travels in Scotland. After Dr. Johnson gave up wine for tea, Boswell still tried to win him over. But the Doctor was stubborn. Meals, on the other hand, they often shared together. A common breakfast was tea and buns. On an Easter Day Dr. Johnson invited Boswell to dinner. Boswell anticipated a crude meal—even without knives or forks, and only an 'uncouth, ill-dressed dish.' But—he apologized heartily—'I found everything in very good order': soup, boiled leg of lamb and spinach, a veal pie, and rice pudding.

Laird of Auchinleck, professional lawyer, cosmopolitan traveller, *coureur de filles*, indifferent father and husband, literary amateur—Boswell was all these; but beyond all this—as even his portraits testify—he was a man who relished the delicacies of life—but just a little too much.

(Harry E. Wedeck)

LE CURÉ DE BREGNIER

When we read in early literature, of the preparations made for the entertainment of two or three persons, and the enormous quantity of food offered to a single guest, it is difficult to avoid concluding that the men who lived nearer than ourselves to the cradle of the world were endowed with appetites far larger than our own. Appetites, in those days, were held to increase in proportion to the dignity of individuals; and he whose share of the feast was the entire back of a five-years-old bull would drink from a cup so massive that he might scarcely lift it to his lips.

Certain persons have lived among us in more recent times to bear witness to what may have been done in the past; and examples of almost incredible voracity are on record, applied, moreover, to the most unpleasant objects. I will spare my readers a recital of disgusting details, and instead relate two particular feats of which I myself was a witness, and which require no blind faith to be believed.

Some forty years ago I paid a flying visit to the curé of Bregnier, a man of great stature, whose appetite was renowned throughout the district. Although it was hardly midday when I arrived, I found him seated at table. He had already made a clean sweep of the soup and *bouilli*, and to this invariable prelude a leg of mutton *à la royale* succeeded, together with a sizeable capon and a large dish of salad.

The moment I appeared he offered to have a place laid for me, but I declined and rightly, as it turned out; for alone and unaided he easily worked his way through

the entire supply, namely, the leg of mutton down to
the ivory, the capon to the bone, and the salad to the
bottom of the dish.

A large white cheese was then placed before him, in
which he made an angular breach of ninety degrees,
washing it down with a bottle of wine and a jug of
water; then he rested from his labours.

What particularly pleased me was that throughout
the whole operation, which occupied the best part of
three-quarters of an hour, the venerable priest was
perfectly at his ease. The huge mouthfuls which he cast
into his mighty maw by no means prevented him from
laughing and talking, and in fact he made no more
to-do than if he had been eating a brace of larks.

(Brillat-Savarin. *The Physiology of Taste*. Meditation
IV. 25)

GREAT EATERS

Philoxenus of Cythera, Archytas, and other gluttonous
Greeks, washed their hands and rinsed their mouth in very
hot water the better to seize and eat hot viands as soon as
served and before other guests. Cromylus, the comic poet,
makes one of them say:

> I've fingers Idaean to take up hot meat,
>   And a throat to devour it too;
> Curries and devils are my sweetest treat,
>   Not more like a man than a flue.
>
> (*Athenaeus*. 1. 9)

Another greedy poet whom Aristotle calls 'Philodeipnos',
that is 'Feast-lover' had fingerstalls made to protect his
fingers from the hot meat he was always the first to grab;
also a covering made of fine fish skin to protect his tongue.

Galba could taste nothing if he was not served with
inconceivable profusion. His stomach imposed limits
upon him, but his eyes knew none; and when he had

gloated to his heart's content upon the magnificent spectacle of innumerable viands for which the universe had been ransacked, he would have the imperial dessert taken slowly round the table, and then heaped up to a prodigious height before the astonished guests.

(From Suetonius as quoted by Alexis Soyer in *The Pantropheon*, 1853. p. 340)

The ingenious Fuller speaks of a man, named Nicholas Wood, to whom the County of Kent proudly claims the honour of having given birth, who once ate a whole sheep at one meal. One day three dozen of pigeons were placed before him, of which he left only the bones. Another day, being at Lord Wootton's, and having a good appetite, he devoured eighty-four rabbits and eighteen yards of black pudding for his breakfast.

(From Fuller's *Worthies*, quoted by Alexis Soyer in *The Pantropheon*, 1853. p. 341)

Marshal Villars had a house-porter who was an enormous eater. 'Franz', said he one day, 'tell me, now, how many loins you could eat?' 'Ah, my lord, as for loins, not many; five or six at most.' 'And how many legs of mutton?' 'Ah! as for legs of mutton, not many: seven or eight perhaps.' 'And fatted pullets?' 'Ah! as for pullets, my lord, not many: not more than a dozen.' 'And pigeons?' 'Ah! as for pigeons, not many: perhaps forty–fifty at most, according to the appetite.' 'And larks?' 'Ah! as for that, my lord, little larks, for ever, my lord, for ever!'

(From Berchoux' *La Gastronomie*, as quoted by Alexis Soyer in *The Pantropheon*, 1853. pp. 341–2)

David was a great painter; he was also apparently a great eater. An English traveller who had occasion to call upon him during his exile in Brussels observed that he looked the image of an ogre while devouring the following articles for his breakfast:—Four dozen of Ostend oysters, washed down with two-thirds of a bottle of Sauternes; four mutton chops; one *bif-tek, aux pommes de terre*; two whitings; half a dozen smelts;

four large bunches of grapes; as many peaches, and bread enough to have supplied an English family of eight individuals. A bottle of Burgundy or Claret was engulfed during this gastronomical operation, and the whole repast terminated with a *tasse de café* and a *petit verre de Curaçao*! Allowing for a certain amount of exaggeration, it would appear that David was no mean performer with knife and fork as well as with palette and brush.

(This information was conveyed in a letter to *The Times* by Mr. A. Shaw Mellor, who had come across it in an old magazine *La Belle Assemblée*, of May, 1830)

FAMILY DINNER IN TRINIDAD

Mangrove oysters served on ice with pepper-vinegar
and limes
Puree of lentils with toasted bread
Boiled red snapper with mayonnaise sauce
Blue crab farci
Stewed lappe served with akee
Avocado salad
Morocoy with pigeon peas
Coconut ice
Guava preserve and cream
Dessert
Cheese
Coffee   Liqueurs

The mangrove oyster is one of the finest of the oyster class, and is brought in direct from the swamps with the bivalves still clinging to the root, and opened fresh for the table. The pepper-vinegar must also be freshly made. The blue crab is a species of land crab which needs special preparation. The crabs are kept in a 'crabbery' which is attached to the kitchen, and are fed on a special diet in which capsicums enter largely. At the end of a month they are fit for the table. The crab is boiled and the flesh from its big claws and legs carefully removed, the shells being kept. This flesh is then fried, after being mixed with bread crumbs and spices, and the farce thus prepared is replaced in the empty shell, in which it is served up. Lappe is the Creole name for the pacca (*coelogenys pacca*), a species of *agouti*, which is one of the most succulent morsels of game that any gourmand can wish for. Akee is the boiled fruit of *blighia sapida*, and is an excellent vegetable to accompany the game dish when plainly boiled in milk. Morocoy is a land-tortoise (the Brazilian tortoise, *testudo tabulata*), the preparation of which is very elaborate, since it must be stewed in Bordeaux wine with spices. The liver of this animal is highly esteemed and surpasses in flavour the best qualities of *foie gras*. Pigeon peas are derived from an Indian shrub, and replace in Trinidad the ordinary young new peas. Coconut ice as prepared in the West Indies is a delicacy which no one who has only tasted the imitations made on this side of the Atlantic can presume to know the full value of. It is prepared from the milk and jelly found in the tender young nut, which are boiled and mixed with cream and then slowly frozen. Guava preserve is obtainable in England, and, served with cream, is an admirable dessert dish. The cheese figuring on this menu is the flaky *queso de mano* which comes from Venezuela, and which has a mild and agreeable flavour.

(*The Belly Book*, by C. Louis Leipoldt. London, 1936)

DINNER SERVED AT A SOUTH AFRICAN FARMHOUSE

Bean Soup
Bredie of tomatoes and mutton
Soesaties with sweet pilau
Beetroot salad
Roast francolin partridge
Stewed sweet potatoes
Stewed fruit
Coffee

The bean soup demands no special description. The bredie corresponds very closely to the olla as served in Oporto and Andalusia. Its basis is a good meat stew, with which is incorporated peeled tomatoes and certain spices. The whole is carefully 'smothered' for several hours at a simmer, so that the meat, which is cut into small portions, is thoroughly impregnated with the tomato flavour, and the dish as it finally appears on the table is of an even red colour. Usually rice—not boiled in the oriental fashion, but made into a more cohesive mass—is served with it. Soesaties are small bits of mutton and pork which have been laid in a pickle composed of coriander seeds, allspice, laurel leaves, and various other spices, including curry powder, onions, and vinegar for several days. When the meat has been well pickled it is taken out of the liquid and strung on tiny bamboo skewers, which are grilled over a sharp fire. The pickle, well boiled, is served with it in a separate dish. This, like the pilau, is an Indian dish, but has become thoroughly naturalized at the Cape. The pilau is rice, slightly sweetened, coloured yellow by the addition of turmeric, and mixed with raisins. It is an admirable accompaniment to the rather sharp flavour of the curried kabobs. The beetroot salad is made with boiled beets sliced thinly and dressed with vinegar and salt; oil hardly ever enters into the dressing, but the dish is ornamented with slices of hard-boiled egg. The sweet potatoes are stewed with the addition of sugar and cinnamon, and is really an *entremet* and not to be considered as a vegetable dish pure and simple, although it is taken with the roast. The stewed fruit is prepared from sun-dried peaches, peeled, with the addition of wine, sugar, and a small portion of tangerine peel, which helps to bring out the exquisite flavour of the fruit done in this way.

(*The Belly Book*, by C. Louis Leipoldt. London, 1936)

STATE GASTRONOMY

The President of the French Republic and Madame Lebrun paid an official visit to King George VI and Queen Elizabeth, in March, 1939. They were the guests of the King and Queen at Buckingham Palace on Tuesday evening, 21st March, soon after they had reached London. On Wednesday, 22nd March, they were entertained to Luncheon at Guildhall by the Lord Mayor and Corporation of London, and they entertained the King and Queen at the French Embassy the same evening. The next day, which was their last, they lunched with the King and Queen at Windsor Castle, and they dined with Lord Halifax, H.M. Principal Secretary of State for Foreign Affairs, at the Foreign Office. At all five functions there were important speeches delivered by important people, speeches which have been duly reported in all the principal dailies for the benefit of generations to come; but, as it is quite possible that generations to come may evince greater interest in gastronomy than in oratory, it is only right and proper that the fare and wines served at each of those ceremonious meals should also be recorded.

1. STATE BANQUET AT BUCKINGHAM PALACE

21st March, 1939

The fare: Consommé Quenelles aux trois couleurs
Filet de truite saumonée roi George VI
Rouennais à la gelée Reine Elizabeth;
   Garniture Buzancy
Mignonnette d'Agneau Royale; Petits
   Pois à la française; Pommes nouvelles
   rissolées au beurre
Poussin Mercy-le-Haut; Salade Elysée
Asperges vertes; Sauce maltaise

Bombe l'Entente Cordiale; Corbeille
  Lorraine
  Cassolette Bassillac

The wines: Sherry 1865
      Madeira Sercial 1834
      Piesporter Goldtröpfchen 1924
      Deidesheimer Kieselberg 1921
      Perrier-Jouët 1919
      Château Haut-Brion 1904
      Château Yquem 1921
      Port: Royal Tawny
      Port 1912
      Brandy 1815

2. GUILDHALL LUNCHEON

22nd March, 1939

The fare: Clear Turtle
     Casserole of Lobster Chablis
     Mousse of Duckling Périgord
     Baron of Beef; Baked Potatoes in skins;
      Lettuce salad
     Roast chicken and peas
     Orange Jellies; Passion Fruit Ice Soufflé;
      Maids of honour
     Dessert

The wines: Punch: Birch's
      Sherry: Domecq's Onoroso
      Dry Graves: Château Lion d'Or
      Claret: Château Margaux 1929
      Champagne: Bollinger 1928
              Veuve Clicquot 1928
      Port: Offley's Boa Vista 1923
      Brandy: Rouyer Guillet
      Bénédictine D.M.O.
      Whisky; Vichy; Perrier; Apollinaris

c

3. DINNER AT THE FRENCH EMBASSY
22nd March, 1939

The fare:　Consommé Chevreuse
Coulis de Langoustines
Saumon de la Loire Régence
Noisettes d'Agneau Châtelaine
Dindonneau rôti à la broche; Petits Pois au
beurre d'Isigny
Foie Gras glacé au Porto; Salade Marigny
Bombe Valentinois; Corbeille de fruits

The wines:　Meursault 1929
Château Lafite-Rothschild 1928
Romanée St. Vivant 1928
Château d'Yquem 1928
Pommery Brut 1929

4. WINDSOR CASTLE LUNCHEON
23rd March, 1939

The fare:　Homard Bagration; sauce verte
Poularde poëlée Mascotte; Haricots verts
nouveaux au beurre; Pommes fondantes
Mousse de Jambon à la gelée; Salade
princesse
Bombe glacée Victoria; Bonbonnière de
Petits Fours
Dessert

The wines:　Sherry; Fino La Ina; Sherry 1865; Corona-
tion 1911
Berncastler
Deidesheimer Kieselberg 1921
Château Lafite-Rothschild 1923
Port: Royal Tawny
Brandy 1830
Kümmel; Crème de Menthe

5. FOREIGN OFFICE BANQUET
23rd March, 1939

The fare: Caviar; Huîtres de Colchester
           Consommé aux quenelles
           Filet de Sole Montaigne
           Selle d'Agneau Empire
           Petits Pois frais
           Poussin rôti; Salade de Romaine
           Asperges de Lauris: Sauce Mousseline
           Soufflé Glacé Devonshire; Fraises rafraî-
             chies; Petits Fours
           Café
           Pêches

The wines: Amontillado
           Grand Chablis Valmur 1929
           Château Palmer Margaux 1875
           Krug 1928
           Chambertin Clos de Bèze, Vieux Cépages
             1915
           Château d'Yquem 1920
           Port: Allnutt 1897
           Grands Fins Bois 1820
           Liqueurs
                     (*Wine and Food*, No. XXII)

POINT DE GÊNE

Point de gêne dans un repas;
Table, fût-elle au mieux garnie,
Il faut, pour m'offrir des appas,
Que la contrainte en soit bannie.
Toutes les maisons où j'en voi
Sont des lieux que j'évite;
Amis, je veux être chez moi,
Partout où l'on m'invite.
               (Panard, 1691–1765)

Meaning that:

    'The first duty of a good host.
    Is to make his guests feel at home.'

MEMORABLE MEALS

MEALS MAY be called 'memorable' when either the food or the wines served, or both, were of outstanding quality and excellence; and also when we shared them with either hosts or guests, or both, whose personality was such as to impress us. The Lord Mayors of London have to attend dinners practically every day during their year of office, fine dinners all, no doubt, when both the fare and the wines are plentifully supplied and very well served, but if we were to ask any past Lord Mayor of London which were the 'memorable meals' of his year of office, he would most likely tell us that he cannot remember any one, in fact that he was only too anxious to forget as soon as possible the nightmare of the compulsory feasting of his year of office. The true 'memorable meal' is the one which deserves its place in our memory because it was a happy occasion, one which it gives us pleasure to call to mind and recount to others in after years. Good food alone, however good it may be, is not enough. The company present, what was said, what happened, and above all our mood and disposition at the time, all are contributory factors, and some of these are most difficult to share with others. Hence the fact that we often fail to make others appreciate why we call 'memorable' a meal which does not appear to them remarkable.

I

The date: 24th April, 1934.
The place: 5 St. Andrew's Place, Regent's Park, London.
The host: Eustace B. Hoare.

The guests: Lord Bearsted, Anthony de Rothschild, C. M. Wells, C. J. Brocklebank and A.L.S.

The menu: Plovers' Eggs.
Consommé.
Boiled Salmon.
Chicken en Casserole.
Savoury.
Fruit.

The wines: Château La Lagune 1900.
Château Margaux 1900.
Château Mouton-Rothschild 1900.
Château Pichon-Longueville 1899.
Château Margaux 1899.
Château Haut-Brion 1899.
Taylor's 1896.
Hine's 1906.

A truly memorable evening, and a most interesting match—in three rounds—between the two most famous of the post-phylloxera Claret Vintages, 1899 and 1900.

Thirty years ago the question was not so much 'Which is the best?' but 'Which will be the best?' Opinions were divided. The 1899's were firmer; the 1900's had more charm. From the purely commercial angle the '99's cost more, and the 1900's were more plentiful as well as cheaper. Both were excellent. Most of us agreed that the '99's would last longer, and all who were wise drank 1900's freely, before the war, when 1900's were delicious and inexpensive.

After the black-out of the war, both '99's and 1900's became rare and dear, but whenever I had the good fortune to meet them both together, the 1900's showed no sign of falling behind the '99's. I certainly had given up all hope of ever assisting at so noble a tug-of-war as our young host staged for us tonight between three of the giants of both years.

The first two wines to be served were the Pichon-Longueville 1899 and the La Lagune 1900. The 1900 won. It was not so good as it had been once: it showed signs of fatigue, but it still had great charm and distinction; it still retained some sweet memories, some sugar. The Pichon had none left. It was perfectly sound, but thin and dry. It had not stayed the course nearly so well as the 1900.

The second bout was between the two Margaux, the '99 and the 1900, and again the 1900 won. But it was a much closer fight. There was not very much to choose between them. Both were very good, and there was an unmistakable family likeness between them both; the 1900, however, had greater freshness and was more pleasing. We all agreed again that the 1900 should be given the palm.

Then came the last round, and for the first time we failed to agree. The Mouton-Rothschild 1900 was easily the best 1900 of the evening: it had a finer bouquet and more body than the other two; a truly beautiful wine. But the Haut-Brion '99 was, I thought, finer still. It had greater breed and greater charm too. A wonderful wine, showing no sign of fatigue, no blemish, and perfectly balanced.

Our young host asked us whether pre-phylloxera Clarets, when thirty-four or thirty-five years of age, were better or different from the '99's and 1900's, which we had been discussing, a question which only C. M. Wells and I were old enough to answer. They were better, undoubtedly, and chiefly because they were fresher, younger, with a fuller measure of life and liveliness. In 1904, for instance, the Margaux 1869 was as black as ink, and with an extraordinary intensity of fruit entirely different from the languidly charming Margaux of 1899. As to the 1870's, in 1904 they were hardly fit to drink, so big were they, almost hard.

Today most 1920's are too old, and '23's at their best, whilst I know some '26's that are quite ready to drink. We all are in a hurry—God only knows why—and Clarets apparently mature more quickly.

The Port was good, and the Brandy quite remarkable: a Hine distilled in 1907 from 1906 wine, shipped

to England in 1908 and left untouched until 1933,
when it was bottled; its bouquet altogether delightful,
intensely clean, and so penetrating.

II

The date: 2nd May, 1934.
The place: The Savoy, Mikado Room.
The host: Louis E. Harfeld.
The guests: Col. the Hon. Osbert Vesey, Sir Walter
Schroder, A. W. Folks, E. Price Hallowes,
Frank Ratto and A.L.S.

The menu: Les Perles du Volga.
La Bisque d'Écrevisses.
La Truite Saumonée au Court Bouillon
accompagnée d'un beurre blanc.
Le Baron d'Agnelet à la broche par-
fumé aux Morillons de forêt.
La Caille dodue dans sa Gelée tremb-
lante.
Le Cœur de Palmier Riviera.
Le Fenouil Braisé Flamande.
La Coupe de Fraises des Bois
rafraîchies.
La Crème d'Ananas Voilée. Les
Gourmandises.

The wines: Macharnudo La Riva Fino.
Vin Nature de Rilly-la-Montagne 1929.
Berncasteler Doctor 1925.
Domaine de Chevalier 1923.
Le Grand Musigny 1923.
Oestricher Eiserberg 1920. Feinste.
Trockenbeeren Auslese.
Quinta da Paz 1845. Madeira.

A rare feast and perfect gastronomical symphony—
the perfect dinner. The cooking, Latry's best—there is
no better. The wines, each one better than the last, and
all in tune. The setting and service, the Savoy's best—
and again there is no better.

The Fino Sherry, which was served before we sat to table, was both light in colour and body, but it possessed great breed and was free from the quininy after-taste that is so unpleasant a characteristic of some dry Sherries. It struck a very gentle—*pianissimo*—note which was to swell in volume and power with every wine that followed until we came to the *furore* of the 1845 Madeira.

After the unctuous and pervasively delicious *Bisque*, the 1929 still Champagne came as a sharp anticlimax, a fuller wine than the La Riva, but a commoner fellow and as such better suited to introduce the next wine, a somewhat delicate but very pretty Moselle which came in with the fish. It was a Berncasteler Doctor of 1925, shipped by Deinhard, its bouquet most alluring, its body flimsy without being in the least angular, and its farewell just a little sweetish.

Then came the most perfect baby lamb ever reared in Dorset, as tender as tender can be, and free from the encumbrance of potatoes and other vegetables, except that most refined of all edible wild fungi, the *Morillons de Forêt*. And with it we scaled two steps at one bound with a magnum of Domaine de Chevalier 1923, a sweetly scented Graves of a vintage that was not nearly sufficiently appreciated at first. It possessed everything that Claret should possess: balance, fruit and simplicity. The bouquet was more discreet than that of the Moselle, but it was so entirely free from all trace of artificiality that its appeal was, to me at any rate, greater. The body was so perfectly proportioned that it gave one the impression of being light and full withal—a soap-bubble gently floating in the air. A really delightful wine.

The next course, a fat and richly stuffed quail, introduced a much bigger wine, a Grand Musigny 1923, shipped by Bouchard Aîné, which was a far better match for the stuffed quail than the lighter Claret would have been. Its bouquet was not so attractive as that of the Chevalier, but it had a stouter frame, a greater volume of fruit, and a most attractive freshness.

Instead of the asparagus, which is almost inevitable in May, Latry then gave us some braised fennel, which was not only excellent and more original, but also supplied a very good background for the next wine, a giant, one of the finest, if not the very finest hock, made in that remarkable year, 1920, the glory of which has been so unfairly eclipsed by the larger and better advertised 1921 vintage. It is a truly magnificent wine, and our host told us that we had gone up and up, from better to best, but that we had now reached the top. The concentrated perfume of this wine's beautiful bouquet; its richness of colour and texture; its exquisite flavour, were such that it did seem impossible to go 'one better'. And yet we did.

The last wine was the finest, and so it ought to have been, considering that it had a seventy-five years' start, a whole lifetime during which to improve and think it all over again and again. It was a wine made from the grapes of one vineyard—Quinta da Paz—on the south shore of Madeira, back in 1845, before both the Phylloxera and the Oïdium, and carefully matured in demijohns by Tarquinio da Camara Lomelino, by whose heirs it was bottled in 1926. No mere words can do justice to such a wine as that. A poet in his least sober moments might attempt it, but the only man whom I know—by name only—who might do it, would be Mr. Brock, and 'say it with fireworks'.

The menu of this exceptional gastronomical feast was worthy of the occasion; it was not printed, but engraved on music paper, each course and its accompanying wine being described under its appropriate tune—the first bars of it only—written in by Mark Hambourg.

III

The date:　4th June, 1934. 1.30 p.m.
The place:　The Café Royal, London.
The host:　P. H. Muir.
The guests: Hugh Walpole, A. J. A. Symons.
c*

The fare: Hors d'œuvre.
           Purée d'Epinards aux Croûtons.
           Consommé Sévigné.
           Turbot Bouilli, Sauce hollandaise.
           Blanchailles au Naturel et à la Diable.
           Selle de Mouton Rôtie.
           Salade à la française.
           Poulardes Rôties.
           Petits Pois au Beurre.
           Glaces à la Vanille et aux Fraises.
           Canapés d'Anchois à la Windsor.
           Dessert.

The wines: Liebfraumilch Stifstswein 1921.
           Château Margaux 1924.
           Château Gruaud-Larose-Sarget 1870.
           Corvo Blanc 1929.

This menu is not intended as an example of that gastronomic balance so wisely recommended by the President of the Wine and Food Society. It offended against his axiom that soup should not be served after hors d'œuvre. But there was a reason for the choice of dishes. The occasion of the lunch was the host's desire to bring together two book-collectors sharing a fanatical interest, not only in the writings of Baron Corvo but in the literature of the eighteen-nineties generally. Accordingly he had the amusing notion of serving a replica of a meal set before the Sette of Odd Volumes in 1895, on the occasion when Mr. Max Beerbohm first dined with that entertaining body. And certainly the Café Royal responded nobly: the choice of dishes may have been open to 'the higher criticism', but the cooking and serving of each was beyond reproach. The two Clarets provided an interesting comparison. The Margaux was excellent, and had that promise of long life which we associate, at present, with its vintage; but it seemed almost slight when contrasted with the robust, undiminished, altogether excellent 1870 Gruaud-Larose-Sarget. The Corvo Blanc was

altogether unworthy to follow such wines, and was
chosen only because, in its title, it reflects the pseudo-
baronial dignity of the eccentric genius in whose
memory the luncheon was given.

(A.J.A.S.)

IV

The date: 30th July, 1935.
The place: 4 Fitzroy Square, London.
The host: Curtis Moffat.
The guests: J. Murray Easton, Montague Shear-
man, André L. Simon, Bruce Todd.

The fare: Truites au Four.
Mayonnaise de volaille.
Foie Gras.
Wensleydale.
Fruits.

The wines: Berncasteler 1929.
Pommery and Greno 1884 (Magnum).
Grand Montrachet (Baron Thénard)
1929.
Erbacher Markobrunn 1917. Schloss
Reinhartshausen Cabinet.
Berncasteler Doktor Trockenbeeren
Auslese 1921. Fuder 24.
Hine's Fine Champagne 1870.

A baked trout and a cold chicken salad, nothing
could have been better or half as good on a hot summer's day, in London. Both were perfect of their kind.
A glass of fresh Berncasteler was all that the most
fastidious connoisseur could have wished for and would
have been grateful for. We had a glass of fresh 1929
Berncasteler, a wine of Feldheim's shipping, just the
sort of wine for such a fine day. But we did not stop
there. It was followed by a Magnum of 1884 Pommery
which was wonderful. Its cork was covered up with a
thick blob of yellow wax which took a lot of time to
knock off, and when it was off, the head of the cork
also came off, the wire that once upon a time held it

down having been eaten up by rust. But the 'cheville'
inside the neck of the bottle still held on like grim
death; it had to submit to the indignity of a corkscrew
after fifty years of good service, and when it came out,
the wine within sent out a distinct bang of pleasure.
It poured out with life and bubbles and it drank very
well indeed. It had no 'old stink' on the nose, but a
sweet caramel-like smell, absolutely clean and free from
any sign of decay. The colour of the wine was deep
yellow gold, without any trace of mahogany red in it.
It had both body and power and it finished sweet to the
last: quite an incredible *tour de force* of Nature. After
such a wine, there was nothing to do but say Grace
with due gratefulness. Our host had other views. He
was anxious to have our help in deciding which was
the better of the two, a fine white Burgundy and a
first-class Hock. The Burgundy was a bottle of the real
Montrachet, from Baron Thénard, and of the 1929
vintage. It was beautiful and above all perfectly
balanced, just right, the bouquet very fine but the
body and flavour and the very farewell of the wine
quite equal to the bouquet, equal and not greater.
The Magnum of 1884, which had just preceded it, did
not upset it in the least: it may have made it taste a
little fresher than if it had followed a very young wine,
but that was all to the good. It deserved and received
fuller marks than the 1917 Marcobrunn, a remarkable
wine indeed, but one with so superb and so much of a
bouquet that the wine itself failed to live up to it: its
noble nose had worn out its less noble body. Of course,
the more we assured Curtis that we had been only too
happy to give him the benefit of our opinion in the most
disinterested spirit, the more he insisted upon rewarding us for our valuable assistance, and he gave us a
bottle of one of the most extraordinary, as well as
rarest, wines which millionaires could still buy today,
had not their sense of beauty been dulled by a surfeit
of money. It was a Moselle like a light tawny Port
in colour, like an Yquem in sweetness and more like
a Tokay in its concentrated essence of grape. It was the

last wine made by the Widow Thanisch's son, in 1921, from the famous Berncasteler Doctor vineyard, from the sun-dried last berries—Trockenbeeren Auslese—and much more of a liqueur than a wine, although it could not be called a liqueur, it was too gentle; to call it a freak would be an insult: let us call it a miracle.

V

The date: 27th November, 1935.
The place: 'Bachelors', Ockham, Surrey.
The hosts: Mr. and Mrs. Eustace Oldham.
The guests: Colonel Ian M. Campbell, Robert Gray, Major A. M. Cheeke, André L. Simon and Donald J. Wardley.

The fare: Consommé.
Œufs Brouillés aux Rognons.
Perdreaux Rôtis.
Foie Gras en Croûte.
Salade.
Cox's Orange Pippins.

The wines: Amontillado.
Domaine de Chevalier 1920 (Magnum).
Cockburn 1908.
Fonseca 1908.
Graham 1908.
Taylor 1908.
Hine 1906.

The menu speaks for the occasion, a *dégustation*—would 'tasting' or 'judging' be the correct English word to use?—of 1908 Ports, which, incidentally, went far to reinstate that vintage in the estimation of one at least of the assembled company. It was a remarkably interesting experience: but there were other memorable features of the evening—the grace of our hostess; the charm of the little country house; the agreeable talk, and, then, the excellence of the pâté, the succulence of the birds, and the sweet but incisive fragrance of the Graves—a magnum. Nothing could have been more acceptable than this as an accompaniment to the dinner. It was delicate and lovely: no great body, but possessing quite definitely the promise of something to give after its first charming bow before nose and palate—and giving it.

The ports were served from numbered decanters into numbered glasses, without the identity of the wines being revealed until all had had time to make up their minds quite impartially. They were soon sifted into 1, 4, 2 as candidates for first place, with 3 nowhere in the running. Then 2 settled quite firmly into third place, with no loss of personal prestige. It was full of virtues which had not yet perfectly coalesced into their final and harmonious relationship. There were many of the same characteristics in 4, but it had achieved a more perfect balance. And yet, I venture to prophesy that it will be a better wine still some years hence. It was voted the best until the limpid ruby, full body and discreet harmony of 1 proclaimed it the best of the four at the moment, and probably the best absolutely. A wellnigh perfect bottle.

The identity of the wines was then disclosed and it was discovered that 1 was Graham; 4 was Taylor, which ran it very close; 2 was Fonseca, the youngest tasting of the four; and 3 was Cockburn, the only one that appeared to be tired and to have passed its best, but it is quite possible that this particular bottle, although in no manner of way faulty, was not quite as good as it should have been.

To finish with—and reward us for giving him very freely our views and opinions upon Port in general and *his* Ports in particular, our host gave us a brandy that was very pale, very clean and very delicious, a 1906 shipped in 1907 and bottled recently.

(D.J.W.)

VI

The date: 28th February, 1936.
The place: Mid-Atlantic,   on   board   M.V. *Champlain.*
The excuse: My birthday.
The hosts: My wife and myself.

The guests: Mr. and Mrs. A. Connett, of New York; M. and Mme. Michel Weil, of San Francisco; M. and Mme. L. Charton, of Montreal; Comte Serge Fleury and M. Roditi, of Paris.

The fare: Miniatures de Bouchées Bayard.
Velouté Forestière.
Suprêmes de Poulardes de Bresse Champlain.
Le Filet de Bœuf en Chevreuil Grand Veneur.
La Langouste en Bellevue.
L'Ananas glacé et voilé à l'Orientale.
Corbeille de Friandises.

The wines: Le Cristal Vouvray Extra Dry, in place of cocktails.
La Réserve Riesling Dopff, with the Hors-d'œuvre.
Le Pontet-Canet 1924, after the Soup.
La Côte Rôtie 1926, with the Entrée.
Le Corton Grancey 1928, with the Roast.
Le Krug 1921, with the cold Langouste, in place of Salad.
L'Ayala Goût Américain, with the ice.
La Fine Normandin (20 ans), with the coffee.

What will make this Birthday Dinner ever memorable is not so much the food and the wines, good as they were, but the weather, which could not possibly have been worse. A terrific gale from the north-west was blowing us along and almost over, at times; it made it very difficult for us to keep to our seats and impossible to keep any wine in our glasses; but that made the dinner all the merrier. What was so wonderful was that the people in the kitchen managed to cook such an elaborate dinner and that the stewards managed to serve it. I shall never forget the look of relief on the face of the man whose duty it had been to keep the Langouste en Bellevue standing up on its tail when all the white *médaillons*, with their truffle black eye in the centre, were safely transferred from the back of the Langouste to our plates.

That such perfectly cooked food could be obtained in mid-Atlantic for the asking, without any special notice nor a penny extra charge, was quite a revelation to me. The wines were young, for obvious reasons, but very good indeed.

VII

The date: Saturday, 3rd April, 1937.

The place: The Hind's Head Hotel, Bray-on-Thames.

The host: Mine Host, Barry Neame.

The fare: Giblet Soup.

Tay Salmon; Cucumber; Hollandaise Sauce.

Saddles of Newbury Lamb; Worthing Beans; Creamed Mushrooms; New Potatoes.

Asparagus.

Cheese Soufflé.

Coffee.

The wines: Solera 1858 (José Ramirez).

Bâtard Montrachet 1929 (Louis Poirier).

Château Ducru Beaucaillou 1924 (Imperiale).

Château Gruaud Larose Faure 1924 (Jeroboam).

Château Haut-Brion 1924 (Jeroboam).

Château Lafite 1924 (Jeroboam).

Château Margaux 1920 (Jeroboam).

Hine's Grande Fine Champagne 1900, landed 1901.

I have omitted to set out the guests; there were about thirty of us, nearly all the Old Gang and a few

THE MELON EATERS *by Bartolomé Estéban Murillo* 1617–1682

THE COOK

by

Jan Vermeer of Delft

1632–1675

ALEXIS SOYER

by

Emma Soyer

1813–1842

THE PICNIC

by

James Tissot

1836–1902

THE TEA PARTY

by

Hilda Fearon

1879–1917

INVALIDS' DIET by *Thomas Rowlandson* 1756—1827

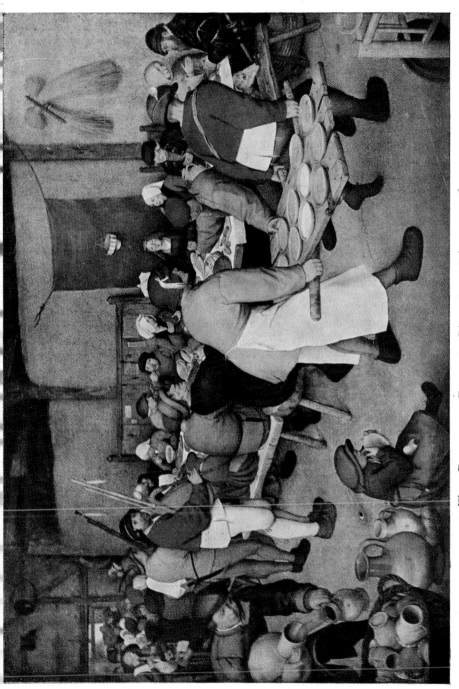

THE BAKEHOUSE FEAST *by Pieter Brueghel* 1530—1569

THE BREAKFAST TABLE *by Vincent Van Gogh* 1853–1890

new faces. The occasion was Barry's birthday: his twenty-fifth (or was it the twenty-fifth celebration of his fiftieth? Anyway, it doesn't matter so long as he's spared to us). As usual, he met us, bottle in hand (Krug's 1928, in magnums: delightfully full and fresh, with a real winy flavour), and showed us proudly his regiment of jeroboams (the imperiale had suffered a disaster, but only the receptacle; the wine was saved, having been decanted before the accident), faced by a bevy of Beauty, disguised as Hebe and her assistants. We were a cosmopolitan gathering; besides two Cork men, I noticed representatives of England, Scotland, Wales, France, Belgium, Italy, and Chile. The other Corkman was specially designed by Providence to play the part of Sir Henry Curtis in a film of 'King Solomon's Mines'; but the wretched man won't hear of it, and proposes to go on sculpturing in Berkshire, as if he were an ordinary-looking citizen.

I shan't waste words praising Barry's good food, delicious as ever; it was the wines we were after. The Sherry was a stately herald, quite like a venerable Madeira; it went admirably with the giblet soup. The Bâtard, like his namesake in 'King John,' had an easy carriage; he didn't give a damn about the bar-sinister, and spoke his piece with the assurance that he had the ear, or palate, of the assembly. I was surprised to find an after-bouquet of Sauternes; but there was no suggestion of sweetness or heaviness in the flavour.

Then came the Clarets. The Ducru seemed a little light at first, but held its own splendidly; I thought it better than the Larose, which was firmer, but not so elegant, and I put the latter last of the five, with the Ducru fourth; but I am only giving my own view, which was not generally shared. I don't think I have ever tasted the Haut-Brion '24 in better fettle. He swung into the procession with the stride of a conqueror and, to my mind, achieved the primacy at a blow. The Lafite promised to be a more stylish wine, and Lafite '24 commands my homage in many quarters,

notably at 'The Rag'; but on this occasion it seemed
to me not to stay the course, and even the Ducru stood
up to it very well towards the end. The Margaux '20
gave the Irishman his best fight; had its sugar lasted
a little better it would have taken first place, but it
seemed to me a little dry, and more than a little tired.
And so it was my Haut-Brion that I kept until the last.
The Hine put a noble crown upon the feast.

But what an occasion! Where else could one sit down
to a table at which four jeroboams and an imperiale
of first and second growth Clarets adorned the feast?
Was it any wonder that a spate of oratory was let loose,
encouraged rather than governed by Ian Campbell,
who constituted himself chairman, and kept the current
of good humour flowing? And it was grand to hear that
nice lad, Aneurin Bevan, shouting with laughter like
a delighted schoolboy (I wonder what Sir Ronald Storrs
was telling him!) and showing as firm an allegiance to
Red Wine as to the Red Flag. It was a noble evening:
thirty happy people thanking God for Barry Neame
and the other gifts so generously provided; and even
if we had to crawl home through a pea-souper of a fog,
more appropriate to November than to April, it only
fixed in our minds the difference between the atmosphere within the Hind's Head and the atmosphere
anywhere else.

(M.H.)

VIII

The date: 5th April, 1937.
The place: Scott's   Restaurant,   Haymarket,
                London.
The hosts: John and Charles Gardner.
The guests: Sir Hugh Walpole, André L. Simon,
                J. C. Ionides, and A. J. A. Symons.
The fare: Whitstable Natives.
                Grilled Fillet of Beef.
                Grilled Mushrooms.
                Jacket Potatoes.
                Lauris Asparagus and melted butter.
                Blue Cheshire Cheese.

The wines: Graacher Himmelreich 1934.
Château Rausan-Ségla 1929.
Château Lafite 1920.
Cockburn's 1912.

This halcyonic luncheon had been primarily arranged in order to remind Hugh Walpole, freshly returned from Los Angeles, where he had presided over
one of the entertaining dinners held by our Branch
there, and been guest of honour at others, that simple
English fare need fear no transatlantic or Continental
comparisons. After a preliminary glass of excellent
Alambra Sherry, dry and cold, we were ready for the
oysters for which Scott's are famous—Whitstable
Natives served in the English tradition, on the flat
shell; firm, substantial, and tasting of the sea.

To find a wine that really suits the oyster is always
a problem, but our hosts solved it handsomely by the
Graacher Himmelreich 1934; one of the most attractive
Moselles I have ever drunk, as well as surprisingly
inexpensive. It was dry enough to be refreshing, while
not hiding that delicious, unabashed grapiness whose
secret no chemist has yet penetrated. What a pity
that most of them have such faith in sulphur!

The grilled fillet of beef that followed was perfect.
Perfection is easily claimed; but here the term is used
with intention. Our President, critical and widely experienced though he is, could not recollect meat more
tender, or of an equal flavour; and all the rest of us con-
curred. The fillets were served with a couple of grilled
mushrooms, and nothing else save their noble juices,
though, on another plate, we were given one potato,
plainly baked in its jacket, with a pat of farmhouse
butter in its middle. A simple but in every way memorable course. With it we drank Rausan-Ségla 1929;
young, but already displaying all the graces of its
nature: fragrant, full flavoured, and sweet.

The asparagus were excellent, but did not help the
beautiful Lafite 1920 passed round just before they

arrived. I reserved my glass for the cheese, which was
also perfect—and here again I use the word with
intention. Blue Cheshire, as students of the Society's
Cheese Catechism are aware, starts by being red, but,
instead of maturing early and remaining mild, it loses
its carroty colour and develops a blue system of veins
which spreads all over the cheese, much to the streng-
thening and improvement of its flavour. I have known
many fine examples at the Savile Club. But this remarkable cheese was a *white* Cheshire turned blue;
not the usual crumbly Blue Cheshire, but a wonder of
rich, creamy softness: an undying gastronomic
memory. Of such cheeses, I hope, is the Kingdom of
Heaven. The Port was perhaps worthy of it; the
President said it was, but the Claret decanter was not
empty, and I kept to the Lafite.

A memorable, a superlatively good meal, which
we enjoyed thoroughly, listening, quite without envy,
to Walpole's account of the feasts he had taken part
in at Los Angeles, including one whereat all the courses
had been prepared during a whole day by private
members of the Society, and the whole had been
crowned by wines as carefully selected as the dishes.
We envied no one. I have never agreed that man
wants but little here below; but for one glorious hour
it was true.

(A.J.A.S.)

IX

The date: 28th April, 1937.
The place: 'Quinto's', Arlington House, London.
The host: A.L.S.
The guests: Colonel Ian M. Campbell, F. P. Robin-
            son, and Donald Wardley.

The fare: Crème Forestière.
            Turbotin au four.
            Tournedos Rossini.
            Pommes Purée.
            Petits Pois nouveaux.
            Soufflé au Parmesan.

The wines: Château Margaux 1926.
Château Haut-Brion 1920.
Château Cheval Blanc 1911.
Grande Fine 1847 'Comte de Béarn'.
Fine Champagne 1809 'Comte de Genet'.

Memorable may be too big a word for this little dinner; it was certainly notable for its quiet perfection. It was perfectly ordered, perfectly cooked, and perfectly served. Who shall say whether it was perfectly appreciated? One of the company, at any rate, thinks that it was.

The soup was perfectly—the word seems inescapable—seasoned, quite a rare achievement, so much so that the passing of the salt to one's neighbour as soup is served has become second nature to most of us. What followed, an excellent turbot, a succulent tournedos 'done to a turn', and the cheese Soufflé, a miracle of upstanding lightness, bore the unobtrusive but unmistakable hall-mark of the master hand. And yet all those good things were merely there to help the Clarets display their many charms.

The Margaux was definitely one of the good latter-day Margaux, it was also one of the good 1926's. Good but not great; rather light, too light for its age and not likely to grow old gracefully, but fully able to give pleasure and to prepare the way for its elders. The Haut-Brion which followed was more immediately attractive: it had more colour and more sugar; a more winy wine, but by no means a big wine, and towards the end of dinner, when both '26 and '20 had had time to breathe—or should it be inhale?—I was surprised to find that the Margaux not only stood its ground manfully, but it pleased me more than the Haut-Brion. As to the Cheval Blanc 1911, it was in a class by itself and simply wonderful. It was light in colour, of course, but it had more body and greater sweetness than I had expected, and that touch of cedary after-flavour which is so puzzlingly attractive. There was in this

1911 the unmistakable high aristocratic quality which
no other wine possesses to the same superlative degree
as a really fine Claret. All three Clarets were decanted
at the table by Quinto himself, or should Quinto not
be his real name, by the Boss himself; they were
poured ever so gently from the bottle into four large
glasses set in a row and then passed on to each one of
us; this method certainly avoids the double beating of
wine that passes from the bottle to the decanter and
from the decanter to the glass. The two rare old
Brandies which Mine Host produced from his private
'Réserve' were as 'perfect' as the rest of the feast.

(D.W.)

X

The date: 10th February, 1938.
The place: 'Boulestin's', Covent Garden.
The hosts: X. M. Boulestin and Francis Toye.
The guests: The Hon. Harold Nicolson, Sir Hugh
Walpole, André L. Simon, A. J. A.
Symons.
The fare: Lamproie Bordelaise.
Rôti de Porc Périgourdine; Pommes
Parisienne.
Salade de pissenlit à l'huile de Noix.
Fromage.
Tarte de Famille.
The wines: Château La Lagune 1922.
Château Ausone 1914.
Château Climens 1929.
Fine Champagne 1830.

Ever since at school I read of the English king who
(by a fate comparable to that of the Malmsey-
drowned Duke of Clarence) died of a surfeit of
lampreys, I had been eager to taste this dangerously
seductive fish; and at last Marcel Boulestin's kindness
satisfied my curiosity of twenty years by making the
lamprey the opening dish in one of the most interesting
feasts I have ever eaten, heard, or dreamed of. The
lamprey, it seems, resembles the eel in shape, and in

having no scales; it has a mouth like a sucker, pouch-like gills, and seven spiracles on each side of its head. But none of these icthyological details need concern the fortunate feaster at M. Boulestin's table. Presented in a rich, dark, wine sauce, the succulent and boneless lamprey had a consistency midway between the sweet-bread and the turtle-fin, with a delicate taste in which the sea played little part. But where is the vocabulary for taste? I must content myself, if not my readers, by saying that it was one of the most delicious dishes I have ever eaten.

Next came the principal course, a speciality of our host's home province: meltingly-tender, symmetrical circles of roast pork, with a centre-piece of truffle and an undertaste of garlic and the jellified gravy from the joint. M. Boulestin had spent three hours that morning at work on this masterpiece of seeming simplicity— a compliment to his friends—and it received full recognition in our avidity and enjoyment.

The richness of these dishes was relieved by the salad that followed, a salad of unbleached, common gardener's dandelions dressed with very little vinegar and some fresh walnut oil.

With the lamprey we had been drinking a modest Claret of a year marked at '3' in our vintage chart. My own experience of the 1922's is that they are fuller to the nose than the tongue; the La Lagune was no exception, though with more fullness of flavour than those I remembered. But now, with the pork and the cheese, we soared higher. The Ausone of 1914 was a magnum. Light, yet well-balanced, aromatic, smooth and yet *brisk*, it was a wine perfectly suited to be the benignant dictator at luncheon. For dinner it would perhaps have been placed as the centre of a sequence; here it was an enjoyable veteran, with an assured, de-served mastery of the table. The Camembert set it off admirably, and was itself admirable. The rind had been removed; instead, a coat of fine breadcrumbs com-fortably invested its tasty surface.

What ending could be chosen for so notable a con-
course of various excellences? M. Boulestin modestly
announced the Tarte de Famille. But what a family
his must have been if it ate such tarts! Imagine crème
brûlée mounted in a croûte, lined with thin slices of
fresh pineapple; a sweeter, more intense and yet not
cloying interior, and a more delicately brittle and tasty
top. An Empress among tarts! And with it came the
most remarkable wine of the day, which I rejoice to
know is still to be had on M. Boulestin's list: the
Climens of 1929. The wines of Sauternes hold a high
place in my affections, though Climens has never been
one of my favourites. But *this* was Climens transfigured;
a perfect wine, already showing that wonderful tan-
gerine-marmalade flavour which usually graces the old
age of the Sauternes. Yet there is nothing *old* in the
radiance of this wine; it has the honeyed sweetness and
strength of complete maturity, the beauty of the blonde.
After its perfection, the Brandy, excellent though it
was, could hardly help being overlooked. (A.J.A.S.)

XI

The date: 4th March, 1938.
The place: 4 Fitzroy Square, London.
The host: Curtis Moffat.
The guests: Mr. and Mrs. Christopher Sykes, A.
              Duff Cooper, Hilaire Belloc and
              André L. Simon.
The fare: La Mijourée de Matata.
              Les Tagliatelli à la Crème de Champig-
              nons.
              La Salade de Légumes verts truffés.
              Le Fromage de Monsieur Fromage.
The wines: Gonzalez Nectar.
              Tavel Rosé.
              Domaine de Chevalier 1923 (Magnum).
              Château Pichon Longueville 1875.
              Château Cheval Blanc 1921.
              Fine Champagne Hine 1904.

A model and pattern for a meatless luncheon, whether it happens to be Friday or any other day. The first dish was both soup, hors d'œuvre and fish: an excellent stew of fish and vegetables, served in its own savoury gravy, too highly seasoned and flavoured to be fair to a serious wine; but our host knew it and he gave us a fresh-looking and fresh-tasting young Tavel Rosé, which was delicious as a long drink with the fish. The next course was a large dish of fresh Tagliatelli profusely sauced with a fine *purée* of fresh mushrooms and cream, a truly admirable combination as well as a very fine background for so gracious a wine as the Domaine de Chevalier 1923, still rather frail but not more so than five or six years ago when wine-wise prophets announced that it could not last. The 1875, which came next, was no longer sound—and no wonder after its sixty years' solitary confinement. But the 1921 Cheval Blanc which stepped in its place was simply and splendidly stupendous. It possesses a superabundance of everything that makes a wine really great, and the wonder of it is that it is so full of colour, of body, of life without having lost any of its charming poise: it is an outstanding example of a wine that is absolutely complete as well as perfectly balanced. The 1904 Hine was as delicate and delicious as ever, as well as a very agreeable anti-climax.

XII

The date: 10th March, 1938.

The place: Ley On's Chop Suey Restaurant, Wardour Street, London.

The host: Mr. Kenneth Cantlie.

The guests: Dr. C. C. Wong, Mr. André Simon, Jnr., Lieut.-Col. R. H. Ingham Clark, Mr. Keith Murray, Mr. Hamilton Readman, Mr. Russell Beverley, Mr. Ralph Keene.

The fare: Pee Dan Chung Kog Salad.
            Gai Yung Yin Wo.
            Shui Arp.

Houng Shui Yue.
Subgum Yuk Pen.
Gor Yuk.
Jung Jar Min.
Gum-gut and Chow-chow.
The liquids: Moey Quai Loo.
Loong Cheng Tea.
Hung Yuen.

This was a particularly interesting luncheon, arranged by Mr. Cantlie to demonstrate the delicious flavouring and charm of Chinese food, and novel to all of us but three.

It represented a typical Chinese luncheon, and the menu had been carefully arranged by Dr. Wong and our host some days before.

We started with Pee Dan Chung Kog Salad, which consists of bean and bamboo shoots and one-hundred-year-old eggs, which, despite their unprepossessing look, are most delicious, though perhaps to some of us a little sweet.

The second dish was the famous Chinese Bird's-nest Soup, and we learned for the first time that the bird concerned was about the size of a humming bird, and the nest is comparable to the honeycomb of a bees' nest, formed with the saliva of the bird. In taste it is comparable to a rather thick chicken broth, but with a particularly delightful sweetness to it.

With this we drank Moey Quai Loo, which is served slightly warm and is in the nature of an *apéritif*. It is a grain spirit and slightly reminiscent of 'Marc'. (From Dr. Wong I learned that the Chinese are practically teetotallers, generally drinking but a small cup of wine at the commencement of their meal.)

We then had placed before us five dishes, from which we helped ourselves, using the traditional chop sticks. These dishes must be tasted to be really appreciated, and no words of mine can adequately describe them —delicious flavours so entirely different from what we are used to. The Shui Arp is roast duck, and is prepared so that the skin and fat resemble slightly the crackling in our English roast pork. The skin is considered by the Chinese as *the* delicacy—the meat is not thought so much of. The Houng Shui Yue is a coarse fish of the perch or carp type, cooked in a rich brown gravy flavoured with special herbs and vegetables. The Subgum Yuk Pen is a mixed vegetable dish, with which a number of herbs and small pieces of fat pork have been mixed.

The Gor Yuk is possibly the most delicious of the three dishes, being pork cut in slices with the leaf of some herb between each slice, packed together, and cooked in a way which renders the crackling, fat and lean, all of a similar texture.

In place of potatoes we had Jung Jar Min, which is a type of noodle fried quite crisp. By the side of our plates there was a small dish of brown liquid called Soya, which is made from the soya bean, and takes the place of salt.

To complete the meal we were served with Gumgut, *anglice* Cumquat, which are preserved oranges about the size of a pigeon's egg, and Chow-chow, which is a mixed fruit preserve, flavoured with ginger.

After the meal we drank two different teas. Both were freshly infused and tasted quite unlike any China tea procurable in this country.

Dr. Wong informed me that the Chinese method of cooking is considered by a number of scientists as the most digestible, and for that reason obesity is almost unknown in China.

The highest praise must be given to Mr. Ley On for his interest in the preparation of the meal, and for the way in which it was served.

(R.H.I.C.)

XIII

The date : 1st September, 1938.

The place: 'Scotts', Haymarket, London.

The hosts: Major A. D. S. Rice, John E. Gardner, Isidore and David Kerman.

The guests: Viscount Leverhulme, Lord Sempill,
Miss Frances Day, Maurice Healy,
Israel Sieff, Henry Horne, A. P. Her-
bert, M.P., Sir Lionel Earle, Ralph
Lynn, Douglas Fairbanks, Barry
Neame, Tom Webster, Sir David
Hughes Morgan and others.

The fare: Scotts' Imperial Natives.
Roast Partridge.
Scarlet Runners.
Scotts' Special Savoury.

The wines: Bâtard Montrachet (Poirier's) 1935.
Château Mouton-Rothschild 1920.
Grande Fine Champagne 'De la
Maison'.

A truly remarkable function, memorable socially as
well as gastronomically: truly may it be said that oysters
are a sure bait to net big and small fish, lawyers and law-
givers, Press magnates and gossipers, actors and ac-
tresses, stars and aces, big business and Civil Service,
old and young, rich and not so rich, and all possessed
of the same devouring passion for oysters, all but the
Chairman, Major Rice, who does not eat oysters.
Smoked salmon was his consolation whilst every one of
his guests had a large plate placed in front of her or of
him, and on each plate there were three perfect rows
each of eight oysters on the flat shell, plump, artless
and dignified in their bearded nudity, quiescent and
resigned to their fate. They may be larger in a few
weeks' time, but they cannot be any better. The wine
that was served at the same time was a Bâtard Montrachet of Louis Poirier's shipping and of the 1935
vintage. It was delicious. It had far greater breed than
any Chablis can ever hope to possess; in a year or two
it will have acquired greater body, power and dignity,
more bouquet and a little deeper colour; it will be a
finer wine, certainly, but no longer so suitable for such
an occasion when its youth, freshness and charm
provided a perfect background for the oysters.

After the oysters, the first of the season, we were each given a partridge, the first of the season also; but whereas the oysters had left their beds overnight to be with us today, with the morning's dew, so to speak, still fresh upon their scaly cheeks, the partridges were not shot till dawn today, and how they could have been shot, hung, quartered and roasted between sunrise and lunch time is one of those mysteries which I, for one, do not feel called upon to probe. Why should I bother about what is no business of mine when I can be so much more profitably occupied disjointing the little creature before me and enjoying its warm and tender body?

With the partridge, Claret was served and a splendid wine, the Mouton-Rothschild 1920, beautiful of colour, a little bashful, perhaps, on the nose, but simply radiant on the palate, light of body because so lithe and smooth; its flavour sweet to the end with a lingering coddle in it for the little taste-buds of the palate.

Scotts' special savoury was another one of those mysteries which it is so much wiser to accept with faith and gratitude rather than take to pieces. It was a little substantial, perhaps, but full of goodness, and an excellent excuse for yet another glass of Claret. With the coffee and very fine cigars we had some very good Cognac brandy and a great flow of oratory.

(A.L.S.)

XIV

The date: 15th September, 1938.
The place: 'Princhetts', Chelsworth, Suffolk.
The hosts: Eustace and Lady Peggy Hoare.
The guests: Mr. and Mrs. C. G. Brocklebank, Vyvyan Holland, and A. J. A. Symons.
The fare: Consommé Edouard VII.
Turbotin poché, Sauce hollandaise.
Mousse de Foie Gras.
Perdreaux rôtis.
Champignons à la crème.

The wines: Verdelho 1779.
              Château Lafite 1874.
              Château Lafite 1870.
              Château Lafite 1865.
              Château Lafite 1858.
              Cockburn 1863.
              Moët & Chandon 1889.

There are many wine-lovers to whom the cult of pre-phylloxera Clarets seems an almost affronting folly, in which the superstition of antiquity triumphs over good sense. And it may be admitted that such survivors of the '70's as now remain are to be appraised as curiosities rather than examples for the present day. Yet, even when full allowance has been made for this objection, it remains undeniable that these veterans do survive; and that though some of them have passed their best, the majority remain remarkably good. No host has a finer collection of these rarities than Mr. Eustace Hoare; and the memorable meal now chronicled proved once again what superlative wines were made in Bordeaux sixty and more years ago.

The Verdelho 1779, with which our feast began, is a notable wine which has been preserved till recently in cask at Madeira. Evaporation has been made good by the same wine: and though it lacks the fumosity of bottle age, it has the fire, the dryness, and the deep, burnt flavour which are the characteristics of the great Madeiras of the past. A hundred and fifty years had left its vigour unimpaired; it glowed red, gold and brown in the even older glasses, a delightful, though perhaps exacting, prelude to the battery of Lafites.

The first gun misfired. The 1874 had promised badly when decanted, failed to improve in the decanter, and was removed to the vinegar vat. But the magnum of 1870 hit the mark at once. Its bouquet greeted the nose with sweet authority; its flavour delighted first the tongue, then the nose, then the throat; it was a perfect wine, outstanding in sugar, taste and smell, with the heavy grace of rich red velvet in a peer's robe.

It has been my good fortune to meet this wine frequently; not frequently enough, but still, frequently;
but I have never known another bottle or magnum to
attest in such superlative degree the slow maturing
qualities of its year.

The Lafite 1865 which followed was from a bottle,
not a magnum. If the first wine was red velvet, this
was worn brocade; as beautiful, perhaps, but with
more trace of time's wear in its fabric. In my view it
showed less flavour, less sugar, and less bouquet than
its predecessor, but the general judgment was much
divided, and both the ladies (exceptionally good
judges) preferred the older wine.

Next came a wine I had never expected to see again.
My previous acquaintance with Lafite 1858, the oldest
Claret I have ever drunk, was confined to one bottle,
presented to Col. Ian Campbell, and shared by him
with the President and myself. My recollection was
clear, and led me to expect great charm and breeding;
but this magnum outran my anticipation by a mile.
It was pure cloth-of-gold. To say it was 'sound' is too
tame a term; it was perfectly proportioned, with the
abstract perfection of an architectural drawing or a
quadratic equation. I meditated poetry as I drank that
wine; in the spirit of Stevenson I pondered over the
vicissitudes it had successfully endured from the time
when the château sent it forth, the merchant sold it,
the butler binned it, the auctioneer knocked it down,
and who knows what beside, till now, when it graced
this Suffolk house, and gladdened this pleasant company. Sitting abstracted, I thought of those novels
with an object as hero which our forefathers used to
love: *The Adventures of a Guinea, The Adventures of
a Gold Watch, The Adventures of a Phaeton.* Why not
The Adventures of a Magnum of Lafite? With a start I
was recalled to reality—just in time to secure the last
glass of this 'incomparable' wine—by a question from
my host.

It was not incomparable: I had carefully compared

it with the two wines which preceded it. In actual sweetness and in volume of flavour it came behind the 1870,
but in bouquet, and in that air of perfect proportion
already mentioned, it seemed to me to surpass any
Claret I have ever enjoyed.

Next came the Port—Cockburn 1863—as good as
its reputation and its year. But what wine could over-
throw that astonishing Claret? The Cockburn was
too discreet to try; but it gave a charming finish to a
great dinner.

The dinner itself, simple and satisfactory, would
have reflected credit on any chef. The partridge was
outstanding; as tender as it could be, and, with the
mousse de fois gras, provided a stimulating back-cloth
for the three principal actors in this gastronomic
drama—to which there was an unexpected epilogue,
for after dinner, the talk turning on old Champagne,
our host brought up for us a bottle of Moët & Chandon
1889 (from Lord Coventry's cellar), which belonged
to the best cuvée—cuvée 36—of that outstanding vintage. Still sparkling, fruity in flavour, but not at all
madérisé, it was a worthy companion to the great
wines we had enjoyed, and the most fitting of all con-
clusions to a meal which, for its just description, calls
for the pen of Brillat-Savarin.

(A.J.A.S.)

XV

The date: All Saints' Day, 1938.
The place: Bonaly, Oxted, Surrey.
The hosts: Mr. and Mrs. Ernest H. Cockburn.
The guests: Colonel and Mrs. Ian M. Campbell,
            Mr. and Mrs. Frederick Cockburn,
            Mrs. Harold Cox, Mr. Barry Neame,
            Mr. and Mrs. Eustace Oldham,
            Mr. and Mrs. André L. Simon.
The fare: Turtle Soup.
            Dublin Bay Prawns.
            Sasarties; Fried Pumpkin.
            Roast Pheasant.
            Chocolate Soufflé.

Portuguese Tongue on Toast.

Dessert.

The wines: Solera 1872, bottled 1928 (John Harvey & Sons).

Piesporter Goldtröpfchen 1935 (A. Hellmers & Sons).

Château Latour 1878, Magnums (Findlater, Mackie, Todd & Co.).

Château Léoville 1878, Magnums (Cockburn & Campbell).

Château Lafite 1870, Magnums (Cockburn & Campbell).

Krug 1928.

Cockburn's 1887 (Winterschladen & Co.).

Cockburn's 1858 (Carr & Quick).

Martell 1904 (Corney & Barrow).

Hennessy 1906 (G. F. Grant & Co.).

Resplendent and gorgeous in the centre of the dining table was a large bowl of exquisite single dahlias, of an apricot shade of colour: their name was 'Peggy Wood'. The Turtle Soup was excellent, and that Harvey's Old 1872 Solera played up to it most admirably. The Dublin Bay Prawns were the largest and best I have ever come across. They must have flown over from Dublin that day, they were so fresh and tender. A rather lightly-flavoured mayonnaise sauce was served with them, and they were accompanied by the 1935 Piesporter Goldtröpfchen, which was also lightly flavoured and very happy in its selection. The puzzle and pleasant surprise were the Sasarties. One might have feared the worst under such an outlandish name, but if anybody present had entertained any fears, they soon faded away when a perfect piece of broiled beef appeared with a faint aroma of bayleaf and as tender as tender can be. We learnt that although the name is a Malay name the article is a South African native dish, consisting of slices of meat and fat in alternate layers on a skewer left overnight in a strongly herb-scented

D

marinade and then quickly broiled in front of a blazing wood fire. The result was very good, and the slice of fried pumpkin upon which the beef was served just added a sweet note that was as unexpected as it was agreeable.

I confess I was a little afraid that the sweetness of the pumpkin might spoil the 1899 Château Latour, but my fears were groundless, as this famous Claret, mature full of flavour and charm, came away with flying colours.

The pheasant, hung to the day and roasted to the second, was accompanied by the 1878 Château Léoville and 1870 Château Lafite. It was hard luck indeed on the magnum of '78 that it found itself sandwiched between a superb magnum of '99 Latour and a quite remarkable magnum of '70 Lafite. If we had had it alone its soft velvety mellowness would have brought it well deserved eulogies, but on this occasion, in spite of showing, with the others, excellence of condition and perfection of temperature, it was outclassed. I have enjoyed, occasionally, an 1878 of which the bouquet and flavour and sweetness were reminiscent of 1875 itself, but as a rule the vintage lacks the breed and quality of its predecessors in that wonderful decade.

Our Host, great lover and student of wine, was wise enough to give us a young cool Champagne between the majestic old Claret and the princely Port that followed, neither of which, moreover, might have relished being served with Chocolate Soufflé! The 1887 Port was princely indeed. Never can any of us have tasted a finer specimen of Victoria's Jubilee year. Of brilliant colour, full of the fine flavour of the grape and the joy of living, this fifty-year-old wine has just celebrated its own jubilee and would seem to have many years still ahead of it. As perfect a Port as can be found today, not even excluding the 1896 and the younger giants of the present century.

The 1858, alas! fine old fellow though he was, suffered by comparison. A great aristocrat and holding himself up with grace and dignity, he was unable to stem the flight of time or overcome the handicap of his eighty years.

The choice of two young, unspoilt, pale coloured brandies brought this never-to-be-forgotten dinner, *Regum, mensis arisque deorum*, to a close.

A marvellous evening, made joyous and memorable, not only by the bounteous hospitality we enjoyed, but also by the unaffected and genial kindness and courtesy of our Host and Hostess.

(I.M.C.)

XVI

The date: 2nd March, 1939.
The place: 2 Gloucester Street, Boston, Mass.
The hosts: Mr. and Mrs. Augustus P. Loring, Jnr.
The guests: Mrs. Charles Codman, Messrs. Philip
           Dexter, Robert Dodge, Sohier
           Welch and A.L.S.
The fare: Cape Cod Oysters.
           Cream of Veal Soup.
           Saddles of Lamb.
           Green Peas and New Potatoes.
           Salad and State of Maine Sage Cheese.
           Strawberries.
           Coffee.
The wines: Pale Rainwater Madeira, bottled 1922
           by Harvey.
           1934er. Scharzhofberger Auslese.
           (Wachstum von Appolinar Kock.
           Original Abfüllung. Fuder Nr. 35.)
           Amontillado selected by the late Francis
           R. Harte at Jerez in 1929, at Gon-
           zalez, Byass', and bottled by Fort-
           num & Mason.
           Grands Echézeaux 1915, bottled by
           the Comte R. de Vaulchier.
           Château Climens 1929.
           1865 Cognac (Hedges & Butler).
           Old Rhum Villejoint, Haïti. (Bottled
           in December 1932 at No. 2 Gloucester
           Street, Boston.)

'Belle of Nelson' Kentucky Whiskey
1875. (Used in U.S. Government
hospitals for the insane.)

This meal, by no means the most sumptuous of those
which I was privileged to attend during my last visit
to New York and Boston, deserves to be placed on
record among more elaborate but no more memorable
meals, as an example of princely simplicity. Just six
oysters, small ones and very good ones, as an appetizer,
with a glass of young, fragrant and delicious Saar wine
of real breed. Then a plate of hot soup, home-made and
full of goodness, and a small glass of a very pleasing
Amontillado. Two charming heralds, gracious and
modest, to introduce the prince, the joint, the *pièce
de résistance*. The saddle was placed before our host,
who stood up and carved seven long fillets from the
middle of the back, seven perfectly cooked long strips
of pink meat, one for each one present. What was left
of the saddle was then taken away. Vegetables were
passed round, and the finest 1915 Burgundy that I
have tasted for many months: it had retained all its
fruit and grace, which is, unfortunately, not the way
with the great majority of 1915's: a perfect glass of
Burgundy, its colour as rich as ever, its bouquet more
attractive than ever and its lithe body showing no
trace of fatigue. The lamb was excellent and excellently
mated. All was well. All were happy. Then quite a simple
thing happened. Another saddle was placed before our
host: a second saddle, just the same as the first, but
it had been put in the oven twenty minutes after the
first so that the second helping should be just as pink
and just as hot as its predecessor.

The Sage Cheese from Maine, with the salad, was
new to me, and I did not care for it, but the Florida
strawberries were delicious, and the Climens 1929
that came with them was exceedingly agreeable. Then
we went upstairs for coffee and liqueurs. The coffee
was exceptionally good and the spirits various: the
most amusing of all, speaking of the label, was the

bottle of Whiskey, and here is the exact copy of the label from neck to punt: '*The finest Whiskey in the world. Used in U.S. Government Hospitals for the Insane. Contract awarded after Chemical Analysis establishing our claim that the BELLE OF NELSON is the finest Whiskey on Earth. No other can be used for the purpose. 1875. BELLE OF NELSON, Bartley, Johnston & Co. Louisville, Ky. Guaranteed to be superior to any Whiskey distilled in Kentucky. None genuine without our signature. The Whiskey that made Kentucky famous. This is an old fashion hand made sour mash Whiskey distilled from carefully selected Kentucky grain by the BELLE OF NELSON DISTILLERY Co.*

XVII

The date: 29th March, 1940.

The place: Savage Gardens, in a City Cellar.

The host: 'Tubby' Ionides.

The guests: Michael Richards, J. Kenyon Gregory, Charles Durrant, J. D. Finch Noyes and A.L.S.

The fare: Chicken Turbot.
Steak and Kidney Pudding.
Blue Cheshire.

The wines: Bâtard-Montrachet 1937.
Corton Charlemagne 1933.
Grands Echézeaux 1929.
Corton 1911.
Romanée St. Vivant 1904.
Hine's 1906, landed in 1907 and bottled in 1939.

Simple fare, simply excellent: the fish flaky and firm, free from all fishiness and suitably gingered up by a Sauce Tartare. The pudding, meaty, unctuous and comforting, its steaming hot message of peace and plenty most welcome below the belt. Yet, good as fish and pudding were, and good also as the Blue Cheshire cheese was, the whole of the limelight was reserved for a wonderful trio of red Burgundies.

Fine wine is so rare and so good that it deserves and repays the compliment of being introduced with some ceremony. With the fish, which blunted the edge of our appetites, two white Burgundies removed all fear that thirst might interfere with the leisurely enjoyment of the princely Reds that were to follow. The first wine, Louis Poirier's 'baby', a 1937 just weaned and bottled, was very pleasing, and showed every sign of living up to the reputation of its elders. Then, coming up one step nearer to the great ones, we had a Corton Charlemagne of 1933, a fine wine with greater bouquet and body than the youngster. And then, in unhurried, dignified order, came the three noble princes of Burgundy, each bringing precious gifts to gladden our hearts. The first, a 1929 Grands Echézeaux, brought the pure gold of perfect balance of wine at the top of its form, the second, a 1911 Corton, the frankincense of its sweet bouquet, and the third, a 1904 Romanée St. Vivant, glorious rubies the brilliance of which age could not dim. A truly wonderful sequence of Burgundies at their best.

(A.L.S.)

XVIII

The date: 25th December, 1941.
The place: Soho.
The hostess: Mademoiselle Chicou d'Argences.
The guests: Forty-three destitute old French men and women.
The fare: Crème de tomates.
               Dindonneau farci à la mode de chez nous; Haricots verts.
               Pêche de mes rêves.
               Café.
The wines: Un doigt de Porto.
               La Piquette de la Cigale.
               Les Cerises de la Fourmi.

Mademoiselle Chicou d'Argences was born in 1858 and she has been an honoured guest at many rich men's tables in her native France as well as in the United

States, where she had once upon a time many friends, most of them dead by now and the others unaware of the fact that she has no income whatever today. Her old ship is at the bottom of the sea but she is not down-hearted! Like the rest of the company on that happy Christmas Day, she still lives and bobs up and down on the choppy sea of misfortune, safe enough on that old raft, the French Benevolent Society in London. And she still has 'le sourire'; she also has 'le mot pour rire'. She was the most lively and delightful hostess imagin-able when she presided over a Déjeuner de Noël, pro-vided by a generous French Restaurateur, who does not wish his name nor that of his restaurant to be mentioned. The restaurant was closed to the public on that occasion and the little band of aged and poor French people, stranded in London, were given a meal such as they had lost all hope ever to enjoy again. The welcoming *Verre de Porto* which awaited them on arrival set everybody at ease and set tongues wagging. Then the steaming hot soup, the chestnut-stuffed turkey and the *haricots verts* tossed in butter were so good that a hush fell upon the babel of tongues whilst jaws were busy. *La Piquette* was unstinted, and what a joy it was for all these old French people to see once again wine in a glass before them; most of them looked at it with moist eyes before drinking it. To be penniless in a strange land and to be given wine when wine is so difficult to buy, even when you are as rich as rich can be! 'Quel miracle!' Toasts began to be drunk before coffee was served, and with the coffee there was another miracle. 'Des Cerises à l'eau-de-vie, ma chère! Tout comme chez ma grand'mère', confided a guest of close upon ninety years to her neighbour. When the com-pany dispersed, not without gentle hints that it was time to be making for home before blackout time, some of the old legs may have been a little less steady than before lunch, but all the hearts were younger. And they all promised the kind host to come again next Christmas, when he took leave of them with '*À l'année prochaine*' as a parting gift. Was there ever a more memorable meal?

A NIGHTMARE LUNCH

An epic lunch—partaken in a dream—
With André Simon and Mr. Neame,
(Maurice Healy of legal fame
And A. J. Symons also came).
Wines and meats and little fishes
Combined to make delicious dishes
To put before these famous men—
Appended is a list of them.

Birds' nest soup and hot hors-d'œuvre
Accompanied by Clicquot (Veuve):
The blending sounds a trifle curious,
Only one guest found it injurious:
Indeed he was so indisposed,
He murmured with his eyes fast closed,
'A this year's bird in last year's nest'—
Then died upon his neighbour's breast.

The chopped-up tails of mountain goats
Pounded with mint and quaker oats,
Proved a very favourite dish
('Twas handed round before the fish).
The trout was cooked in Corton Blanc—
At least one guest burst into song—
Then oysters from the Apennines
Served with a novel blend of wines.

For fear the wine should not go round—
The reasoning was very sound—
A 1919 Montrachet
Was wedded to a 'vin du pays'.
From childhood's days we've learnt to know
Rough with the smooth must always go,
The only comment made was 'Reely!'
It came from Mr. Maurice Healy.

Sausages (Swiss) with cream and spice,
Garnished with snips of edelweiss.
Crocodiles' livers, a dainty rare,
Carefully packed and sent 'by air'.
Caviare served with the port,
Oh, surely an unusual thought,
Proclaimed a genius was the host,
The subject of a special toast.

Epilogue

The guests retired with thankful hearts,
And even fuller other parts.
They were not seen for days and days,
Alas! the gourmet always pays!

(B. P. Metcalfe)

D*

COOKS AND COOKERY BOOKS

THE OLDEST known English cookery book is the one which was written by the Master Cook of King Richard II at the end of the fourteenth century; it has been edited and published in 1791 by the learned Samuel Pegge. A few other books were written in England during the fifteenth and sixteenth century by experts, for princes and noble families, but more importance appears to have been given in those days to etiquette and ceremonial details than to gastronomy as such. A number of other treatises were written by doctors who prescribed for their patients or for the instruction of their pupils; in such books remedies and receipts are often mixed up together in a most surprising manner. These were the books first to be printed, and, to judge from their extreme rarity, they were printed in very limited numbers for the comparatively small number of people who were not only interested in cookery but also able to read. By the time of the Restoration, however, not only was education far more general but many more people showed a lively interest in gastronomy than it had been possible or advisable to show during the austerity days of Cromwell's grim rule. Hence the spate of cookery books issued from English presses at the time, books which have by now become quite rare.

Robert May, who was the son of a cook and a good royalist, was trained in France: he returned with Charles II to London, where he published, in 1660, *The Accomplisht Cook*, because, so he tells us in the preface, 'God and my

Conscience would not permit me to bury these experiences in the grave'. We have his portrait as a frontispiece which is that of a youngish and intelligent man, although there is no deception as regards his age: 'Ætatis Suae 71, 1660' being perfectly legible in the background. Under the portrait the following lines appear:

> What! woulldst thou view but in one face
> all hospitalitie, the race
> of those that for the Gusto stand,
> whose tables a whole Ark command
> of Nature's plentie, wouldst thou see
> this sight, peruse May's booke, tis hee.
>
> Ja. Parry,
> (For Nathaniell Brooke, att the Angell in Cornhill)

In spite of 'his attendance on several Persons of Honour' during his 'fifty years of experience and industry', Robert May had evidently lived in France too long to produce a book likely to be popular in England: his recipes for preparing frogs and snails for the table were not likely to rouse the enthusiasm of conservative Englishmen for these French delicacies.

A far better book was published in London the following year, in 1661, under the title *The whole body of cookery dissected, taught, and fully manifested, Methodically, Artificially, and according to the best tradition of the English, French, Italian, Dutch, etc.* The author, whose name does not appear on the title page, was one William Rabisha, who signs the preface and describes himself as 'Master Cook to many honourable families before and since the wars began, both in this my Native Countrey, and with Embassadors and other Nobles in certain forraign parts'. Some well-meaning but poor rhymster friend of the author contributes a piece of verse beginning with:

Cooks burn your Books, and vail your empty brains;
Put off your feigned Aprons; view the strains
Of this new piece, whose Author doth display
The bravest dish, and shew the nearst way
T''inform the lowest Cook how he may dress,
And make the meanest meat the highest mess.

and ending thus:

'Therefore brave Book, into the world be gone,
Thou vindicates thy Author; fearing none
That ever was or is, or ere shall be,
Find the parallel of thee'.

In the same year, 1661, there was another cookery book
published in London, called *The Ladies Directory*, written by
Hannah Woolley, who was a remarkably precocious child,
if we are to believe her own statement, in the introduction of
another one of her cookery books, 'Before I was fifteen, I
was intrusted to keep a little School, and was the sole Mistress thereof'. In 1664, she published another book, called
The Cook's Guide, or rare Receipts for Cookery, which she
prefaced in these words:

'I would not willingly dye while I live, nor be quite
forgotten when I am dead: therefore have I sent forth
This book, to testifie to the scandalous World that I
do not altogether spend my Time idely.'

In 1666, presumably when a widow, she married one
Francis Challoner, but she retained to the end of her author-
ess' career the name of Hannah Woolley or Wolley, that is
the name of her first husband, whom she had married at the
age of twenty-four. Her best book was the one published in
London in 1670 under the title: *The Queen-like Closet, or
Rich Cabinet: stored with all manner of Rare Receipts for Pre-
serving, Candying and Cookery. Very Pleasant and beneficial to
all Ingenious Persons of the Female Sex*. There is very little
that can be called either original or very helpful in this little

book, but it has a very charming frontispiece which alone makes the book a desirable item for collectors. There are four other editions of the same book; they were published in 1672, 1675, 1681 and 1684.

This indefatigable Hannah brought out in 1672, a new edition in one volume of *The Ladies Directory* and *The Cook's Guide*, with the same frontispiece as that of the 1662 edition of *The Ladies Directory*, but she gave it a new title: *The Ladies Delight*. The book was translated in German and published at Hamburg in 1674.

In 1673, Hannah Woolley published her last and most comprehensive book, a kind of 'know-all' entitled: *The Gentlewomans Companion: or a Guide to the female sex: containing directions of behaviour, in all places, Companies, Relations, and Conditions, from their Childhood down to Old Age*. There were several editions of the book, during the latter part of the seventeenth century, and it was reprinted, in 1711, as a new book altogether, of which nothing was new except the title: *The compleat Gentlewoman*. By that time Hannah Woolley was no more, and Hannah Glasse had not appeared yet.

There were more than a score of cookery books published in London alone during the first half of the eighteenth century, mostly by chefs, such as Henry Howard, who describes himself as 'Free-Cook of London, and late Cook to his Grace the Duke of Ormond, and since to the Earl of Salisbury, and Earl of Winchelsea.' His book was called *England's newest Way*, and it was published in 1703, other editions following in 1708, 1710, and 1726;

T. Hall, also a 'Free-Cook of London', whose *Queen's Royal Cookery*, was published in 1709;

Patrick Lamb, who was 'near 50 years Master-Cook to their late Majesties King Charles II, King James II, King William and Queen Mary, and to her present Majesty

Queen Anne.' This surely must be a record among the royal chefs of all times. His book was called plainly *Royal Cookery;* it was first published in 1710, and other editions followed in 1716, 1726 and 1731;

R. Smith, a pupil of Lamb, who published, in 1723, a *Court Cookery or, the Compleat English Cook;* he describes himself on the title-page as: 'Cook (under Mr. Lamb) to King William: as also to the Dukes of Buckingham, Ormond, D'Aumont (The French Ambassador) and others of the Nobility and Gentry';

John Nott, 'Cook to his Grace the Duke of Bolton', published *The Cook's and Confectioner's Dictionary: Or, The Accomplish'd Housewife's Companion,* in 1723;

Charles Carter, 'lately Cook to his Grace the Duke of Argyll, the Earl of Pontefract, the Lord Cornwallis, etc.', published *The complete practical cook: or, A New System of the Whole Art and Mystery of Cookery,* in 1730, and a shorter book of the same nature, in 1732, under the title *The compleat City and Country Cook;*

Vincent La Chapelle, Chief Cook to the Right Honourable the Earl of Chesterfield, published, in 1733, *The Modern Cook,* in one volume, the second edition of which appeared in 1736 in three volumes fully illustrated;

Henry Howard, in 1734, 'revised and recommended' the *Five Hundred New Receipts* of John Middleton, Cook to His Grace the late Duke of Bolton.

All these and a number of other cookery books apparently met with a fair measure of success since there were several editions called forth in many instances. There were therefore no shortage of cookery books available when, in 1747, yet another cookery book was published anonymously 'By a Lady', under the title of *The Art of Cookery made plain and easy.* The 'lady' disclosed her identity when the second edition appeared in the same year as the first, 1747. She was a Mrs. Hannah Glasse, not a professional cook, but the wife of an attorney residing in Carey Street. It is true that some evil-minded people had spread the rumour that the real author of the book was Dr. Hill, but Boswell tells us that Dr. Johnson refused to believe it and that no shred of evidence had ever been produced in support of the statement. The fact which baffles understanding but must be accepted is that Mrs. Glasse's book was constantly re-published for over a hundred years, the last edition bearing the date of 1852. Today, when *The Art of Cookery made plain and easy* has long been both out of print and out of date, it is still remembered chiefly because of 'First catch your hare', which never was printed in the first nor any of the many subsequent editions of the book. What Mrs. Glasse wrote was 'First case your hare', which meant at the time 'First dress your hare'.

The great popularity of Mrs. Glasse's book did not discourage publishers from accepting cookery books by other authors. On the contrary, the interest in cookery appears to have been stimulated to such an extent that more cookery books than ever came forth year after year, and the majority of them were written by women. Thus, in 1750, Mrs. Fisher, of Richmond, published *The Prudent Housewife*, which she qualified as 'Instruction that relates to the pleasing of the palate, and the preservation of that inestimable Blessing, Health';

In 1753, Mary Johnson, 'for many years a Superintendent of a Lady of Quality's Family in the City of York', published, in London, *The young woman's Companion or the Servant Maid's Assistant*, which ran to six editions. In that same year, Arabella Fairfax's *The Family best friend* was published. In 1754, Sarah Jackson published, in London, *The Director: or, Young Woman's best companion, collected for the use of her own family, and printed at the request of her friends;*

In 1756, *The Ladies Companion or, the Housekeeper's*

Guide was published in London by 'a Gentlewoman who has been a Housekeeper to several noble Families many years'. Her name still is her secret.

More remarkable by far than any of these, there was a Mrs. Raffald who published a book entitled *The Experienced English Housekeeper*, at Manchester, in 1769. It ran to many editions between that date and 1825. Thanks to the *Manchester Collectanea*, published by the Chetham Society, in 1867, we know a good deal about her. She was a Miss Whittaker, of Doncaster, and was housekeeper to the Lady Elizabeth Warburton, of Arley Hall, Cheshire; she married the head gardener, Mr. Raffald; they went to live in Manchester and were blessed with sixteen daughters in eighteen years, but never a son. Mr. Raffald had a florist and seedsman's stand in the market place, whilst Mrs. Raffald kept a confectioner's shop, at the corner of the Old Exchange Alley. There she received pupils whom she taught how to pluck poultry, skin hares, cook them and carve them; also how to make all manner of confectionery. Later she took the Bull's Head Inn in the market place, and ran that so well that the officers of the regiments stationed at Manchester had their mess table at the Bull's Head, and when the Raffalds moved to the King's Head, Salford, the officers' mess moved there too. Mrs. Raffald must have been exceptionally active as well as gifted, for she brought out a *Manchester Directory* for the first time in 1772 and for the last in 1781, in which year she died. Her cookery book was the first to challenge seriously the popularity of Mrs. Glasse's *Art of Cookery*, which had had no real rival during the preceding twenty-two years.

It is highly probable that every man and woman who has published a cookery book has been accused of copying out some recipes out of some other cookery book or books; this is inevitable: it is quite impossible to expect thousands of original and different recipes for boiling an egg or roasting meat, for instance, in the thousands of cookery books which have been published already and those to be published in years to come. Thus, Mrs. Mary Cole, who describes herself as 'Cook to the Right Hon. The Earl of Drogheda', in the preface of her book, *The Lady's Complete Guide: Or Cookery in all its Branches*, published in London, in 1788, roundly accuses Mrs. Glasse, Mrs. Raffald and Mrs. Charlotte Mason of being, like herself, mere compilers of recipes, whilst, she, unlike them, is honest enough to give after each recipe she has 'lifted' the name of the author from whom she has borrowed it. This, after all, is the principle upon which all anthologies are presented to the reading public, and provided the selection is a good one, the anthology serves a useful purpose. But it is difficult—not to say impossible—to find any excuse for passing off one's book under the more popular title of somebody else's book. This is what happened to Mrs. Raffald. A certain Catherine Brooks published, in 1762, a cookery book under the title *The Complete English Cook: Or prudent housewife*, with the following four lines on the title page:

> In cooking Fowl, or Flesh, or Fish,
> Or any nice, or dainty Dish,
> With care peruse this useful Book,
> 'Twill make you soon a perfect Cook.

As a cookery book of the period it is quite a good book, but good books do not always get the reception which they deserve and this book evidently failed to attract public favour since two later editions appeared—and one of them was published at Manchester—under the title *The Experienced English Housekeeper*, the title of Mrs. Raffald's very popular book. To make matters even worse for the collector of cookery books, whilst Mrs. Catherine Brooks was pinching

Mrs. Raffald's title, she was robbed herself of her original title by Ann Peckham—another Ann—of Leeds, 'well known to have been for forty years one of the most noted cooks in the County of York'—as she describes herself. She published several editions, between 1767 and 1790, of a cookery book under the title *The Complete English Cook: or, Prudent Housewife*, which undoubtedly was Catherine Brooks' original property.

Some of the minor or shooting stars to appear in the firmament of cookery book writers during the last thirty years of the eighteenth century were, in order of seniority:

Caroline Butler, 'who has practised Cookery in all its various branches, and in the best Families, upwards, of Thirty Years': *The New London and Country Cook*, c. 1770;

Mrs. Martha Bradley, late of Bath: *The British Housewife: Or, the Cook, Housekeeper's and Gardiner's Companion'*, c. 1770;

Mary Smith, 'late Housekeeper to Sir Walter Blackett, Bart. etc.': *The Complete House-keeper, and Professed Cook*, 1772;

Elizabeth Marshal: *The Young ladies Guide in the art of Cookery*, 1777;

Elizabeth Price: *The New Book of Cookery; or every woman a Perfect Cook*, c. 1780;

Ann Cook, 'teacher of the true art of cookery': *Professed Cookery*, London, c. 1780;

Mrs. Ann Partridge: *The New and Complete Universal Cook*, c. 1780;

Susannah Carter: *The Frugal Housewife: or, Complete Woman Cook*, 1795;

Eliza Melroe: *An Economical and new method of Cookery*, 1798;

Mary Holland: *The Ladies Best Companion: or, A Golden Treasury for the Fair Sex*, 1880.

During the nineteenth century a constant stream of cookery books flowed from English presses, but we do not propose to notice more than three of the most successful among the large number of women who published cookery books: Mrs. Rundell, Miss Elizabeth Acton and Mrs. Beeton.

We know very little about Mrs. Rundell, except that she was born in 1745 and died in 1828; also that she was the author of an anonymous book called *A New System of Domestic Cookery; Formed upon Principles of Economy, and adapted to the use of Private Families. By a Lady.* The earliest recorded edition is dated 1807, whilst the 65th edition came out in 1841 and an amended edition was published as recently as 1893. It was by far the most popular cookery book in England during the second, the third and part of the fourth decades of the nineteenth century; and not in England only: it was also very popular in the United States. The third edition published in Philadelphia was dated 1810; the first New York edition appeared in 1814 and others followed up to 1869. It was also published in Baltimore in 1819. According to the preface of her book, Mrs. Rundell did not intend to publish it at first, having written it for the private instruction of her daughters (there is no record as to their numbers as in the case of Mrs. Raffald), in their married homes; she declares that she was persuaded to publish her notes in book form but that it had not been written for professional cooks nor with any idea of pecuniary gain. However, it must have proved a little gold mine until the appearance of Eliza Acton's *Modern Cookery in all its Branches*, which was first published in 1845, in London, and had reached its 14th edition by 1854. Eliza Acton's success proved that in all arts, the art of cookery included, the amateur has as good a chance to attain fame as the professional: she was not a cook, nor a housekeeper, nor an innkeeper, nor even a housewife; she was a poetess whose poems had a very small number of readers whilst her cookery book was a best seller during full twenty years, that is until Mrs. Beeton's *Book of Household Management* had established itself as the greatest classic among modern English Cookery Books.

Eliza Beeton was born in 1840 and died in 1869: if one compares what she achieved in so short a life, she deserves to be placed at the head of all the Englishwomen who helped others to be better cooks and enjoy cooking. She married a publisher, Samuel Orchardt Beeton; she was beautiful, a good cook, a clever journalist, and accomplished musician and a devoted wife and mother: she died at twenty-nine, yet her name liveth still and cookery books are still being published under her name.

Two English women, born during the latter part of the nineteenth century who became famous as cooks in the twentieth, deserve a few words of grateful recognition here: Florence White and Rosa Lewis. Both have told us their own stories, Florence in *A Fire in the Kitchen: the Autobiography of a Cook*, published by Dent, in 1938; Rosa in a series of interviews, recorded by Mary Lawton, and published in 1925 by Boni and Liveright, of New York, under the title *The Queen of Cooks—and some Kings* (The Story of Rosa Lewis).

Florence White was a school mistress, a journalist, a traveller and an artist before becoming a professional cook, during the first world war. She wrote *Good Things in England, Flowers as Food*, and other books, and she founded the English Folk Cookery Association. She learnt not only how to cook but to love cooking from her mother and when forty years of age, in 1903, she went to Paris where she spent every spare afternoon at the Cordon Bleu, in the Faubourg St. Honoré, attending not the classes for 'ladies' but those for professional cooks.

> My education in cookery was progressing side by side with my academic education, and this is as it should be. The renaissance of learning in Italy went hand in hand with the renaissance of good cookery.

When the first world war broke out, in 1914, Florence White was engaged to teach in an English school, but she gave up teaching in 1915 because, she tells us herself:

> It seemed to me that now was the time to act up to what I had always preached, that is, that no occupation was so good as domestic service, and no service so valuable to the nation as good cooking. It was up to me to show that I really believed what I had said and written, and could prove its truth. Accordingly I went to two servants' registry offices and entered my name as a woman of fifty-two, who could cook well and wanted a situation as working cook-housekeeper in a house where a young girl was kept, and I added that I preferred to be housekeeper to bachelor gentlemen.

She was offered and she accepted a situation as working cook-housekeeper to a Catholic priest, in a large but very poor parish, with two assistant priests.

> It was here that I first began to realize the full value of good food and cookery. All these priests worked very hard, and they couldn't possibly have done their duty properly if they had not been properly fed and had a happy, comfortable, peaceful home to which they could return and rest, beginning again refreshed. I honestly felt that in looking after them I was not merely attending to the fire in the kitchen, but that I had a share in the sermons they preached, the parish work they did, and the comfort they gave to the sick and

sorrowful. It is true my work was like the seed sown in the earth, hidden and unnoticed, but it was very well worth doing. I began to wish every girl and woman could realize what a fine vocation domestic service is. I saw that it was the finest national service one could possibly render, whether in peace or war.

Her health, which never was really good, was responsible for enforced periods of rest which became more and more frequent as she grew older, but she never changed her mind as regards the value and interest of cooking.

'The longer I live,' she writes in the last chapter of her biography, 'the more convinced I become that the home and its work are the most important, as well as the most interesting, things in life, and the kitchen fire the hub of the universe, far more important than any mere parliamentary vote, which might well be left to men.' She was then seventy-four years of age, an unrepentant Victorian, with oldfashioned views on sex equality, perhaps, but there is no denying her crystal clear sincerity when she declares that she has had wonderful happiness in serving others, adding: 'There is nothing in the world to equal it, and it isn't as if I have never known worldly pleasures. As a journalist I have done every worldly social thing that was worth doing, and a few that were not!'

Florence White was not merely a good cook; she had that much greater and rarer gift of attracting disciples, making converts and passing on to others her enthusiasm and knowledge. She said that she never knew a girl really dislike cooking if she were given a chance of learning from a teacher who loved her job, and she was convinced that there was much culinary talent wasted in England because its existence was not suspected.

Rosa Lewis was a very different kind of woman and it may be said that she was a cook all her life, since she tells us that she was a general servant at the tender age of twelve, in a small suburban villa, and at thirteen washer-up and kitchen maid at Sheen House, the Comte de Paris' residence at Mortlake. It was there, she also tells us, that she learnt to think 'that it was not a stupid thing to cook. I saw', she adds, 'that the aristocracy took an interest in it, and that you came under the notice of someone that really mattered. It struck me that it was far more interesting than a factory life; that you were not just one of a number of sausages! I saw that they took an interest in me, their chefs and other people. I picked up what I could there—I taught myself. I worked every spare moment—I helped everybody else, and by helping everybody else I helped myself, because I picked the brains of the other people, and what they had got I soon got, so between the two I made a wonderful success.'

Rosa Ovenden, as she was then, was the only English person in the kitchens of the Comte de Paris, and that of his son, the Duc d'Orléans, at Sandhurst, and although everybody was very kind to her she knew that there was no chance whatever of her being given the position of chef, so she left and began her very successful career as working cook and caterer in the West End of London. Lady Randolph Churchill, Winston's mother, one of London's greatest hostesses during the 'Nineties, was one of the first to recognize and use Rosa Lewis' genius for cooking, and whatever her own servants might think of it, Lady Randolph must have Rosa to cook the dinner whenever Edward VII, then Prince of Wales, honoured her with his presence, as well as on other important occasions. Other fashionable hostesses naturally followed Lady Randolph Churchill's lead, and Rosa was soon the most sought after cook in London. If we wish to know how and why she became so great a favourite, we only have to listen to her own words:

I used to go—when I first started catering—at six in the morning. In those days I used to make the bread, the rolls and the salt sticks—buy everything and do everything in the house for ten pounds or ten shillings—anything they liked to give me. I cooked because I loved to cook—the money didn't matter.

What I have always done (which no other cook ever does) is to cook the potatoes, and the beans, and the asparagus *myself*. I do not give these to the char-woman or to the scullery maid—or a person without brains—because they are more expensive than the meat, and more essential than anything else in the dinner. I would take more trouble with the cabbage than most people would with a chicken. I would take trouble with the chicken, of course, but would not take trouble to chop it up or decorate it. I can't waste time on stuff that is not going to be used. If it is a chicken, you want it to taste like a chicken—you don't want it to taste like a rabbit or a duck; if you have asparagus you must have asparagus, but you must have all these perfectly cooked and treated just the same way as if they were gold; and no cook in England understands this—they give the vegetables to the last person who comes into the house to ruin. That has been one of the reasons of my success—not to mess things up.

Perhaps the greatest compliment that was ever paid to Rosa Lewis was when she was asked, in December, 1899, to run the kitchen of White's Club, which she did for a few months, until she acquired the Cavendish Hotel, in Jermyn Street. It was also about then that she married a Mr. Lewis, whom she divorced some ten years later. It was the one and only failure in her highly successful and colourful life. She tells us:

In those days, I had twelve girls in my kitchens, all experienced girls. All their photographs were in the *Daily Sketch*. I would take the entire staff with me for these dinners, the food prepared as far as possible at the hotel, and would finish off at the various houses where I was catering. I would go to a house and take entire charge of the kitchen, and none of their own servants were there. I took *full* charge. I had complete authority —as though it were my own house, like a general in command. We used to take all our own pots and pans and dishes, and so forth—gilt chairs, washers-up, carvers, everything taken from here, the hotel, to wherever the dinner was. The cold dishes and so forth would be prepared here and taken down cold, and kept till wanted. The hot dishes were taken in hot boxes, and oftentimes I supplied the waiters, the wines and the flowers, too, if wanted. In addition, I used to go away for week-end parties, to take charge of the kitchen, and would take two or three of these girls with me to the country. In those days we used to have a lot of people send their cooks to me to learn cooking.

Rosa had certainly made a wonderful success of her professional life and we must not forget that she started from scratch if ever a cook did, a poor slavey at twelve to some obscure suburban family. No Cordon Bleu school for her, but what her wits enabled her to pick up when she chanced to be taken in the kitchen of the Comte de Paris at thirteen. She had brains, of course, and intense vitality, and she had some original notions about good cooking. We may or we may not agree with her always, but even when she fails to be convincing she always is entertaining. Only one more quotation: 'Some people's food always tastes better than others, even if they are cooking the same dish at the same dinner. Now I will tell you why—because one person has much more life in them—more fire, more vitality, more guts—than others. A person without these things can never make food taste right, no matter what materials you give them, it is no use. Turn in the whole cow full of cream instead of milk, and all the fresh butter and ingredients in the world, and still that cooking will taste dull and flabby—just because they have nothing in *themselves* to give. You have got to throw *feeling* into your cooking.'

These two highly intelligent Englishwomen, as different in education and mentality as it is possible to be, not only were good cooks both, but loved cooking and believed that there was no greater nor any better profession. May their example be a tonic for those today who cook because they must: let them try Rosa Lewis's tip: 'throw feeling into your cooking.'

CARÊME

Marie-Antoine Carême was born in June 1783, in Paris, Rue du Bac, in the gutter, the sixteenth child of an itinerant stonemason.

He died in Paris, in 1833, the most illustrious chef of the nineteenth century, having known and served Napoleon I, George IV, the Emperor of Russia, and a host of illustrious people in Paris, London, Vienna and St. Petersburg.

He cooked and he taught, and he left at his death a number of books on cooking and the art of good living which have been a source of inspiration for cooks and all students of the art of good living during the last hundred years.

His writings are signed *Antonin Carême de Paris*, and there is every reason to believe that Antonin was the name by which he was known during his life, and not Marie-Antoine, the name given him at birth.

Carême was a true apostle. Apostles cannot be beaten. They have great confidence in themselves and greater confidence still in their cause. They know no fear, no defeat. They must win.

Carême was not yet ten years of age when he was turned out of home, in 1792, the year One of the Republic and of the Guillotine, the year of Valmy and Jemappes, a year of famine and glory for France, when poor and poorest alike—there were no rich left—were all but starving, all but hapless Louis in his prison, who had lost his kingdom and was soon to lose his life, but who never lost his royal appetite.

In the autumn of 1792, on the threshold of one of the blackest winters ever known, 'Go,' said Carême senior to Marie-Antoine, 'go and fare thee well, my child. The world is large; chances are many. Leave us to our squalid poverty; it is our lot; die we must as we have lived; penniless. But this is an age of quick fortunes; there are splendid opportunities for all who, like thee, have a ready wit!'

A strange speech, indeed, for an unemployed, itinerant mason to make to his barely fledged sixteenth child when pushing him off the nest. But they were strange times.

Marie-Antoine left; he wandered about in search of food and shelter and found both. A man who kept a modest eating-house in the Rue du Maine, close to where the Gare Montparnasse now stands, gave Marie-Antoine his first start in life as boy of all work. During six years, six of the most fateful years in the history of France, young Carême slaved away for his master, washing, serving, sweeping, fetching and watching until old enough to do some of the cooking also.

In 1798 Marie-Antoine left the Montparnasse Quarter, crossed the Seine, and offered his services as pastrycook apprentice to Monsieur Bailly, the fashionable pastrycook of the day, in the Rue Vivienne.

Bailly was kind to young Carême, who was ever after deeply grateful to him. 'I shall never forget', he wrote, 'how kind this good Monsieur Bailly was to me and how he gave me time to go to the Cabinet des Gravures, where I taught myself drawing. But he did even more for me when he entrusted me with the making of the *Pièces Montées* which his clients ordered, for of what use would all my drawings have been had it not been for the opportunities given me of making them in confectionery and being then able to judge of their looks and appeal? All these first *Grosses Pièces* were much to everybody's taste and I could not have had greater encouragement. I was indeed greatly attached to this highly respectable man who was the first to give me the means of becoming proficient in my profession.'

Carême remained with Monsieur Bailly nearly four years, four important years during which he was taught all about the handling of sugar and fish-glue, and taught himself drawing and the rudiments of architecture. It was only then, strange to say, that he also taught himself to read and write. His chief object in doing so, he tells us himself, was to read cookery books, but when he was able to read, great was his disappointment at the existing cookery books: they were of so little help to him that he made up his mind there and then to fill the gap himself and write books that would be really helpful for the young cooks of generations to come.

Carême's love for elaborate table decorations, sugar ships in full sail, or marzipan Greek temples, which must have cost considerable time and labour, appears to us out of all proportion to their gastronomic or ornamental worth. There is something childish in making our edibles pictorial, but Carême did not introduce the taste for table structures: it was a legacy from the *ancien régime;* he inherited it, accepted it and improved it. Thus, in *Kettner's Book of the Table*, we read that 'Horace Walpole describes how in the last century the Intendant of Gascony gave a magnificent banquet on the birth of the Duke of Burgundy. The centre-piece was covered with wax figures moved by clockwork, which at the conclusion of the feast were set in motion, and gave a representation of the labour of the Dauphiness and the happy birth of an heir to the monarchy. He also tells an anecdote of Lord Albemarle's cook in this country, who prepared a middle dish of gods and goddesses 18 ft. high, and complained bitterly because Lord Albemarle would not demolish the ceiling of his dining-room for the gorgeous structure. In the previous century an English cook, Robert

May, contrived an astonishing trophy—a ship with
guns charged with veritable powder, and a castle of
pies full of live frogs and birds. After the guns were
fired the ladies were directed to take eggshells full of
perfume and throw them at each other, "to sweeten the
stink of powder". Then the lids were to be removed
from the castle of pies; the frogs would jump out,
making the ladies shriek; the birds would fly forth,
putting out the candles; and nobody knows what kisses
and struggles and pretty adventures might happen
when the lights were out. When the candles were lit
again, the company might proceed to the more serious
business of mastication.'

There flourished in Paris, at the same time as Bailly,
Carême's master, a remarkable man, Beauvilliers, who
was the first to open a restaurant as we understand it
today, a well-appointed establishment where one can
enjoy a well-cooked meal and good wine in comfort, in
pleasing surroundings, and being waited upon by a
well-trained staff.

Until Beauvilliers' advent, one used to invite one's
friends to one's house, where there was no question as
to one's cook being able to supply an excellent soup,
a fair entrée and a good *rôti*. To do honour to distinguished guests, however, the host had to send to some
pâtissier of repute for Entremets, Dessert, Glaces,
Pâtisserie or *Pièces Montées*, those ornamental structures of biscuit, lard or sugar, which made the reputation of the young Carême.

Beauvilliers ridiculed all those masterpieces of
picturesque ruins made of lard and Grecian sugar
statuary which Carême called to the end of his life
l'ornement de la cuisine. He wrote in the *Pâtissier Royal*
that his art supplied the necessary food for mind and
heart and filled pleasurably the leisure of modern
gastronomes. *Le sucre porte à la couleur* is another of
Carême's dictates. To which Beauvilliers replied that
the cook's job was not to please the eye but the palate;
not to fill one's leisure but one's belly pleasurably.

'Beauvilliers and Carême may be taken as representative men at the head of two opposite schools of cookery, which have been playfully described by Mr. Hayward as the classical and romantic. "Having spoken," says Mr. Hayward, "of Beauvilliers and Carême as chiefs of two rival schools of art, we may naturally be expected to distinguish them. We should say that Beauvilliers was more remarkable for judgment and Carême for invention—that Beauvilliers exhausted the old world of art and Carême discovered a new one—that Beauvilliers rigidly adhered to the unities and Carême snatched a grace beyond them—that there was more *aplomb* in the touch of Beauvilliers, more curious felicity in Carême's—that Beauvilliers was great in an entrée and Carême sublime in an entremet—that we would bet Beauvilliers against the world for a *rôt*; but should wish Carême to prepare the sauce were we under the necessity of eating up an elephant or our grandfather." (*Kettner's Book of the Table.*)

When Carême had served his term of apprenticeship with Monsieur Bailly, he was sorely tempted to open a restaurant of his own in competition with that of Beauvilliers, but he thought better of it and decided for the much less hazardous task of giving his services to anybody willing to pay for them when entertaining at home.

On the morrow of the Revolution there must have been a great dearth of chefs. Many had followed their aristocratic masters in exile; some had lost their heads on the scaffold, and others had found safety in the rural retreat of their native village. With the Directoire, the Consulat, and much more with the pageantry of the Empire, great chefs came forth, none greater than Carême himself, who were eagerly sought after to *faire des extras*, to prepare dinners *à domicile*.

'In 1802, I was earning quite a lot of money,' Carême wrote later, 'a better proof than all the compliments paid me, that there was in my work something original which pleased and upon which was built my reputation.'

From 1803 until the final exit of Napoleon, in 1815, Carême was the acknowledged master in the art of confectionery, a great artist in sugar, young as he was, and one possessed of a rare power of organization and spectacular display.

Carême has been described as chef to the Prince de Talleyrand during those twelve years, from 1803 to 1815, but he was not. He was Pâtissier, not Cuisinier, pastrycook not chef, not yet. Talleyrand's chef during that period was named Boucher, and it was thanks to Boucher that Carême, Talleyrand's Pâtissier, became one of the world's greatest cuisiniers. When he published the first edition of his *Pâtissier Royal* in 1815, Carême described himself as *Chef pâtissier des grands extraordinaires*, and such was his true title.

There is no doubt that Carême was attached in some capacity or other to Talleyrand's establishment from his twentieth until his thirty-second year, and it is probable that it was owing to this that Napoleon's recruiting sergeants never appear to have troubled him. But it is no less certain that he must have been free to serve other masters at the same time. It is probable that Talleyrand had a prior claim upon Carême's services, whenever he was giving an important dinner, but that he could not, or did not, object to Carême being called to organize or supervise banquets and receptions given by other princes or diplomats, by State officials or foreign potentates.

Carême, in his letter to Lady Morgan, published as an Introduction to his *Art de la Cuisine Française au Dix-neuvième Siècle*, gives her details of Cambacérès' miserly ways as a would-be amphytrion and makes it quite clear that he is not speaking from hearsay but from personal knowledge, adding: 'Mes travaux d' extra m'ont mis à même de travailler dans toutes les grandes maisons de l'Empire'.

But none of the 'Extras', Carême's chief work at the

time, gave him the same pride and pleasure as those of the Prince de Talleyrand. He tells us so himself: 'The finest *extras*, the most perfect that I have seen are the great dinners served in the magnificent gallery of the Foreign Office, which were given by His Highness the Prince de Talleyrand. That was ever the most excellently served table . . . and no other *extra* can ever bear comparison with those of that splendid gallery.' Somewhere else, Carême writes that 'the Minister for Foreign Affairs (Talleyrand) is the sanctuary of modern cooking', and in 1815, writing to Boucher, who was Talleyrand's chef for twenty-five years, Carême says: 'It is because of my co-operation during the last twelve years, under your auspices, to the splendid dinners given by His Excellency to ambassadors, that I made rapid progress in my art.'

Carême's co-operation was chiefly the *ornement de la cuisine*, sugar-and-glue castles and ships, but being remarkably intelligent and ambitious, he took full advantage of the extraordinary chances given him to learn, learning so quickly that he was soon able to teach others.

In 1814, and again in 1815, Carême was Chef des Cuisines of Alexander, Emperor of Russia, in Paris, at Vertus, near Châlons, where the Emperor entertained on a magnificent scale on the occasion of his birthday and at the Congress of Aix-la-Chapelle. The Emperor wanted Carême to come to St. Petersburg, but Carême, who had left his native Paris for the first time, was already homesick and declined the flattering offer of the Emperor Alexander.

On 5th July, 1815, a banquet of 1,200 *couverts* was given in the great gallery of the Louvre to celebrate the return of Louis XVIII. The twelve tables, groaning under ornaments and victuals, each seating one hundred 'warriors', was a magnificent sight in the eyes of Carême, who gives minute details of the feast in Vol. II (pp. 87 *et seq.*) of his *Maître d'Hôtel Français*. There were one hundred cooks lodged for the occasion in the Louvre, and Carême, a born artist, could not help admire the magnificent carved wood ornaments of the ceiling in the apartment which was given him to use as a kitchen.

Vatel's tragedy came very near to being re-enacted on that 5th July, 1815. Some criminal purveyor failed to send the correct weight of fish-glue ordered, which was bad enough, but he failed to warn Carême, which was far worse. The result was that Carême's jellies were known to wobble for the first and last time in his life.

The following year, on 12th February, 1816, a ball was given at the Odéon to 6,000 people. Carême never had had such a chance of showing the world what an artist he was as an architect as well as a cook. He had a splendid buffet erected, with nine wide rising shelves, and he gives in his *Maître d'Hôtel* the full list of all the cold dishes, pastries and jellies which stood on that monumental stand, all according to size and colour, a sight to melt the heart of all men and women of feeling. Alas! a terrible thing happened on that night. The king and the royal party watched the dancing from the Royal Box whilst Carême, presumably, was watching his buffet. But no sooner had the king and the royal party left the Odéon than a rush was made for the buffet, and in no time it was reduced to a very sorry sight indeed. Jellies did not wobble—they disappeared altogether, and for ever.

It was soon after this gargantuan affair that the Prince Regent sent to Paris a trusted friend in search of the best French chef willing to come to England. The Prince's emissary asked the Frères Robert, two brothers who owned the most famous Paris restaurant of the day: they named Carême as *facile princeps*. Louis XVIII's brother, the future Charles X, was then consulted and his own chef summoned, who endorsed the choice of the brothers Robert. Would Carême accept and leave France? He had declined the offer of the Emperor of Russia a year before, but he

E

accepted the Regent's offer and arrived at Carlton House in time to prepare the banquet given in honour of Grand Duke Nicholas, the Emperor of Russia's brother. However, Carême was not destined to remain long in England. The Prince Regent was particularly gracious to his French chef, if we are to credit Carême's own accounts of his informal conversations with his royal master, but Carême wanted to come back to Paris: he was homesick, and he left London early in 1817 for Paris.

He had only been a few weeks in Paris when Lord Charles Stewart, who was on his way from London to Vienna, where he was to attend the Peace Congress as British Ambassador to the Austrian Court, asked him to accompany him to Vienna and Carême accepted. He returned to Paris in 1818 and went to Russia, at his own expense, he tells us, in 1819. He spent the summer of 1819 at St. Petersburg and returned to Paris before going to Vienna again, where Lord Charles Stewart was still apparently willing to welcome his wandering chef.

In 1820, Lord Collingham came to Paris commissioned by George IV to offer Carême £500 a year, fifteen days of rest and freedom in every month and a pension for life if he would come back to London. Carême refused. The 'pension for life' made him fear that he was expected to give up his native land for ever. His health was failing and he was very anxious to complete the series of works on cooking which he had undertaken. He refused George IV's offer, tempting as it was, and accepted the offer of the Baronne de Rothschild to be her chef and remain in Paris. It was to be his last place; he died in 1833, at the age of fifty, never having had any holidays, never having played any games, never having saved money, but having during his short life learnt much and taught more. He certainly was an artist and he also had a spark of that divine gift we call genius, the intuition and enthusiasm which alone achieve lasting results.

He certainly had the apostolic as opposed to the mercenary spirit. Food and drink meant little to him, but he was all his life anxious to increase other people's appreciation of food and to improve its preparation so that it might give greater pleasure and be more profitable; last, but by no means least, he was bent upon helping all cooks who were to come after him to be masters of their art and, as such, deserve and secure both respect and rewards.

Apostles are men of action: rarely men of letters. Only one of the Twelve was also an Evangelist. Carême was certainly a man of action: he was also an Evangelist. At any rate, the Gospel of Good Living, in several volumes—*Le Pâtissier Royal, Le Pâtissier Pittoresque, Le Maître d'Hôtel Français, Le Cuisinier Parisien, L'Art de la Cuisine Française au Dix-neuvième Siècle*, have gone into the world under the name of Carême. Whether or not Carême had the benefit of Dardant's, Fayot's—some even mention Balzac's—literary assistance, his books are full of his own culinary knowledge, of his philosophy of the table and of his own interesting personality, sometimes childishly vain-glorious, but, because of its obvious sincerity, never offensive.

PROSPER MONTAGNÉ (1865-1948)

Prosper Montagné died at Sèvres, near Paris, on 22nd April, 1948, in his eighty-third year. Born at Carcassonne, and a typical little Frenchman of the Midi, quick-witted and quick-tempered, an indefatigable worker and a pugnacious fighter, he was also a great artist and an even greater apostle. Which is why he died a poor man, as all must who live to give, and to share with others the faith that is in them. Prosper Montagné was proud of the fact that ever since 1545, which was as far back as he could trace his ancestors, there had always been among them some *aubergistes, traiteurs* or *maîtres-bouchers*. His own father, however,

had a drapery shop, at Carcassonne, when Prosper
was born, but his heart was not in it : he used to
put up the shutters with the notice '*Fermé pour
cause de Cassoulet*', whenever he wanted to prepare
and enjoy in peace this favourite dish of his. Whether
his father gave up the shop or the shop gave up his
father, Prosper was too young to remember when the
family moved to Toulouse and settled in a very ancient
hotel, the Hôtel des Quatre Saisons, where Prosper had
his first taste of work in the kitchen. It was not at all
to his liking; his ambition at the time was to be a
painter, and he managed to rig up a kind of studio at
the top of the hotel: callers were few, but they must
have been duly impressed by the Latin inscription and
the self-granted coat-of-arms which the budding artist
had painted on the door: '*Aspice Prosperus Montagne
pictor coquusque*', whilst a rampant saucepan, knives,
forks and spoons were displayed escutcheon-wise.

The Hôtel des Quatre Saisons was not a financial
success and Prosper soon had to fend for himself. He
first of all worked for a Toulouse *pâtissier*, then for a
relative of his father's, who owned the Hôtel d'Angle-
terre, at Cauterets; then, in Paris, for a short while until
called back to Toulouse for his *service militaire*. During
the three years which he had to serve in the army,
although he did not rise in rank, he nevertheless rose
from colonel's cook to chef of the Brigadier, then of
the Divisional Commander, and finally of the Corps
Commander.

It was only after he had been demobbed that he had
the good fortune to come under the direction of one of
the best chefs of the nineties in France, M. Giroix,
who was in charge of the kitchens of the Casino de
Luchon during the summer, and of those of the Grand
Hôtel, Monte Carlo, during the rest of the year. Giroix
was the first chef to introduce Prosper Montagné to
La Grande Cuisine, and also to fire his enthusiasm for
it. But the disciple very soon staggered his master and
all the older chefs who had been brought up in the
Carême tradition and still clung to the *décor* of the table,

the *socles*, *bordures*, *attelets*, all manner of wax, mutton
fat and silver ornaments, the cost of which, in skilled
labour and time, was very great, and their food value
absolutely nil. Prosper Montagné began then and went
on writing profusely and vehemently in the most widely
read French culinary magazine, *L'Art culinaire*, plead-
ing ardently for greater simplicity in the preparation
and service of perfectly cooked dishes, arguing that
whatever was brought into the dining-room should be
artistically displayed and made to look its best, but
that every inch of the dish should be given to *food* and
not *décor*. Escoffier, who was nearly twenty years older
than Prosper, and who had published, in 1885, *Les
Fleurs de cire*, of which a second edition appeared in 1892
and a third in 1902, was quite indignant that this
youngster, merely *sous-chef* of the Grand Hôtel,
Monte Carlo, should have the audacity of laying down
the law and pretending to modernize the technique of
the kitchen. Philéas Gilbert, the then acknowledged
master of the decorative art in the kitchen, was at first
equally hostile, but he had the good sense to recognize
that the young Prosper was right, and his was also the
self-imposed and difficult task to convince his friend
Escoffier, that they should both back Montagné and
adopt his views—which they did.

Montagné's book, *La Grande Cuisine illustrée*, which
he wrote in collaboration with Prosper Salles, his friend
and chief at the Grand Hôtel, Monte Carlo, was published by Flammarion in Paris in 1900. Its authors
approached from an entirely new angle the art of the
Cuisine, claiming that the basis of all good cooking
must be good taste and common sense, and not mere
fancy and make-believe. Montagné believed and never
tired of repeating that sauces and garnishes were not
meant to camouflage, cover, hide, or make acceptable,
fish or flesh or whatever the food was which they
sauced or garnished; their function, he claimed, was
to help and not to hide, to add to the flavour, taste, or
consistency of the food which they adorned, and to do
it discreetly.

Soon after the publication of this, the first of his more important books, Prosper Montagné left Monte Carlo and was chef at the Restaurant Ledoyen and at the Pavillon d'Armenonville, in Paris, and, after a short spell in Brussels, during the Centenary Exhibition, he took charge of the kitchens of the Grand Hôtel, Paris, where he remained until 1907.

He then gave up professional cooking and much of his time was devoted to the *Société technique de l'alimentation*, of which he was one of the founders, and to the organization of various culinary exhibitions. He also did much to improve catering conditions in the French Army, at the request of the then French Minister of War, and he published two culinary guides for the feeding of men in barracks and in the field. This work became more absorbing as well as more important during the First World War, at the end of which the French War Office sent him to the U.S.A. to find out whether there was anything to be learnt from American catering methods.

In 1920, a group of capitalists who admired the professional ability of Prosper Montagné and his disinterestedness, offered to finance a restaurant where he could practise what he had preached for so long in his books and the many articles he had written for all sorts of journals and magazines. Montagné accepted, and presently gastronomes from every part of the civilized world repaired to the Rue de l'Échelle, off the Avenue de l'Opéra, Paris, to Montagné, Traiteur. There never was better food nor better service anywhere in Paris, but it was a case of *la mariée est trop belle:* Montagné served neither *grillades* nor *fritures*, none but the finest classical dishes, lovingly *cuisinés* by his chef, Maurice Magisson, and vetted by Montagné himself before being served. Everybody did go *Chez Montagné:* it was a *must*. Everybody who went was enchanted, and would not have missed it for anything, but the memory of such wonderful meals was quite enough for most people to cherish, and they did not go again for quite a long time, if they ever went again. By 1927 Prosper Montagné had lost every penny he had ever saved, and he had to sell his beloved collection of cookery books, to pay for the mistake he made when he decided to give nothing but the best. He was penniless but by no means broken-hearted, and he managed to live very simply and quite contentedly on the moderate income brought in by his books, his articles in the press and his lectures. In 1934, when I started the magazine *Grandgousier*, I asked Montagné to be responsible for the culinary articles published in it, which he was, right up to the time of his death.

It was also at about the same time that M. André, one of the most important dealers in Burgundy wines, acquired the famous Paris restaurant La Rôtisserie de la Reine Pédauque, and he asked Prosper Montagné to be his *conseiller culinaire*, a post which the veteran chef held to the end of his days.

Prosper Montagné never was hailed as *Emperor of Chefs* by the Kaiser, nor called the *King of Chefs* by Edward VII, nor saluted as *Officier dans l'Ordre National de la Légion d'Honneur*, as Escoffier was, but it would be a grave mistake to label him a failure because he amassed no riches and received few honours. The fortune that he has left to us all, and to the generations that will come after us, is indeed very great: one has only to look at the list of the books which we owe to him to realize that his name shall live and be honoured whenever and wherever there will be men and women of good taste to appreciate the art of good living.

(Dr. A. Gottschalk)

A LIST OF SOME BOOKS BY PROSPER MONTAGNÉ

La Grande Cuisine illustrée, en collaboration avec Prosper Salles.
Bonne chère pas chère, ou La cuisine sans viande.
Le Manuel du cuistot et de la bonne ménagère.

La cuisine militaire en garnison, en collaboration avec
Philéas Gilbert.
La cuisine militaire en manœuvres et en campagne, en
collaboration avec Philéas Gilbert.
La cuisine diététique.
Le petit bréviaire des gourmands, en collaboration avec
Auguste Escoffier et Philéas Gilbert.
Le Grand Livre de la Cuisine, en collaboration avec
Prosper Salles.
Le festin occitan.
Les délices de la table.
Le Larousse Gastronomique, avec la collaboration du
Dr. Gottschalk. Préface de A. Escoffier et Philéas
Gilbert.
300 *Recettes culinaires, pour MON MENU,* par Dr.
Gottschalk.
Recettes modernes, added to the latest edition of Gouffé's
Livre de cuisine.

THE WORLD'S OLDEST COOKERY BOOK

The first printed cookery book is the 1474 edition of
J. B. Platina, but it is by no means the oldest cookery
book in the world. Platina himself was no professional
cook; he was the Vatican Librarian and a gifted amateur
in matters pertaining to gastronomy, whose book was
merely an adaptation of *The Art of Cookery,* written by
Maestro Martino, Master Cook to the Patriarch of
Aquileia, a manuscript of eighty-six leaves written in
medieval Italian, which has now arrived in Chicago,
the most highly treasured manuscript in my collection.
But even Maestro Martino's book is modern when
compared to the *De Re Culinaria* of Celius Apicius, the
fons et origo of both ancient and modern cookery.
Whoever wrote Apicius' treatise we do not know and
it is immaterial; it certainly was not Apicius himself,
a rich epicure who lived in Rome under the reigns of
Augustus and Tiberius, during the first century of the
Christian era, when the power and the cookery of Rome

were at their zenith. I am inclined to believe that the ten Books of the Apicius which have reached us are really Greek monographs upon different aspects of cookery—Athaeneus speaks of such—each one of them having retained its original Greek title, but with a number of recipes and interpolations introduced by different Roman cooks in the course of the ages. The fact that some of the recipes were given the names of Vitellius, Trajanus and Commodus, just as we still name new dishes after Melba or Princess Marina, proves that the *De Re Culinaria* was added to long after the death of the last Apicius known to history, M. Gabius Apicius.

The two oldest Apicius manuscripts (Vatican Urb. Lat. 1146 and Cheltenham, Bibl. Phillipps, 275, now in New York) are both of the ninth century and refer to an earlier one at Fulda, now lost. The original Apicius manuscript was certainly more complete than the ten books which have reached us, and we have a proof of this in the thirty-two excerpts from Apicius by one Vinidarius, in the Codex Salmasianus (Paris, Bibl. Nat. Lat. 10318) dating back to the fifth century and not included in the ninth-century copies.

The bibliographical interest of the oldest cookery book in the world is considerable, but greater still, in my own estimation, is its gastronomical value, its professional merit as a guide to the preparation of food. Many have been the Latin editions of Apicius and it has been translated into different languages, although never into English until I set myself the task of translating it, but the learned men who have hitherto edited Apicius, good Latinists as they undoubtedly were, had no technical knowledge of cookery and kitchenry. Their knowledge of Latin may have been, and probably was, greater than mine, but I venture to think that none could have done what I did, and that is not only translate Apicius but prepare, cook and taste the majority of the recipes given in the oldest cookery book in the world. Of course, some of the recipes are wholly

E*

unintelligible, probably due to faulty copying or mutila-
tions; the majority of the directions given, however,
are perfectly clear and eminently sound. Quite a
number of Apician recipes are still in constant use in
the south of Italy, in Provence and as far north as the
Baltic; typical Jewish cookery is full of them, and many
very modern dishes have merely been rediscovered
by cooks who have never heard of Apicius.

The Romans had the pastures, woodlands, rivers
and seas which supply us with table necessaries and
delicacies. They had quite as much common sense as
we have to make the best use of all Nature's gifts. They
had or made time and they certainly had the advantage
over us in the matter of labour. They excelled in vegetables and sea-food. They knew all about mineral salts
and how to save them. Let us take cabbage as an
example of the superiority of Roman cooks. In
America, and for that matter in England also, cabbage
is quartered, boiled or steamed and the water in which
it has been cooked goes down the drains. By the time
that the ribs of the leaves and the strunks are done,
the tender leaves are cooked to death. The choice is
between indigestible strunks or leaves or both. The
Roman way was very different. Ribs and strunks were
separated from the leaves, cut into small pieces of
uniform size and boiled in very little water. The leaves
were cooked separately and only very lightly, being
kept green by the addition of a little baking soda. Then
a sauce was made of the water, well seasoned with pepper, salt, fresh rue, coriander, etc., and thickened with
a *roux* of olive oil and rice flour. Both the leafy and
pulpy parts of the cabbage, cooked to a point, were
combined in this sauce; no mineral salts were thrown
away; no flavour lost.

Asparagus is another example of the superior genius
of the Roman cooks. We cook asparagus mostly without any trace of common sense, boiling in the same
water and manner stems and heads. Not so the Romans.
They bunched the peeled asparagus, inserted it into

boiling water in a tall vessel, stems down, the heads protruding out of the water, to be cooked by the rising steam. Thus stems and heads were cooked to perfection simultaneously.

Perhaps the most maligned because the least understood of Roman delicacies was the *Garum*, which has made translators shudder, only because they have never attempted to follow the directions given in the Apicius for making it. Had they done so, as I have, they would have found a great similarity between the Roman *Garum* and the modern anchovy sauce. The basis of this culinary adjutant sounds horrible when we are told that it consisted of the entrails of fish none too fresh, but the fault is the translator's, not the Roman cook's. He used the *Garus's* liver dried in the sun. The *Garus* was probably tunny fish, treated as cod liver is treated today, exposed to ultra-violet rays to obtain Vitamin D in liquid form, and the reason why the Romans valued liver has only lately been rediscovered by modern scientists.

Indeed, there is nothing new under the sun, and Apicius reminds us that proud as we may rightly be of all we have learnt, there is much that we have forgotten that is of far greater value than some of our newly acquired knowledge.

(Joseph D. Vehling)

But now the Cook must pass through all degrees,
And by his art discordant tempers please,
And minister to health and to disease.
Homer, less modern, if we search his books
Will show us that his Heroes all were Cooks:
How lov'd Patroclus with Achilles joins
To quarter out the ox, and spit the loins.

V

BREAD AND MEAT

BREAD, WINE and oil, that blessed trinity of the kindly fruits of the earth, have been, ever since biblical times, the symbol of peace and plenty, the reward promised by angels in heaven to men of goodwill upon earth.

In all times and among all nations bread has been regarded as the staff of life, the foundation upon which all kinds of different diets have been built, according to age, climate, and custom. Among free and civilized peoples the head of the family is known as the breadwinner. And for close upon two thousand years Christians of all denominations have had and still have one prayer in common—the Lord's Prayer: they all ask, as they were divinely enjoined to do, that they may be given their daily bread, even before asking to be forgiven their trespasses, to be delivered from evil and not to be led into temptation.

BREAD

The name of the commonest, oldest and best form of human food: it is made of the flour or meal of one or more sorts of cereals, as well as from the flour or meal obtained from various grasses, roots and seeds. The quality of bread, that is its nutritive value, appearance, and flavour, depends in the first place upon the quality and nature of the grain or grains from which the flour or meal is obtained. Then there is the 'milling' or extraction of the flour, which comes second in point of timing, but is of capital importance.

The grains or seeds of all cereals—and cereals are the chief source of flour for breadmaking—consist of four main parts: (1) the outer covering or husk; (2) the superficial layers of the grain itself—these are known as the bran layers; (3) the tiny embryo or germ from which the young plant springs on germination; and (4) the main mass of the grain known as the endosperm. The latter contains the starch and protein reserves upon which the young plant lives during its early days after germination. By contrast with the endosperm, a food reserve, the germ contains the building material of the plant itself. It is rich in protein, fatty constituents and certain vitamins as important to man as they are for the development of the growing plant.

The vitamins in cereal grains are not entirely concentrated in the germ, at least not in the case of wheat, which is the cereal of greatest importance in Great Britain and the U.S.A. There is quite a good proportion in a layer of protein—rich cells, known as the aleurone layer which underlies the innermost coat of bran. Modern research has shown the importance of trying to get as much as possible of the aleurone into the flour.

During centuries beyond count, bread was made from flour obtained by the crushing of grain between two stones: such flour contained all but the coarsest part of the outer covering, the whole of the starch and the whole of the germ present in the grain. In colour it was any shade from light brown, in the case of wheaten flour, to black, in the case of rye flour. That was the bread which was deservedly known as the 'staff of life'.

Then came the roller-mill from Hungary during the last quarter of the nineteenth century: it made it possible to crush the grain between revolving metal cylinders much more rapidly and economically. It also made it possible to

separate fairly completely and easily the outer covering or
bran, from the kernel or starch and the germ or vitamins
storehouse. At the time, the vitamins were not yet understood and the chief merit(?) of the roller-mill was the pos-
sibility it gave to the millers of offering to the public a more
attractive-looking loaf because of its snow-white crumb, at
the same time as having more and better 'offal', i.e., left-
overs in the shape of bran-cum-germ to sell as feed for cattle
or poultry. Another fact that made the roller-mill popular
with millers and bakers was that by removing the germ,
flour kept longer without showing rancidity. Actually stone-
ground flour containing germ keeps well if it is milled dry and
kept dry, but in milling 'roller' flour the grain has to be more
moist. It is the relatively high moisture content of flours containing germ, made by the roller-mill, that results so often in
an early onset of rancidity. Doctors and scientists warned
the public that whilst the pure white flour was better than
the brown for stiffening linen, being largely starch, it was a
much poorer article as regards its food value. They were
not listened to, and in the British Isles and the U.S.A., the
public went on demanding white bread in preference to all
others.

The discovery of the vital importance of vitamins, during
the past twenty-five years, should have made the inclusion of
the germ of the grain in the people's bread a moral as well
as a legal obligation for the millers. But nothing of the sort
happened. The separation of the germ was made even more
complete in order to provide raw materials for valuable cattle
foods and for a variety of 'health products' to be sold to the
public as proprietary articles.

Whole grain bread is more wholesome, more toothsome
and just as handsome as white bread, but all brown breads
and all the so-called wholemeal breads are not necessarily
whole grain: they may be brown because they contain bran,

without any significant amount of germ. Such breads will not have the vitamin value of those containing germ.

There cannot be any question of scrapping the modern roller-mills and returning to the old and picturesque windmills; nor is there any need of going 'back'. On the contrary, there are indications that the modern roller-mill can be adapted to produce a flour acceptable by the mass of the public and at the same time almost as rich in nutriment as wholemeal. A new type of flour produced in Canada known as 'Canada approved' has these qualities and is proving very popular. The new National Wheatmeal now being milled in Great Britain is rapidly approaching the same character.

On the other hand, there are also new milling processes already in use and which it is claimed enable for the first time flours containing the whole of the wheat berry to be produced in an assimilable form. In one process, the cells of the berry are exploded by intense air pressure, a process which reduces bran to a fine grist, liberates mineral salts, malt sugar and wheat oil, and produces a meal or flour from which bread is made that is pure, nutritive and digestible and contains the vitamins B_1 and B_2, and E, as well as valuable roughage.

Having secured the right flour for making bread, one must make it into dough with water or milk or both, but water is the more usual liquid used for the purpose; also yeast and some salt. Whatever the kind of bread one may attempt to make, it is important to knead the dough regularly, steadily and thoroughly, so that the fermentation may be satisfactory and the bread free from holes and lumps. The flour must be dried before use and the yeast must be fresh or the bread will taste sour and bitter. All the ingredients should be slightly warmed before mixing. The oven should be raised to the right temperature before the bread is put in, i.e., 350°F., and it should then be gradually slackened or the crust may be too hard and dark.

In old-fashioned brick ovens, which were heated by wood being burnt in them before the bread was put in, the gradual cooling off process was, of course, automatic. Loaves, when taken from the oven, should be placed on a sieve or leant against something so that the air can circulate round them. If they are left lying flat the steam will condense into moisture and the bread becomes heavy.

MEAT

Meat, in its widest sense, means food, any food. In its more restricted sense, meat means butcher's meat, beef and veal, mutton and lamb; also pork. It also means any and every part of any of the mammals which we consider as fit food for man.

Whether man's diet was wholly vegetarian before the Flood is a question for biblical students, upon which we are unable to throw any light. Since the Flood, however, and surely this is as far back as we can reasonably be expected to search for evidence, the business of shepherds and goatherds has been to ward off danger from their charges, not that they might reach an honourable old age, but to keep the wolf from the door.

Although man has killed man in this our enlightened generation upon a scale quite undreamt of by our savage ancestors, we do not kill to eat our enemies, which is to the cannibals plain logic. Nor is there any record that the English were at any time of their history so sentimental as to emulate those eastern tribes where dead relatives were eaten by the surviving members of the family, thus to be endowed with a fuller life. We know, of course, that there are individuals and whole nations who live and love, work and rest, and are strong of body and alert of mind, in spite of a wholly meatless diet. Vegetarians would say 'because' instead of 'in spite of', but we cannot agree. We maintain that since man was given teeth capable to tear, champ, and cut, he was intended to use them, just as any of the other animals, carnivorous all, with similar or the same teeth. Of course, there is this difference between man and either shark or tiger: the flesh that man eats is cooked and dressed by him or for him. This makes a great deal of difference: flesh is both more appetising and more easily digested when suitably cooked, seasoned and carved. Let us always bear in mind that meat has a grain, just like wood has, so that it is very important to carve meat according to its grain, never to tear it away from it. Sharp knives are also of real value to avoid the tearing of meat and to ensure its proper enjoyment.

BEEF

Beef has meant meat *par excellence* in England for the past thousand years. Sheep were reared for their wool until modern times; they were slaughtered and eaten in large numbers, chiefly because of the lack of grazing and winter keep, but oxen were bred for the one and only purpose of Beef.

And because Biefe of all flesh is most usuall among English men, I will first entreat thereof. I need not to show how plentifull it is through-out this land before all other countries, and how necesserary it is both by sea, for the victualling of Shyppes: and by land, for good house-keeping, insomuch as no man of honour or worship can be said to have good provision for hospitalitie, unless there be good store of Biefe in readinesse. And how well it doth agree with the nature of Englishmen, the common consent of all our nation doth sufficiently proove.

(Cogan, *Haven of Health*, 1589. p. 113)

CONSTABLE OF FRANCE: ... give them great meals of beef and iron and steel: they will eat like wolves and fight like devils.

DUKE OF ORLEANS. Ay, but these English are serewdly out of beef!

(*The life of King Henry V*. Act III. Sc. 7)

TO THE OLD BEEF-STEAK CLUB

'May beef long bless our favoured coast,
    Where no despotic ruffian
Has dared a brazen bull to roast,
    With men inside for stuffing!
Where never Jove, a tyrant god,
    Who loves fair maids to purloin,
As a white bull the billows rode
    With madam on his sirloin.
Like Britain's Island lies our steak,
    —A sea of gravy round it.—
Shalots, in fragrance scattered, make
    The rock-work which surrounds it:
Our Isle's best emblem here behold,
    Remember ancient story;
Be, like your grandsires, just and bold;
    So live and die in glory.'

(Charles Morris, Laureate, in 1785)

Beef and mutton, and mutton and beef, no matter what their price, John Bull will not dispense with; and although they are 40 and 50 per cent. dearer now than they were ten years ago, and although we import animals largely from abroad, and our cattle-breeders do their best to meet the demand, cattle and sheep will not increase and multiply fast enough to bring down the price for the consumer.

A writer in *Household Words* thus alludes to our national weakness: 'Next to the Habeas Corpus and the Freedom of the Press, there are few things that the English people have a greater respect for, and a

livelier faith in than beef. They bear year after year
with the same interminable, unvarying series of wood-
cuts of fat oxen in the columns of the illustrated news-
papers; they are never tired of crowding to the Smith-
field Club cattle show; and I am inclined to think that it
is their honest reverence for beef that has induced them
to support so long the obstruction and endangerment of
the thoroughfares of the metropolis by oxen driven to
slaughter. Beef is a great connecting link and bond of
better feeling between the great classes of the common-
wealth. Do not Dukes hob and nob with top-booted
farmers over the respective merits of short-horns
and Alderneys? Does not the noble Marquis of Argent-
fork give an ox to be roasted whole on the village green,
when his son, the noble Viscount Silvercoral, comes of
age? Beef makes boys into men. Beef nerves our
navvies. The bowmen who won Cressy and Agincourt,
were beef-fed, and had there been more and better beef
in the Crimea a year or two ago, our soldiers would
have borne up better under the horrors of a Chersone-
sean winter. We feast on beef at the great Christian
festival. A baron of beef at the same time is enthroned
in St. George's Hall, in Windsor's ancient Castle, and
is borne in by lacqueys in scarlet and gold. Charles the
Second knighted a loin of beef, and I have a shrewd
suspicion that the famous Sir Bevis of Southampton
was but an ardent admirer and doughty knight-errant
in the cause of beef. And who does not know the tradition that even as the first words of the new-born Gar-
gantua were: 'A boyre, à boyre', signifying that he
desired a draught of Burgundy wine—so the first intel-
ligible sounds that the infant Guy of Warwick ever
spake were 'Beef, beef!' When the weary pilgrim
reaches the beloved shores of England after a long
absence, what first does he remark—after the incivility
of the customs-house officers—but the great tankard
of stout and the noble round of cold beef in the coffee-
room of the hotel? He does not cry 'Io Bacche! Evöe
Bacche!' because beef is not Bacchus. He does not fall
and kiss his native soil, because the hotel carpet is

somewhat dusty, and the action would be, besides, egregious; but he looks at the beef, and his eyes filling with tears, a corresponding humidity takes place in his mouth; he kisses the beef; he is so fond of it that he could eat it all up; and he does ordinarily devour so much of it to his breakfast that the thoughtful waiter gazes at him, and murmurs to his napkin. 'This man is either a cannibal or a pilgrim grey who has not seen Albion for many years.'

(Peter Lund Simmonds. *The Curiosities of food*. London. Bentley. 1859. pp. 374)

Beef is the flesh of the Ox (*bos taurus*), a bovine quadruped domesticated (and usually castrated as well), reared for food, when a year old or over, and fattened for the market before it is slaughtered. It may also be the flesh of a cow or of a bull used for breeding or for work on the farm as a beast of burden, in which case it never can hope to be prime beef.

Prime beef is firm to the touch, the lean is of a brilliant red colour, pleasing to the (butcher's) eye, and the fat is nearly white: the lean should be 'peppered' with small flecks of white fat. The quality of prime beef depends upon the breed of the ox, its age, its mode of feeding and fattening, and the manner of its slaughtering. The quality of any individual joint or piece of beef depends upon the 'cut', or the part of the carcase from which such joint or piece was cut.

'Ox-beef is the largest and richest; but, in small families, and to some tastes, heifer-beef is better, if finely fed,'— EX. B.

All the main joints and best pieces of beef are known by their Norman-French name Beef, but all titbits which were presumably left by the Norman lords to their Anglo-Saxon menials have retained their original Anglo-Saxon Ox prefix: here is a list of them with their corresponding names in culinary French:

Ox brains	*Cervelle de bœuf*
Ox cheek	*Joue de bœuf*
Ox head	*Tête de bœuf*
Ox heart	*Cœur de bœuf*
Ox kidney	*Rognon de bœuf*
Ox liver	*Foie de bœuf*
Ox marrow	*Moëlle de bœuf*
Ox muzzle	*Museau de bœuf*
Ox palate	*Palais de bœuf*
Ox pith	*Amourettes*
Ox tail	*Queue de bœuf*
Ox tongue	*Langue de bœuf*

In culinary French, *bœuf* means meat from either ox, heifer, bull or cow. The more usual 'cuts' and *abats* of *bœuf* are the following:

Sirloin	*Aloyau de bœuf*
Steak	*Bifteck*
Rib of beef	*Côte de bœuf*
Rump of beef	*Culotte de bœuf*
Rump steak	*Entrecôte*
Fillet of beef or 'undercut'	*Filet de bœuf*
Belly	*Gras-double de bœuf*
Shaft or handle	*Hampe de bœuf*
No English name for it	*Onglet de bœuf*
Shoulder blade	*Paleron de bœuf*
Brisket	*Poitrine de bœuf*
Tripe	*Tripes de bœuf*
Leg of Beef	*Trumeau*

MUTTON AND LAMB

The best mutton is the flesh of a well-bred, well-fed sheep three or four years old, and kept in an airy, cool place from two to three weeks after the sheep has been slaughtered. As in the case of beef and pork, the Norman name *mutton* is used for the best parts or joints of the sheep, whilst the innards and less *recherchés* parts have kept their Saxon name, *sheep*. Thus:

Mutton-chop	*Côte de mouton*
Mutton Cutlet	*Côtelette de mouton*
Breast of mutton	*Poitrine de mouton*
Haunch of mutton	*Quartier de mouton*
Leg of mutton	*Gigot de mouton*
Mutton ham	*Gigot de mouton fumé*
Loin of mutton	*Longe de mouton*
Neck of mutton	*Collet de mouton*
Saddle of mutton	*Selle de mouton*
Shoulder of mutton	*Epaule de mouton*
But:	
Sheep's Brains	*Cervelle de mouton*
Sheep's Head	*Tête de mouton*
Sheep's Heart	*Cœur de mouton*
Sheep's Kidneys	*Rognons de mouton*
Sheep's Tail	*Queue de mouton*
Sheep's Tongue	*Langue de mouton*
Sheep's Trotters	*Pieds de mouton*

A lamb is a young ovine animal that has not acquired its first pair of permanent teeth: when it has acquired those teeth, it becomes a hogget—either a wether hogget, if a male and castrated, or a ewe hogget, if a female—until it reaches the period for clipping. In culinary language, however, there are two sorts of lambs, the baby lamb or *Agneau de Lait*, also known as *Agneau de Pauillac* and the lamb proper, or *agneau*. The first is milk-fed, i.e., fatted off its mother without weaning. The meat is very white and tender, without flavour, but none the less a great and costly gastronomic delicacy. The second, in Great Britain, is either lamb or hogget, that is a sheep not yet twelve months old, after which it becomes mutton. In olden times, however, mutton was the meat of wether or ewe when three, four or five years old; it was darker in colour, better in flavour, with plenty of white fat and very much finer meat than that of the 'old lambs' or yearling sheep of the present day. In the U.S.A., mutton is not mentioned at all in polite culinary society: one never gets anything but lamb.

Breed, age and feeding are the three main factors responsible for the degree of quality of both lamb and mutton, but when none of these important factors is known—and such is the case when one enters a butcher's shop—one has to be guided by the appearance of the meat, and here is the advice given by the Ministry of Agriculture in its Report on the marketing of sheep, mutton and lamb in England and Wales (Economic series, No. 29, p. 102):

'To sum up it may be said that in a lamb or young mutton carcase of high quality, the bone should be fairly soft, the flesh light in colour, fine in grain, firm, well developed and full of sap, the fat of a correct colour and well distributed, and the conformation good. The ratio of muscle to gristle and bone should be relatively high.'

The best joints of both lamb and mutton are the saddle and the shoulder, but they are also the least economical as they carry a greater proportion of bone to meat than other joints; next come the loin, the leg, and then the neck, which is divided in two parts, the 'best end', which is definitely best, and the 'scrag end', which is always much cheaper and about the same price as the 'breast'. From the loin, chops and cutlets are cut off, which are the best 'small cuts'; there are also the innards and the odds and ends, from head to tail.

Lamb Chop	*Côte d'agneau*
Lamb Cutlet	*Côtelette d'agneau*
Breast of Lamb	*Poitrine d'Agneau*
Lamb Kidney	*Rognon d'agneau*
Leg of Lamb	*Gigot d'agneau*
Loin of Lamb	*Longe d'agneau*
Lamb's Liver	*Foie d'agneau*

Neck of Lamb	*Collet d'agneau*
Saddle of Lamb	*Selle d'agneau*
Shoulder of Lamb	*Epaule d'agneau*
Lamb's Sweetbread	*Ris d'agneau*
Lamb's Tail	*Queue d'agneau*
Lamb's Tongue	*Langue d'agneau*

RECEIPT TO ROAST MUTTON

'Gently stir and blow the fire,
Lay the mutton down to roast,
Dress it quickly, I desire,
In the dripping put a toast,
That I hunger may remove—
Mutton is the meat I love.

'On the dresser see it lie;
Oh! the charming white and red;
Finer meat ne'er met the eye,
On the sweetest grass it fed:
Let the jack go swiftly round,
Let me have it nicely brown'd.

'On the table spread the cloth,
Let the knives be sharp and clean,
Pickles get and salad both,
Let them each be fresh and green.
With small beer, good ale, and wine,
O ye gods! how I shall dine!'

(Sydney Smith, quoted in George H. Ellwanger's
The Pleasures of the Table. London 1903 edition. p.
290)

ON BEN TYRRELL'S PIES

Let *Christmas* boast her customary Treat,
A Mixture strange, of Suet, Currants, Meat,
Where various Tartes combine, the greasy, and the
    sweet.
Let glad *Shrove-Tuesday* bring the *Pancake* thin,
Or Fritter rich, with Apples stor'd within:

On *Easter-Sunday* be the Pudding seen,
To which the *Tansey* lends her sober Green:
And when great *London* hails her annual *Lord*,
Let quiv'ring *Custard* crown the *Aldermannic* Board.

But BEN prepares a more delicious Mess,
Substantial Fare, a Breakfast for Queen *Bess:*
What dainty Epicure, or greedy Glutton,
Would not prefer his PIE, that's made of *Mutton?*

Each diff'rent Country boasts a diff'rent Taste,
And owe's its Fame to *Pudding* or to *Paste:*
SQUAB PIE in *Cornwall* only can they make,
In Norfolk DUMPLING, and in Salop CAKE;
But *Oxford* now from all shall bear the Prize,
Fam'd, as for *Sausages*, for MUTTON-PIES.

(The Oxford Sausage, 1764)

OF SWINE

Although swine are accounted troublesome, noisome, unruly, and great ravenours, as indeed their natures are not much different from such qualities, yet the utility and profit of them will easily wipe off those offences; for to speak truly of the swine, he is the husbandmans best scavenger, and the housewives most wholesome sinke, for his food and living is by that which would else rot in the yard, make it beastly, and breed no good mannure, or being cast down the ordinary sink in the house breed noisome smels, corruption, and infection; for from the husbandman he taketth pulse, chaffe, barns dust, mans ordure, garbage, and the weeds of his yard: and from the houewife her chaff, swillings, whey, washing of tubs, and such like, with which he will live and keepe a good state of body, very sufficiently, and though he is accounted good in no place but the dish onely, yet here he is so lovely and wholesome, that all other faults may be borne with.

(Gervase Markham. *The Way to get Wealth.* London. 1648. p. 126)

PIG AND PORK

A young swine of either sex is a Pig before it has reached
the age of sexual maturity, when it becomes a hog. The pig is
an omnivorous mammal and a wonderful converter. Pig used
as food is known by its Norman name of pork, except the
innards and odds and ends. Thus:

Pig's brains	*Cervelle de porc*
Pig's cheek or jowl	
Pig's ears	*Oreilles de porc*
Pig's face	
Pig's feet or trotters	*Pieds de porc* or *de cochon*
Pig's fry	
Pig's harslet	*Fressure de porc*
Pig's head	*Tête de porc*
Pig's kidneys	*Rognons de porc*
Pig's liver	*Foie de porc*
Pig's pettitoes	
Pig's trotters	*Pieds de cochon*

Useless during life, and only valuable when deprived
of it, this animal has sometimes been compared to a
miser, whose hoarded treasures are of little value till
death has deprived them of their rapacious owner.

(E.B.)

Neither is all swines' flesh so commendable, but that
which is young and best of a yeare or two old. Also
better of a wilde swine than of a tame.

(Cogan. *The Haven of Health.* 1589. p. 117)

Pork is the name given to the flesh of the hog, used for
food from times immemorial, in China, and as far as records
go back, in the west. One should always cook pork well:
beef and mutton may be underdone and even 'rare', if liked,
but never pork. One should always bear in mind, when
cooking pork, that it must not be cooked quickly, as it is
likely to be stringy, tough and indigestible if so cooked. For

boiling and roasting, pork should be the flesh of a young hog that is not older than six months, and the leg must not weigh more than from 6 to 7 lb.

BACON

Originally the French name for pig, and its meaning in England in former times was pork: Thus, in *Henry IV* (Act II, Sc. 1),

> 'I have a gammon of bacon and two razes of ginger to be delivered as far as Charing Cross.'

Shakespeare meant 'a leg of pork'. Today, however, bacon means exclusively the back and sides of a pig after they have been cured, dry cured or tank cured, and smoked. The quality of bacon varies in the first place according to the breed, age and feeding of the animal responsible for it and the manner and degree of the curing; in the second place, according to the 'cut' or the part of the carcase. In England the practice is to cut a 'Wiltshire side' into ten different 'cuts', i.e., (1) Fore Hock; (2) Collar; (3) Prime Streak; (4) Thin Streak; (5) Flank; (6) Back Thick End; (7) Back and Loin; (8) Corner of Gammon; (9) Middle of Gammon; (10) Gammon Hock.

Bacon was enjoyed, still is enjoyed in a rationed measure, above all at breakfast time, in the British Isles, either fried, broiled or grilled and by itself, or, preferably, with fried eggs, tomatoes, kidneys, potatoes, etc. One half-pound of prime or thin streaky bacon averages a dozen thin rashers.

Other cuts of bacon are mostly used to boil. Incidentally, a tea-cupful of vinegar and six or more cloves added to the water in which bacon is boiled improve its flavour. Boiled bacon whether hot or cold is a very popular dish for luncheon. Hot boiled bacon is excellent with roast turkey or veal, somewhat dry and tasteless meats by themselves and

greatly benefited by a boiled bacon backing. Cold boiled
bacon, a little mustard, some small onions and a crunchy Cos
lettuce make a meal fit not merely for a king but for the most
fastidious gastronome.

THE SAUSAGE IN ANTIQUITY

There are at least three words in Greek for a sausage
—ἀλλᾶς, φύσκη and χορδή, though all of these mean
something a little nearer to a black pudding than to our
ordinary table sausage; all indeed designate the great
gut of a pig or other animal stuffed with chopped
intestines. From the first of these words is derived one
of the most famous characters of Greek comedy, the
ἀλλαντοπώλης of the *Knights* of Aristophanes, the
sausage-seller, the victorious rival of the odious Cleon.

But of course we must turn to the *Deipnosophists* of
Athenaeus for closer particulars of the sausage. Many
of his mentions of sausages are casual—he speaks of
'a slice of sausage' as a component part of an elaborate
dish or meal, and quotes from a lost play of Aristophanes the surprising fact that the actors in primitive
Greek comedy 'would dance wrapped up in rugs and
bundles of bedding, sticking under their arm-pits
ribs of beef, sausages and radishes'. We also hear a
somewhat improbable story of how, in frugal Sparta,
sausages were nailed to the wall in order that old gentle-
men might come and take a bite at them when hungry.

The English word sausage is derived from a (mediae-
val) Latin term which means nothing more than
'salted viands'; but the classical Latin word is quite
different—*tomaculum*, from a Greek root, and meaning 'that which is cut up'—i.e., mincemeat. It is found
chiefly in the Silver Latin Age, and its occurrences
are not uninteresting. I detail them below.

The word comes twice in Petronius, both in the account of the vulgar and ostentatious dinner given by
the *nouveau riche* Trimalchio. At one of these places

there is a rather elaborate practical joke: a live pig is brought in, approved, and sent to be cooked; it comes back sooner than can be expected, but the cook ruefully admits that he has forgotten to gut it. Threatened with punishment, he is told to perform the process then and there—he rips up the carcass, and out fall *tomacula* and *botuli*. (This latter is another Latin word for a sausage—nearer the Greek kind, perhaps: now of bad omen, since it has given the name to a generally fatal form of food-poisoning, botulism.) At the other place in Petronius we hear that two dishes were brought in, one containing field-mice dressed with honey and pepper, and the other *tomacula super craticulam ferventia argenteam posita, et infra craticulam Syriaca pruna cum granis Punici mali'*. This is interesting, but not very easy: it is certain that there were hot sausages on a silver grill, but a grill is ordinarily an instrument of cookery, and not sent to table. Fortunately we have a gloss adduced by the Dutch scholar Tiberius Hemsterhuys to a passage in the grammarian Pollux which throws some light upon it: 'The "little altar" (*arula*) was a square bronze dish, standing on four feet, on which glowing embers were placed, and above it a grill: and thus they grilled meat.' The silver *craticula* was in fact a portable grill.

There is, I think, only one mention of sausages in Martial. Damning a certain Caecilius, who fancied himself a wit, the poet says: 'What are you? a buffoon. . . .' Like 'the pieman, who bawls aloud as he carries around smoking sausages in hot dishes'. Clearly we have here come again to the Greek idea of the sausage as a vulgar food.

Not so in Juvenal. Here the poet is talking of gifts offered up at a shrine in order to obtain future benefits from the gods, and one of them is—a charming phrase —*candiduli divina tomacula porci*. This is obviously a delicacy: I have personally never eaten sausages made of sucking-pig, but I should much like to!

(Sir Stephen Gaselee, K.C.M.G., C.B.E.)

HAGGIS

Burns' poem *To a Haggis* begins thus:

> 'Fair fa' your honest sonsie face,
> Great chieftain o' the puddin' race!
> Aboon them a' ye tak' your place,
>   Painch, tripe, or thairm;
> Weel are ye wordy of a grace
>   As lang's my arm.'

As a rule one does not attempt to make a haggis; one just buys a haggis and does not inquire too closely as to how it was made. A bought haggis must be simmered in all-but-boiling water long enough to be thoroughly hot and steaming when a slit is made in the paunch for a large tablespoon (previously dipped in boiling water) to be inserted and the haggis scooped out. It is usually served wrapped up in a stiffly starched napkin to cover the none too appetizing bare looks of the sheep's stomach. Neat whisky is the orthodox liquid accompaniment of the haggis, and it should be drunk from a quaich, a kind of shallow wooden drinking cup with two lugs or handles.

Haggis, as the Scotch term it, was a favourite preparation with the Romans; but, instead of mincing the flesh used for this dish, they as often as not brayed it in a mortar, with liquamen and seasonings, till it became a soft pulp. The usual farinaceous ingredient of the Roman Haggis was frumenty; but often no grain was employed. The Apician pork-haggis—esteemed above all other compositions of the same kind—was a boiled pig's stomach filled with fry and brain, raw eggs, and pine-apple, beaten into a pulp, and treated with the never absent sauces and seasonings.

(John Cordy Jeaffreson. *A Book about the Table*. 1875.
pp. 60–61)

VI

FISH

FISH HAS been a favourite food of men from the earliest times. The Greeks even had a name for fish addicts: they were called *Ichthyophagi*. Long before apostolic times, when 'Peter and Andrew fyshed for fode', the fisherman's craft was one of the most flourishing and the anglers of ancient Greece and Rome took the same pains and had the same thrills as our own. Thus Homer:

> Of beetling rocks that overhang the flood
> Where silent anglers cast insidious food,
> With fraudful care await the finny prize
> And sudden lift it quivering to the skies.

And Ossian sang Caracalla's skill with the rod thus:

> A bite, hurrah! the length'ning line extends,
> Above the tugging fish the arch'd reed bends:
> He struggles hard, and noble sport will yield,
> My liege, ere wearied out he quits the field.
>
> See how he swims up, down, and now athwart
> The rapid stream—now pausing as in thought;
> And now you force him from the azure deep;
> He mounts, he bends, and with resilient leap
> Bounds into air! there see the dangler twirl,
> Convulsive start, hang, curl, again uncurl,
> Caper once more like young Terpsichore,
> In giddy gyres, above the sounding sea,
> Till near'd, you seize the prize with steady wrist,
> And grasp at last the bright funambulist.

(*Ancient & Modern Fish Tattle*, by Rev. C. David
Badham, M.D., 1854. pp.3–4)

Gay has given a similar description of the capture of a large salmon, in Rural Sports, a Georgic inscribed to Pope.

> When a brisk gale against the current blows,
> And all the watry plain in wrinkles flows,
> Then let the fisherman his art repeat,
> Where bubbling eddys favour the deceit.
> If an enormous salmon chance to spy
> The wanton errors of the floating fly,
> He lifts his silver gills above the flood,
> And greedily sucks in th' unfaithful food;
> Then downward plunges with the fraudful prey,
> And bears with joy the little spoil away.
> Soon in smart pain he feels the dire mistake,
> Lashes the wave, and beats the foamy lake,
> With sudden rage he now aloft appears,
> And in his eye convulsive anguish bears;
> And now again, impatient of the wound,
> He rolls and wreaths his shining body round;
> Then headlong shoots beneath the dashing tide,
> The trembling fins the boiling wave divide;
> Now hope exalts the fisher's beating heart,
> Now he turns pale, and fears his dubious art;
> He views the tumbling fish with longing eyes,
> While the line stretches with th' unwieldy prize;
> Each motion humours with his steady hands,
> And one slight hair the mighty bulk commands:
> 'Till tir'd at last, despoil'd of all his strength,
> The game athwart the stream unfolds his length.
> He now, with pleasure, views the gasping prize
> Gnash his sharp teeth, and roll his blood-shot eyes;
> Then draws him to the shore, with artful care,
> And lifts his nostrils in the sick'ning air:
> Upon the burthen'd stream he floating lies,
> Stretches his quivering fins, and gasping dies.

Trawling at sea with baited gorge-hook was also practised years ago. This is how Oppian describes a trawler preparing his lines 1,600 years ago!

He holds the labrax, and beneath his head
Adjusts with care an oblong shape of lead,
Named from its form a dolphin: plumb'd with this
The bait shoots headlong through the blue abyss.
The bright decoy a living creature seems,
As now on this side, now on that, it gleams,
Till some dark form across its passage flit,
Pouches the lure, and finds the biters bit.

The same author, however, refers to nets, some of them of enormous size, as by far the more usual and effective means of securing the large supplies of fish in constant demand:

Nets like a city to the floods descend,
And bulwarks, gates, and noble streets extend.

and

A thousand names a fisher might rehearse
Of nets, intractable in smoother verse.

There is one mode of catching eels, however, which has long ceased to be practised, allowing that we accept Ælian's description as fact and not fiction. This is how it is quoted by Athenaeus:

The artful eeler pitches upon a spot favourable for his purpose at the turn of a stream, and lets down from where he stands on the high bank, some cubits' length of the intestines of a sheep, which, carried down by the current, is eddied and whirled about, and presently perceived by the eels, one of whom, adventurously gobbling some inches at the nether end, endeavours to drag the whole away. The angler, perceiving this, applies the other end, which is fixed to a long tubular reed serving in lieu of a fishing-rod, to his mouth, and blows through it into the gut.

The gut presently swells, and the fish next receiving the air into his mouth, swells too, and being unable to extricate his teeth, is lugged out, adhering to the inflated intestine.

From a very early date, men were evidently anxious to make

F

sure of having a more reliable supply of fish than could be speared, hooked, netted, or coaxed from sea, rivers or lakes. So they dug fishponds as breeding places, and other watery prisons for fish which could be relied upon to be always at hand and ready for pot or pan at all times.

The accounts given by Pliny, Varro, Columella, and others provide details of Roman vivaria, leaving nothing for posterity to improve, and all the fishponds of ancient monasteries and lordly houses in western Continental Europe and in Britain were built on Roman patterns. To build a fishpond was a costly business; to stock it with the right kind of fish was also an expensive affair; but to keep the water sweet and the fish in it well fed, was a never-ending task, so that *vivaria* were the privilege of the rich.

ON FISH

Certain sages, with small regard for orthodoxy, maintain that the ocean was the common cradle of all existing things; that the human race itself was born in the sea; and that it owes its actual condition to the influence of the air and the habits which it has been forced to acquire in order that it may live in the unfamiliar element.

However that may be, certain it is that the watery realm contains a vast number of creatures of every shape and size, endowed with vital properties in widely varying proportions, on a system altogether different from that which governs the warm-blooded animals.

It is also certain that at all times and throughout its whole extent, it furnishes a vast quantity of alimentary substances, and that, in the present state of science, it provides our tables with a most pleasing variety of dishes.

Fish, being less nutritious than flesh, more succulent than vegetables, is a *mezzo termine* which suits almost every temperament, and may be allowed even to invalids.

The *Greeks* and *Romans*, though less advanced than ourselves in the art of seasoning fish, nevertheless prized it highly and carried delicacy to the point of being able to tell by the taste in what waters their fish had been caught.

They kept fish alive in tanks; and the cruel story of Vadius Pollio is well known—how he killed his slaves, for eels to feed upon their corpses: a device of which the emperor Domitian strongly disapproved; he ought, however, to have punished the offender.

There has been much argument upon the rival merits of sea fish and fresh-water fish.

The question will probably never be decided, for the truth is contained in the Spanish proverb, *sobre los gustos, no hai disputa*. Everyone is affected after his own manner; such sensations are too subtle to be expressed by any known character, and there is no scale to determine whether a cod, a sole, or a turbot be worth more than a salmon trout, a well-fed pike, or a six- or seven-pound tench.

It is certain, however, that fish is far less nourishing than flesh, whether because it contains no osmazome, or because, being much lighter in weight, it contains less matter in proportion to its volume. Shell-fish, and especially oysters, provide very little nourishment; and this is the reason why so many can be eaten immediately before a meal without discomfort.

Until a few years ago, a meal of any pretension ordinarily began with oysters, and it was no unusual feat for one individual to swallow a gross (twelve dozen, a hundred and forty-four). Wishing to know what was the weight of this advance-guard, I went into the matter, and found that a dozen oysters, water included, weighed *four ounces*, avoirdupois; and a gross, therefore, *three pounds*. Now, I am persuaded that the same individuals, who were in no wise prevented by the oysters from enjoying the rest of their meal, would have been more than satisfied had they eaten a like quantity of meat, though it had only been chicken.

(*The Physiology of Taste*, by Brillat-Savarin)

HOMARD À L'AMÉRICAINE

From time to time, someone writes to the papers to point out that there are still some ignorant people to call *Homard à l'Américaine* a dish the right name of which is *Homard à l'Armoricaine*. It is contended that the Latin name of Brittany was Armorica, and that there are lobsters on the Brittany coast—which is not denied—so that a ragout of lobster should obviously be called *Armoricaine*—which is sheer nonsense. Some claim that it was due to the cunning of an officious Maître d'Hôtel that the name *Armoricaine* was wilfully changed into *Américaine*, 'to please some American customers'. Others blame the bad handwriting of some unknown restaurateur for the change. But they are all wrong. The *Homard à l'Américaine* was never known by any other name from the day when it was so called, in the late 'fifties or early 'sixties, when introduced in Paris at the Restaurant Noël Peters, until after World War I when the *Armoricaine* heresy was first heard of.

Here is the original recipe given by Jules Gouffé in *Le Livre de la Cuisine*, written in 1867 (p. 633, Hachette, 1870):

'Coupez des queues de homard en lames d'un centimètre d'èpaisseur; rangez-les en couronne dans une casserole à legumes; coupez la chair des pattes avec laquelle vous formerez un salpicon pour garnir le milieu de la couronne; saucez avec une sauce que vous ferez ainsi: Mettez dans une casserole des échalotes hachées et lavées; faites-les revenir dans le beurre pendant 2 minutes et mouillez-les avec vin blanc; faites-les cuire, puis ajoutez espagnole et purée de tomates par parties égales avec une pointe de poivre de Cayenne; faites réduire pendant 5 minutes; passez à l'étamine et saucez le homard; Faites mijoter à feu trés doux pendant 10 minutes, et servez.'

During the next fifty-odd years, from the date of Gouffé's recipe, a number of variants were introduced, but they all appeared under the name of *Américaine*, until Curnonsky, so it is said, introduced *Armoricaine*, soon after World War I, an innovation which Maurice des Ombiaux, in his *Traité de la Table*, ridicules very forcibly and quite rightly.

FRESH-WATER FISHES AS FOOD

Save as a means of sport, the freshwater fishes of these islands are entirely overshadowed by the much greater resources of the sea. To those whose interest in freshwater fish extends beyond their mere capture with rod and line, the present-day neglect of these fishes as a food supply is a matter for regret. Indeed, the neglect of freshwater fisheries is the more to be deplored when one considers how far they have fallen from their former high estate. Today in London only the inhabitants of the East End of the Jewish persuasion are large consumers of freshwater fish, and they almost wholly rely upon the Continent for their supplies.

No one who has travelled in Holland can have failed to be impressed by the vast freshwater fish resources of that land. Every town and hamlet of any size has its several live fish shops which consist of a series of large iron cases suspended from the sides of a floating stage in the centre of which stands the shop proper. The housewife reaches this emporium via a gang-plank and the salesman simply nets carp, tench, pike, or whatever she may fancy from the iron cradles in which the fish are graded according to size and species. In France and Italy freshwater fishes are likewise fattened for the market on the grand scale.

One fears the average angler's interest today stops short at bringing the catch safely to the landing net. Izaak Walton, however, had wider views, and one of his chapters in his immortal work is devoted to the 'laying out of fish ponds and how to order them'. The ponds of his days were built up most elaborately of clay and wood interlarded, and the banks were supported with a wealth of trees. As fish food 'bread chippings, curds, grains, and the entrails of chickens or any fowl or beast that you kill to feed yourselves' was recommended.

Save amongst a very small portion of the population there is a general feeling nowadays that freshwater fish, with the exception of the members of the salmon family, are muddy, insipid and otherwise unpalatable. Whilst few compare with the best sea fish, it may be urged that much of this prejudice has its roots in our indifference or inability properly to prepare the harvest of our ponds and rivers for the dinner table. Certainly few can find time or patience to prepare carp as advocated by *The Compleat Angler*. The fish was to be stuffed with sweet marjoram, thyme, parsley, rosemary, savory, onions, oysters, eggs and anchovies. Claret completed the preparation of the dish exceedingly popular in the year of leisure 1644. Pike was the *bonne bouche par excellence*, and after a vastly more elaborate preparation even than that devoted to the carp, was adjudged 'a dish of meat too good for any but anglers or very honest men'.

The carp is still much appreciated on the Continent and in America. Being very hardy, this fish can travel for some hours packed in damp weeds and will survive weeks incarcerated in blocks of ice. In America they are thus transported on a commercial scale. The fishes are first placed in containers of water into which oxygen under pressure has been introduced. After being kept a few degrees above freezing point for two or three days, they are frozen solid. The blocks of ice in which the fish are embedded are then removed from the containers, surrounded by heat-insulating packing, and under such conditions are transported long distances or kept in cold storage until wanted.

(E. G. Boulenger)

EEL FARE

A humourist has observed that eel might be much more popular if it looked less like an eel, and it must be admitted that the creature's serpentine appearance possibly deters many diners from enjoying one of the finest dishes. The delicate-flavoured eel may be cooked in an infinity of ways. Its excellences are, in my opinion, done greatest justice to when the fish is cooked in the manner known as *à la Bordelaise*, but it is also good if merely boiled or smoked. Izaak Walton, as great an expert with the knife and fork as with the rod and reel, recommends stuffing the eel with sweet herbs, anchovies and nutmegs and roasting the whole enclosed in the eel's own skin—a method somewhat suggesting a piscine haggis.

The bulk of eels sold in this country hail from Friesland, and their consumption amongst the comparatively poor classes is greater than many might suppose. That quarter of London known as the New Cut monthly consumes about a hundred thousand eels, and the 'Cut' itself was once actually a narrow path running through a Thames-side swamp swarming with eels. Though this neighbourhood may scarcely suggest wealth, the eel's many devotees cheerfully pay from 1s. 9d. to 3s. per pound for their favourite fish. London's Dutch eels are brought by fast motor launches from Friesland twice a week and stored in quaint schuyts anchored off Billingsgate Steps. These schuyts are huge floating tanks full of living eels. Thames water flows through the holes in the sides of these tanks, and in hot weather the water is clarified and purified by sand filters which tower above the docks. The schuyts' crews serve in three-monthly shifts like the personnel of a lightship.

The ways of capturing eels are almost as numerous as the ways of cooking them. In Lincolnshire eels are ferreted out of the mud where they rest during the day by means of a trident or eel spear called a 'pilgrim'.

Izaak Walton has described in detail the time-honoured procedure of 'sniggling', and in some areas the bait is surrounded by a tangle of twine in which the fish become enmeshed. When to be caught in bulk for market, huge wire or wicker traps known as 'bucks', built on the principle of lobster pots, are placed on the fishes' line of march when they are engaged on their periodic migratory swim. It has long been observed that eels show peculiar liveliness during thunder storms, and Frank Buckland recalls how one old Fenland fisherman used to beat a drum by the streamside in order, as he said, 'to make the eels run'.

Eels of various species frequent all depths of the ocean. Of these, the most notorious off our shores is the conger, which also is excellent eating. Like other eels, this formidable fish, reaching a length of 9 ft. and weighing 160 lb., begins life as a glassy, leaflike creature. By the addition of milk and mussels an excellent soup is made of conger eel in the Channel Islands.

The marbled eel, or muræna, is rarely taken in home waters, but is a well-known food fish in the Mediterranean, and common also in tropic waters of both hemispheres. The muræna is an exceedingly savage fish with long poisonous teeth, but nevertheless of high table excellence.

(E. G. Boulenger)

O, WHAUR HA'E YE BEEN A' THE DAY

O, whaur ha'e ye been a' the day,
    My little wee croodlin doo?
O I've been at my grandmither's:
    Mak' my bed, mammie, noo!

O what gat ye at your grandmither's,
    My little wee croodlin doo?
I got a bonnie wee fishie:
    Mak' my bed, mammie, noo!

O whaur did she catch the fishie,
  My little wee croodlin doo?
She catched it in the gutter hole:
  Mak' my bed, mammie, noo!

And what did she do wi' the fishie,
  My little wee croodlin doo?
She boiled it in a brass pan:
  Mak' my bed, mammie, noo!

And what did ye do wi' the banes o't,
  My little wee croodlin doo?
I gi'ed them to my little dog:
  Mak' my bed, mammie, noo!

And what did your little doggie do,
  My little wee croodlin doo?
He stretched out his head, and feet, and deed'd:
  Mak' my bed, mammie, noo!

(An old Ballad)

HERRING

Lat. *clupea harengus*. Fr. *hareng*. Ger. *haringe*. Ital. *aringe*.
Sp. *arengues*. One of the most nutritious and one of the
cheapest of all the fishes out of the sea. Fresh herrings are
best broiled; salt herrings are best pickled; bloaters and
kippers are best grilled. Herrings travel in schools of millions
of individuals in the more temperate waters of the North
Atlantic. They are in season all the year round, but at their
best from June to December. A closely allied species, the
California herring (*clupea pallasii*), is caught in the North
Pacific Ocean. The thread herring (*opisthonema oglinum*)
is another species of herring to be found in the West Indies
and off the east coast of the U.S.A. Another gastronomically
valuable species of herring, known in the U.S.A. as wall-
eyed herring, is called, in England, alewife.

The herring fisheries of England and Scotland depend
F*

upon the presence of shoals of herrings off different parts of the coasts at different times of the year. In May and June there is great fishing off the Shetlands. Later on, beginning with July, the fishing is carried on from the Shetlands to the Orkneys and at Aberdeen, Peterhead, Fraserburgh and Wick. These fisheries, which last several weeks, are for fish almost ready to spawn. The English drift-net fishery for herring is practically confined to the east coast, and it follows the Scottish fishery. The east coast fishery commences at North Shields, in May, and it goes on at an increased rate during June, July and August, when Grimsby, Hull and Scarborough begin fishing. In September, the landings begin at Yarmouth and Lowestoft, reaching their maximum in November and December.

Were the herring a rare fish, it would be considered one of the greatest delicacies of the table. Its flavour is excellent; its food value very high and its cost very low: it supplies very nearly as much body-building material as the same weight of fresh salmon, but at a tithe of the cost. The fact that herrings are inexpensive is only excuse for their being unfashionable among the well-to-do classes, but it is impossible to find an excuse why they should not be more popular than they are among the masses.

Many people do not like herrings because of their many small, fine bones. If care be taken, nearly all these may be removed with the central bone, but, to do this, the fish must be neatly split, with the fish knife, both sides being separated. Slip the knife under the backbone and gently lever it out, taking care that as many as possible of the small bones come away with it. Naturally, this method applies equally to kippers and bloaters, which are one and the same fish differently treated. The splitting operation may be done before the fish is cooked: it will make it much easier, hence more agreeable to eat.

LAMPREY. LAMPERN

Lat. *petromyzon marinus*. Fr. *lamproie*.
Ger. *lampreten*. Ital. *lampede*. Sp. *lampreas*.
Lat. *lampetra fluviatilis*. The freshwater *lamprey* (q.v.).

Lamperns and lampreys are almost prehistoric creatures: they are eel-like, they have a cartilaginous skeleton, but no limbs, no ribs, no backbone, and no jaws. The lamprey averages about 30 in. in length, and lives in the sea. The lampern is much smaller and inhabits the lower parts of certain rivers. They both live by attaching themselves to fish, and sucking nourishment from them. Lampreys are esteemed by fishermen as the best bait for cod and turbot, and are best left alone by cooks.

Lamperns are by many regarded as a great delicacy. They come into season in October or November, and can be cooked in any method suitable for eels (q.v.). It is usually agreed that they should be served with a sauce made with their blood and that they are especially estimable in a pie with veal stock and mushrooms.

A Lamprey, first a Lampron Grigg, then a lampret, then a lamprell, then a lamprey.
(Randle Holme, p. 324)

Lampreys or lampurnes be partly of the nature of Yeeles, yet somewhat wholsomer, and lesse jepardous, for that they bee not so clammie and so grosse as Yeeles . . . . . . After yeeles and lamprayes, we should drinke good strong wine, as saith Arnold (Arnaud de Villeneuve) and generally with all kindes of fish, wine is very wholsome, for as the French man saith: 'Poisson sans vin est poison.'
(Cogan's *Haven of Health*. 1612, p. 143)

Both lampreys and lamperns have the reputation of being

dangerous as food, which is no doubt because they each have two filaments in the back which are poisonous and which must be removed before cooking.

THE NEGLECTED LAMPREY

A dish well worth reviving is the lamprey, that curious fish, a surfeit of which is supposed to have caused the death of Henry I. It has been pointed out with some reason that the monarch's death was quite as likely due to the apothecary's well-meant efforts to assuage an attack of indigestion. Be that as it may, the lamprey was once much more commonly eaten and was, in fact, in olden days, thought so highly of that King John actually levied an annual toll of lampreys from the burghers of Bristol, heavily fining the authorities one year when the annual gift to the royal table fell short of its usual high standard.

In appearance the lamprey somewhat suggests the eel. It seldom exceeds a foot or eighteen inches in length. It was once commonly taken from autumn to spring in most tidal rivers, but today it is almost confined to the Severn, the Trent and the Ouse.

Lampreys are usually taken in circular basket traps, which are placed in the river near the locks and weirs, the best catches being made when the water rises well above its normal level. The average catch for the season has not been estimated, but it must amount to many hundreds of thousands of fish, all of which are purchased by local customers, with the exception of the happy few who, though living further afield, are wise to the excellence of this delicacy. Lampreys, by the way, will live out of water for many hours and can easily be transported alive for long distances.

Lampreys, after being 'finned' and gutted, can be stewed in milk or jellied like eels. They are possibly best, however, when treated as follows: About three dozen should be placed in a stewpan with five table-

spoonfuls of stock, quarter pint of Port, one teaspoonful
of salt, one of pepper, and a good squeeze of lemon, and
the whole concoction simmered gently for about an
hour.

The lamprey was last sold in London just before the
World War I. About 1910 thousands were washed up
dead at Hammersmith as the result of poisoning, and
the creature has never been seen again in London
waters.

Allied to the edible lamprey, which spends the
greater part of its life in the sea, is the smaller freshwater lamprey, or lampern, and the still smaller brook
lamprey, or pride. Although they differ in their habits
some authorities believe all three to be merely varieties
of one and the same species. These creatures have by
some been described as 'mystery fish', not that such a
description should be allowed to prejudice the diner,
who will find in this ancient dish of kings a *bonne-
bouche* that, once tried, will be often repeated.

(E. G. Boulenger)

MACKEREL

Lat. *scomber scombrus*. Fr. *maquereau*. Ger. *makrelen*.
Ital. *sgombri*. Sp. *escombro*. One of the best, even if one of
the cheapest of all the fishes out of the sea. It is excellent both
hot and cold; hot, in ever so many ways, none better, however, than plain broiled and served with a maître d'hotel
sauce; cold, soused. The one drawback of the mackerel is
that it will spoil more quickly than almost any other fish, a
fact which gained for it the privilege of being the only fish,
once upon a time, allowed to be hawked in the streets on
Sundays, in England. Mackerel are available all the year
round, but they are in their prime in April, May and June,
when they are caught in large numbers along the south coast
of England. In July, August and September, mackerel are

best left alone. At all times, but chiefly during the hot weather, mackerel should be eaten as soon as possible after being caught. When very fresh, they are quite stiff, opalescent, with bright protruding eyes and bright red gills. Beware of the limp mackerel, which is indigestible always, and may be poisonous.

> You may buy land now as cheap as stinking mackerel.
>
> (The first part of *King Henry IV*, Act II, Sc. 4)

OYSTERS

Lat. *ostrea edulis*. Fr. *huîtres*. Ger. *austern*. Ital. *ostrice*. Sp. *ostras*. Any marine bivalve mollusc of the genus *ostrea* of family *ostreidae*. The native, whether Colchester, Whitstable, or from any other Essex or Kentish bed, should always be eaten uncooked and unspoilt by its beard being removed or palate-paralysing vinegars and sauces added to it. A squeeze of lemon is said to be permissible, but it is the thin end of the wedge of heresy. Portuguese oysters, Blue Points, or the large American oysters are the only ones that should be used for cooking.

Oysters must be very fresh, plump and firm, and the shells must be tightly closed. The best way to open an oyster is to insert the oyster knife at the hinge, snap the ligament which attaches the fish to the top, or flat shell and serve the oyster in the deep shell, in its own liquor.

American oysters are sometimes very large indeed and may be cut in pieces when cooking. French oysters have a peculiar savour and are usually small; the best are the *Marennes*, both *Blanches* and *Vertes*, and *the Belons*. Colchesters and Whitstables are the best natives.

When cooking oysters, do no more than allow the edges to curl or they will become tough.

Why, then the world's mine oyster. (*The Merry
Wives of Windsor*, Act II, Sc. 2.)

Although oysters remain so true to type that shells discovered in ruins of the ancient city of Rome are recognizable
as belonging to fish from the Essex rivers, their cultivation
is nevertheless subject to great changes. Despite modern
scientific investigation, there is as yet no certain knowledge
of the method by which the oyster reproduces itself, nor of
the causes of the epidemics which have almost emptied the
beds of Brittany, Holland and England in turn during the
past fifty years. The fisheries thus decimated have been restocked from those which suffered least, and there is in consequence a tendency on the part of those trading in oysters
to confuse together all oysters of the European type (*ostrea
edulis*) under the general name of natives, as opposed to the
American type (*ostrea virginica*). Strictly speaking, however,
the word 'native' is restricted to those oysters spatted and
reared between the North Foreland and Orford Ness. It may
more reasonably be applied to any oyster which is fattened
in the waters in which it was bred; and in that sense it offers
a valuable distinction from the *relaid* oyster, i.e., the oyster
which, for purposes of the market, is transferred from the
original breeding ground to another, so that it may grow and
acquire the flavour of the food in the waters in which it finds
a new home.

The following are among the more popular European
oysters:

Portuguese (*ostrea angulata*). Though these are geo-
graphically a European oyster, they resemble the American
type. As the name implies, they derive originally from Portuguese beds, but the main source of supply is now the Bay
of Arcachon, wherein they became acclimatized through
the shipwreck of a boat carrying a cargo of them. The

Portuguese is much the hardiest of all oysters, and is able to endure long exposure to the sun at low tide without suffering either in health or flavour.

Brittany. The Brittany oyster, excellent in its own native waters, is also the one most suitable for relaying, and it meets that fate in very large quantities. During recent years the beds of Holland, Whitstable, the Helford river in Cornwall, the Yealm in Devon and the Roach in Essex, have been largely restocked from Brittany. The Brittany is a neutral oyster, very ready to assume the local flavour of its adopted ground, and consistently excellent wherever it is laid. It can often be identified by a small trace of lime on the outer side of the shell, at the hinge, owing to the fact that it is laid on tiles, placed in the water for the purpose. The tiles are previously covered with a solution of lime to prevent the oysters becoming so firmly attached that they will be difficult of removal when developed.

Marennes Vertes. These oysters have enjoyed a high reputation on account of their distinctive colour for more than two hundred years. They are cultivated in *claires*, or pits connected together by trenches wherein the tide circulates, and in which a fine green weed is encouraged. Each oyster is given about a square foot of ground, and in due time the beard through which the oyster filters his food collects the spores of the weed and becomes green. The greenness is not due to decay or copper, but to chlorophyl, the colouring matter of vegetables, derived from the weed, together with iodine and other valuable properties. The *Marennes Vertes* are, therefore, usually preferred to the *Marennes Blanches* in France, where the reason for the greenness of these oysters is better understood than in England.

Dutch Natives. The Dutchman is as excellent a cultivator of oysters as of bulbs, and in the past very large quantities of oysters have been shipped from Holland to England.

THE LAND OF COCKAYNE *by Pieter Brueghel* 1530–1569

O The Roast Beef of Old England ! ("Calais Gate") *by William Hogarth* 1697–1764

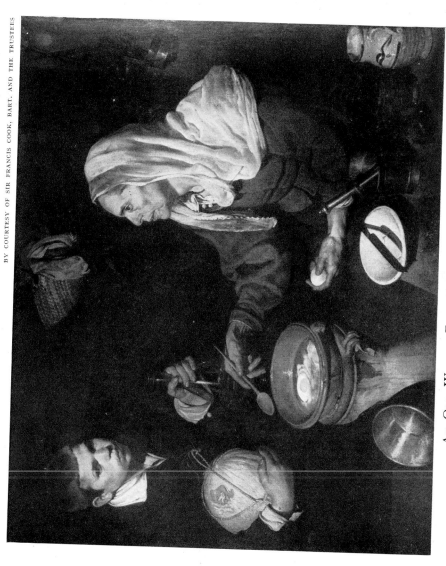

AN OLD WOMAN FRYING EGGS *by Velazquez* 1599–1660

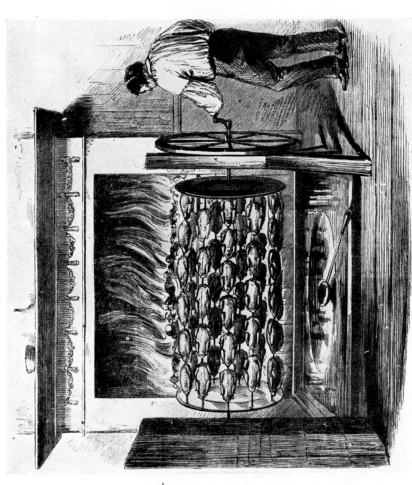

ROASTING FIFTY-SIX GEESE FOR THE OLD MEN'S HOSPITAL, NORWICH

LLOYD'S COFFEE HOUSE, LOMBARD STREET, 1773

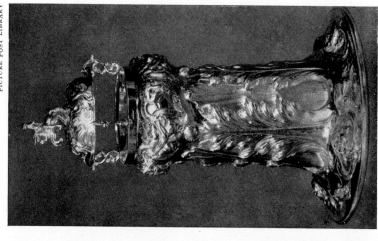

CHARLES II SALT CELLAR, *circa* 1660

THE SALT OF STATE, *circa* 1660

(*The Crown Jewels*)

GOLD SALT CELLAR OF FRANCIS I *by Benvenuto Cellini* 1500–1572

SOYER'S MINIATURE KITCHEN

From a woodcut of the kitchen (8 ft. by 17 ft., capable of cooking for 100 persons)
designed by M. Alexis Soyer, of the Reform Club, for the steam-vessel Guadalquiver
in 1847

1. Roasting fireplace
2. Steam heated Bainmarie-pan for keeping soups, etc., hot.
3. Two charcoal stoves
4. Charcoal stove with movable balance grating
5. Charcoal stove drawers, ventilators and ash pans
6. Hot plate and gridiron

7. Oven with hot closet above for bread, pastry, meat, etc.
8. Pounding pestle and mortar
9. Kitchen table with sliding shelves
10. Small cupboard for condiments
11. Block-tin spoon drainer
12. Shelves for saucepans
13. Vegetable boxes
14. Exit via door leading to the deck

Unfortunately, the Dutch beds were badly hit by the post-war oyster epidemic, and in consequence they have been largely restocked from Brittany. Recent falls of spat, have however, been very good, and there is a probability of increased supplies in the future.

Royal Whitstables. The Kentish beds, like those of Essex, won Roman favour, though the principal supply was then from Richborough, which no longer yields oysters. Shortly before the 1914 war the English spat was so free that Brittany beds were relaid from our own; but since 1921 the reverse course has been necessary. Most Whitstable oysters today are therefore relaid Brittanys or Belons. The oysters known as Royal Whitstables are, however, genuine natives, taken from a breeding ground the boundaries of which were settled by law about 1900, the property of the Whitstable Oyster Company, which alone has the right to call its oysters Royal Whitstables. This Company (strictly, the Company of Free Fishers and Dredgers of Whitstable) has existed from time immemorial; it obtained an Act of Incorporation in 1793, but the Act did no more than confirm the traditional constitution, by which a foreman and jury are elected annually at a Water Court or Court of Dredging for the management of the Fishery for the ensuing year. The freedom of the Company is an hereditary right enjoyed by eldest sons of freemen dredgers. For the time being the supply of Whitstable natives is very small, but there is hope for better abundance for the future. The Whitstable oyster has a particularly pearly shell, a sweet, almost nutty, flavour, and—distinguishing mark of the real English native—a very small beard.

Colchester Pyefleets. Among the many varieties of the oyster, those of Essex in general and the Colne fishery in particular are probably the most famous. There is good ground for supposing that they were exported to Rome during the Occupation, for a great number of shells have been found among the ruins of the ancient city bearing the distinctive characteristics of the Colne oyster. Richard I, in confirmation of previous rights, gave the borough of Colchester by Charter the sole right to the fishery from the North Bridge to the West Ness. The Corporation has ever since successfully defended its claim, and among the treasures of its insignia is a beautifully modelled silver oyster (1804), setting the standard size below which it is illegal to sell Colne oysters. The Colne fishery is about four and a half square miles in extent; the Pyefleet creek is admittedly one of the best fattening grounds in the kingdom, and the rest of the fishery is admirably productive as a spatting ground. Other Essex estuaries share, in a lesser degree, the fame of the Colne, notably the Blackwater, the Roach, and the Crouch. During recent years, and particularly since the American slipper limpet reached England, the relaying of oysters from other parts has been extensively practised in the Blackwater and the Crouch, with excellent results.

All oysters sold on the London market must satisfy stringent tests imposed by the Fishmongers' Company, and there is, therefore, no ground whatever for regarding the oyster as in any way dangerous to health. On the contrary, they are exceptionally rich in vitamins, iodine, and organic phosphorus; and as they are both nutritive and easily digestible they are a healthy food for all save the small minority allergic to oysters.

ON OYSTERS

The discoverer of the oyster's virtues must ever remain anonymous, although the late G. F. Watt painted a hypothetical portrait of the intrepid man which, under the title of 'Experientia Pulchra', ranks amongst the

greatest triumphs of that artist's brush. The poet Gay
has immortalized him in verse:

'The man had sure a palate covered o'er
With brass or steel, that on the rocky shore
First broke the oozy oyster's pearly coat
And risked the living morsel down his throat.'

Oyster feasts and famous oyster 'addicts' have
marked each epoch in the world's culinary history.
Cicero has been described as 'nourishing his eloquence
with the dainty'; whilst in later days Louis XI of France
feasted the learned professors of the Sorbonne once a
year on oysters 'lest their scholarship should become
deficient'. One of Napoleon's marshals consumed 100
oysters as a light prelude to his breakfast proper, and
the late Frank Buckland, father of oyster culture in
these islands, would on occasion excel this gastronomic
feat.

Today great attention has been given to the water in
which oysters are reared in this country, the molluscs
being placed in special tanks where they rhythmically
pump all impurities from their systems before being
dispatched to the retailers. By this means an increasing
number of consumers is being gained, since such
oysters are guaranteed 'safe'.

In the past contaminated beds gave rise to typhoid
scares, and though a recurrence of such disasters is now
practically impossible, the fears then bred have left a
crying evil behind—the practice of sousing oysters in
vinegar. This Philistine custom, once justified as a
fancied safeguard, not only destroys the delicate flavour
of the oyster itself, but deadens the diner's palate.

We are told that on that historic occasion when
Mr. Weller and a party of professional friends con-
cluded some forensic business with an oyster feast,
one member 'took an imperial pint of vinegar with his
oysters without betraying the slightest emotion'. One
can only hope that this practice may eventually be

relegated, with or without emotion, to the dark ages by every self-respecting diner.

Even the establishment of the oyster beds makes fascinating history. The founder of European oyster farming is believed to have been one Sergius Aurata, who established a farm in Italy about the year 100 B.C. The largest oyster farm in the world, that of Arcachon, had its beginning in mere accident. Here the elongate Portuguese oyster became installed as the result of a shipwreck at the mouth of the Gironde. A large consignment of these shipwrecked oysters survived the adventure, and so in time became the founders of a colony covering a vast area.

The oyster is essentially a subject for mass-production, the world's annual crop totalling many millions. Yet there is one case on record of a solitary oyster making fame and fortune for its possessor. A century or so ago the proprietor of an oyster saloon in Drury Lane found himself the possessor of one out of a batch of oysters which had a small hole pierced in its upper shell, with the result that when water was forced through this aperture, as the mollusc breathed, a shrill whistling sound was emitted. At once the distinguished bivalve was segregated and in a single night it set fashionable London alight. Dickens and Thackeray were amongst the stream of celebrities that came to view the musical mollusc and to feast prodigiously on its less distinguished relatives.

In these days oysters are largely a luxury of the well-to-do, but in Dicken's time the situation was reversed. It will be recalled how on Mr. Pickwick's historic journey to Ipswich, Mr. Sam Weller, was prompted to observe 'It's a wery remarkable circumstance, Sir, that poverty and oysters always seem to go together. What I mean is that the poorer the place is the greater call there seems to be for oysters. Here's an oyster stall for every half dozen houses. The street's lined with 'em. Bless it, if I don't think that ven a man's wery poor he rushes out and eats oysters in reglar desperation.'

Alas! Desperation has no such paliative nowadays. Even in the middle of the past century oysters could be purchased 'almost for a song'. The late Sir E. Ray Lankester once told me how as a boy at St. Paul's School, then situated in the City, he daily lunched off a dozen oysters and bread and butter at the price of fourpence. Gourmets may well repine for those vanished days of which one enthusiast wrote: 'Oysters pickled, stewed, baked, roasted, fried and scalloped; oysters made into soups, patties and puddings; oysters with condiments and without condiments; oysters for breakfast, lunch, dinner and supper; oysters without stint or limit; fresh as the pure air and appreciated with all the gratitude which such a bounty of nature ought to inspire'. No nobler epitaph could surely grace the empty shell of *Ostrea edulis*.

(E. G. Boulenger)

In 1798 I was at Versailles as an emissary of the Directory, and had frequent dealings with the Sieur Laporte, who was secretary to the tribunal of the department; he was a great amateur of oysters, and used to complain of never having eaten his fill of them.

I made up my mind to procure him full satisfaction at last, and to that end invited him to dinner.

He came; I kept him company to the end of the third dozen, after which I let him go on alone. He went as far as thirty-two dozen, taking more than an hour over the business, for the servant was a little slow in opening them.

Meanwhile I was inactive, and as that is an intolerable condition to be in at table, I stopped my guest when he was still in full career. 'My friend,' I said, 'it is not your fate to eat your fill of oysters today; let us dine.'

We dined; and he acquitted himself with the vigour and address of a man who had been fasting.

(*The Physiology of Taste*, by Brillat-Savarin)

STURGEON

The sturgeon, *acipenser sturio*, is a fish with a large head and hardly any brains in it; also a great deal of flesh, all of which is fit to eat and used to be much more highly esteemed in the past than it is now: it has no bones, but cartilage, a swim-bladder which is used to make isinglass and a spinal marrow which provides a Russian delicacy known as *vesiga*. Its greatest contribution to gastronomy is its roe, from which caviar is made. It swarms in large schools in the estuaries of the Danube, Dnieper, Don and Volga, and in much smaller numbers in the Elbe, Oder and Rhine. Formerly sturgeon was also caught in the Po, Rhône, Garonne, Loire, Seine and Moselle, and it was considered a great delicacy in Imperial Rome. Cicero, who boasts that he could deny himself murenae and oysters, declared that no man not a Stoic could be indifferent to the excellence of sturgeon. And Ausonius has described the passage of the mighty fish through the placid waters of the Moselle:

'Whom stream and band and silvery shoals admire,
   As on they glide
Parting the rippling waters that recede
   On either side.'

In the thirteenth century *Proverbes* 'Esturgeons de Blaye' are named among the finest fish and during the sixteenth century sturgeon was so plentiful in the Rhône Estuary that it was the cheapest fish sold in Provence. As late as 1782 a sturgeon 6 ft. 7 in. in length was caught in the Seine, in Paris, and sent to Versailles for the royal table. In England sturgeon was a 'royal' fish, which meant that any caught in English waters had to be offered to the King or sold for the benefit of the royal exchequer.

What is quite remarkable is that the flesh of the sturgeon

is not in the least fishy when fresh: that from the back has distinctly a 'veal' quality; that from the under belly is richer and could pass for pork. The whole can be salted, smoked and pickled for storing. Platina, whose book is the earliest of all printed cookery books, considers that 'chine of sturgeon delicately salted, just as it reddens under the operation, is the ne plus ultra for an epicure'. He recommends hanging fresh sturgeon for a few days before cooking and prefers stewing it to any other mode of cooking. 'For this purpose', he adds, 'place your fish in equal parts of water, wine, and vinegar, with a sprinkling of salt, and simmer over a slow fire as long as if it were veal'.

In Imperial Rome sturgeon was served in great pomp at banquets, being carried round the guests, with an accompaniment of flutes and trumpets, by attendants wearing crowns. Alexandre Dumas has related in his *Grand Dictionnaire de Cuisine*, such a banquet given in Paris in the heyday of the Napoleonic Empire by Cambacérès. Orders had gone forth that the finest sturgeon sent to the Paris market on a certain day must be reserved for the *Archichancelier*. It so happened that not one but two were sent, one weighing 162 lb. and the other 187 lb. The maître d'hôtel somewhat perturbed, came with the news to his master to know what to do with the second fish, and Cambacérès told him.

That evening, after the soup course had been served, three musicians dressed as chefs, one playing the flute, the other two the violin, made a spectacular entry followed by four servants bearing lighted torches, and escorting two others who bore on their shoulders a short ladder covered with foliage and flowers, upon which was laid a magnificent sturgeon. The procession went round the guests who rose, cheered, clapped and were thrilled by such a fine sight. As the cortège was leaving the banqueting hall one of the bearers slipped, fell down, and the sturgeon slid to the floor.

There was consternation and commotion among the guests, but their host remained quite calm and in his high-pitched falsetto voice he snapped out the order: '*Servez l'autre.*' A few moments later the same flutist and violinists came in again, followed by the torch-bearers escorting another sturgeon, one bigger than the first, which was borne in state round the amazed guests, before being carved and served.

TROUT

Trout, *salmo fario*. Fr. *truite*. Broadly speaking, the name 'Trout' includes all those *salmonidae* which live entirely in fresh water except grayling and char; and it is applied also to several of the migratory *salmonidae*, including, in Europe, the salmon trout—*salmo trutta*—(in Devonshire, salmon peal, in Wales, sewin). And in America, the rainbow trout (*salmo irideus*) and others.

The common European trout is *salmo fario*, and others, whether or not they have special names, e.g., *levenensis* or *ferox* or Great Lakes trout, are merely varieties of *fario*.

Sea trout are found in all the countries, from Spain northwards, facing the Atlantic. Like salmon also, they are pink-fleshed and their life history is the same as that of salmon—they are begotten and hatched and spend their first two years in a freshwater river, whence they go into the sea, and after an interval of a year or more, during which time they vastly increase in size, they return to their parental river to carry on the cycle of reproduction.

Rainbow trout and similar fish, such as steel-heads, may, quite unscientifically, be classed as half-way between freshwater trout and sea trout, inasmuch as some of them go to the sea, some treat a large body of fresh water as the sea, running to it as two-year-olds, returning to the rivers to spawn and then going back to the lake to regain condition, while still others spend their whole lives in their parent river just like the brown trout.

In the Southern Hemisphere, there are no indigenous *salmonidae* (except a rather rare grayling in New Zealand and—*mirabile dictu*—in the small river in the Falkland Islands), but *salmo fario* and *irideus* have been introduced and have prospered amazingly, especially in Tasmania and New Zealand, and later in Chile, where their average size is far larger than in their native waters. The American Brook trout, so called, *salvelinus fontinalis*, is really a char, and so is the Dolly Varden trout—*salmo malma spectabilis*, and several similar varieties common in American rivers running into the Pacific.

For gastronomical purposes, trout may be divided into two classes—non-migratory and migratory—trout and sea-trout—*truite-saumonée:* char may be included with the former.

As a rule, sea-trout and the large trouts should be treated and dealt with as salmon.

The smaller river or lake trouts are excellent smoked, fried, grilled, boiled and otherwise prepared in many different ways.

RIVER TROUT

The trout is a fish highly valued, both in this and foreign nations. It may be justly said, as the old poet said of wine, and we English say of venison, to be a generous fish; a fish that is so like the buck, that he also has his seasons; for it is observed that he comes in and goes out of season with the stag and buck. Gesner says, his name is of a German offspring: and says he is a fish that feeds clean and purely, in the swiftest streams, and on the hardest gravel: and that he may justly contend with all fresh-water fish, as the Mullet may with all sea fish, for precedency and daintiness of taste: and that being in right season, the most dainty palates have allowed precedency to him.

(Izaak Walton)

'Here comes the trout that must be caught with tickling.' (*Twelfth Night*, Act. II, Sc. 5.)

TUNNY

Tunny, which the Greeks called *amia*, was held in great esteem by them, and Archestratus.

The best part was said to be the tail end of the fish, the liver was also regarded as a great delicacy:

> And after this the luscious intestines
> Of roasted tunnies sail'd upon the table
>
> (Eubulus. Ionian)

> Despise not thou the fat Boeotian eel,
> Nor grayling, nor the entrails of the tunny.
>
> (Aristophanes. The Lemnian Woman)

The smaller tunnies were generally preferred to the larger ones, but not always:

> When that stout Anytus to Pythionica
> Does come, to eat with her; for she invites him,
> As people say, whenever she does get
> Two noble tunnies from Chaerephilus;
> So fond is she of all things that are large.
>
> (Timocles. Icarians)

VII

BIRDS

WHILST THERE are some fishes which are quite unfit for human consumption, and also plants roots, fungi and berries which are not merely unwholesome but actually deadly, there is no bird known to be poisonous. All birds may be fit to eat, but most of them are not good to eat. To begin with there are the thousands of different kinds of sea-birds, from the many 'snippets', tiny visitors to our shores, to the giant solitary albatross, which ranges the southern oceans: their flesh may be safe to eat, but so tough and rank as not to be worth the effort of mastication. And yet there was a time when, in England, seagulls were netted in large numbers when quite young and kept in captivity, fattened on salted beef, and greatly prized as a table delicacy. Why the practice—or should it be called the art?—has not been revived in these days of meat shortage is probably because there is some Order against it. Happily for us there is so far no Order against the collection and sale of gulls' eggs, and these have to some extent replaced the plovers' eggs, the sale of which is now prohibited. As a matter of fact the eggs of all the sea-birds are quite good to eat and not in the least fishy in taste, but most sea-birds are so cunning that they lay their eggs in the most inaccessible places, where they are safe from the greed of man.

Of all other wild birds, it may be said that with the exception of the pheasant, the more beautiful they are to look at the less toothsome to eat. In the good old days of long ago, the days of groaning boards and great displays, swans and peacocks graced the feasts at which barons of beef and boar's heads, legs of veal and saddles of mutton dulled the appetite of guests who were probably fully satisfied with no other part of the birds than a feather for their cap.

ON GAME

The term game includes all animals which enjoy a state of natural liberty in the fields and woods, and are fit to be eaten.

We add *fit to be eaten*, because certain wild animals do not come under the category of game; such are the fox, the badger, crows, magpies, owls, etc., which we call *unclean beasts* or vermin.

Game is divided into three series:

The first begins with the thrush, and includes, in a descending scale, all the lesser birds.

The second ends where the first begins, and includes the snipe, the beccafico, the corncrake, the partridge, the pheasant, and the hare; this is game in the proper sense of the term—ground game and marsh game, feathered game and furry game.

The third is more generally known by the name of venison, and includes the wild boar, the roe deer, and the other hoofed animals.

Game is a prime favourite at table, being wholesome, highly nutritious, and full-flavoured, and easily digestible by all except persons of advanced years.

(*The Physiology of Taste*, by Brillat-Savarin)

In Tudor and Stuart times there were many more wild birds killed for the table, some of them are no longer obtainable whilst others although still with us have ceased to be acceptable.

BITTERN (COMMON BITTERN)

Botaurus stellaris

The bittern is a nocturnal bird, haunting bogs, reedy swamps and marshes, where it hides during the day: it feeds during

the night on fish, grubs and small animals of all kinds. Its
curious call, during the mating season, is responsible for its
different country names such as 'stake-driver' and 'Bull of
the frog'. The bittern was highly prized as an article of food
in England during the sixteenth and seventeenth centuries,
when it was also known as bittour, byttor and betowre. It was
served on numerous occasions to the Lords of the Star
Chamber, and it was so highly prized that, in 1590, for
instance, it cost 5s. when a capon cost but 2s. Its flesh is said
to have much of the flavour of the hare's and none of the
fishiness of the heron's.

> Hearon, Byttour, Shoveler, beying yonge and fatte,
> be lyghtyer digested than Crane, and the Byttour
> sooner than the Hearon   .   .   .   All these fowles
> muste be eaten with muche ginger or pepper, and have
> good olde wyne drunk after them.
>
> (Elyot's *Castle of health*. London. 1539)

The Bittern was at one time common in the British Isles,
but, in the nineteenth century, it became extinct as a breeding species. It has since returned to the Norfolk Broads.

> The flesh of the bittern was formerly in high esteem,
> nor is it despised in the present day: when well fed, its
> flavour resembles somewhat that of the hare, nor is it
> rank and fishy like some of its congeners. The long
> claw of the hind-toe is much prized as a toothpick,
> and formerly it was thought to have the property of
> preserving teeth.
>
> (*Hints for the table: or the economy of good living*. London.
> 1859)

BLACKBIRD

Turdus merula

O.E. *ousel*. Fr. *merle* (*marle*, in Mrs. Glasse's *Art of Cookery*).
A song bird related to the thrush and ranging from
the Outer Hebrides to the Volga, and from North Africa to

Norway. In the British Isles and in Central Europe many blackbirds do not migrate, whilst others do migrate in September or October and return in the following February or March. In England, blackbirds are no longer killed for food, but there was a time when they were considered fit fare for a king. They were served to the Lords of the Star Chamber in 1590, when they cost 2s. per dozen; in 1605, when they cost 3s., and in 1635, when the price had risen to 4s. 6d. per dozen.

> Black byrdes or ousyls, among wyld foule hath the chiefe praise for lyghtnes of digestion.
> (Elyot's *Castle of Health*, London, 1539, p. 30)

> Blacke-Birds, although esteemed by some a good nourishment, yet others are of opinion they are better to delight the eare with their musicke than to feed the belly, being bitter in taste, and hard of digestion.
> (Hart, *The Diet of the Diseased*, London, 1633, p. 80)

BLACK GAME. BLACKCOCK. BLACK GROUSE

Lyrurus tetrix

A game bird related to the capercaillie and to the red grouse: it is smaller than the first and larger than the second: it is also better gastronomically than the capercaillie, but not so fine a bird as the grouse. The male bird is called Blackcock or heathcock (heathpoult in Devon); it weighs about 4 lb. when adult; its plumage is mostly of a rich, glossy black with white wing patches and outwardly curved tail feathers. The female is called greyhen, grayhen or brown hen, and rarely weighs more than 2 lb. when adult: the plumage is mottled and barred. The French culinary name for both cock and hen is *coq de bruyère*. Black game is widely distributed all over Northern Europe and Northern Asia.

There was a time when black game was known as grouse, in England. Thus Henry VIII's 'grows', at Eltham, early in the sixteenth century, were not red grouse but black game. Later they were called black grouse, as a distinction from the red grouse.

In England the season when black game is allowed to be shot is from August 20th (except in Somerset, Devon and the New Forest, where it is 1st September) up to 10th December, but the birds are not really fit to eat before the end of October.

BREWES

The brewe or whimbrel, also called half-curlew (*numenius phoebius*) is a sea-bird which nobody would think of killing for food, but it must have been greatly esteemed in olden times since one brewe, in 1590, in London, cost twice as much as a fat capon; in 1602, eight brewes bought for the Lords of the Star Chamber cost 28s.

They are good for them that live neere the moores and that have not better meate.
(Venner. *Via recta ad vitam longam.* 1628. p. 63)

BUSTARDS

The name of various members of the family *otididae*, but more particularly of:

The little bustard (*tetrax tetrax*), the smaller European species, which is still found in most lands bordering the Mediterranean, in Southern Europe, North Africa and the Near East. It is the best, from the gastronome's point of view, and is known in culinary French as *Bastardau*.

The great bustard (*otis tarda*), the largest of European land birds, ranges from Spain eastwards to China. It used to be found in the British Isles, and it was served to the Lords of the Star Chamber in 1519, when it cost 4s. on one occasion and 2s. 10d. on two other days.

Bustards, some twenty years since, were bred in the open parts of Norfolk and Suffolk, and were domesticated at Norwich. Their flesh was delicious, and it was thought that good feeding and domestication might stimulate them to lay more eggs; but this was not the case. There were formerly great flocks of bustards in England, upon the wastes and in woods where they were hunted with greyhounds, and were easily taken. The bustard is, however, now extremely rare in this country. Three female birds were shot in Cornwall in 1843; on Romney Marsh, in 1850; and in Devonshire in 1851. In January 1856, a very fine male bustard was taken near Hungerford, in Berkshire, on the borders of Wiltshire, this being the only male taken for many years in England; it weighed 13½ lb. and its wings measured from tip to tip 6 ft. 3 in.

(*Hints for the Table*. London. 1859)

CAPERCAILLIE OR CAPERCAILZIE

Tetrao urogallus

This is the largest European member of the grouse family: it is also known as *Cock o' the wood*. It is found in the pine forests of the Jura, Alps, Carpathians and Siberia, and although it became extinct in the British Isles, it has since been re-introduced and is very plentiful in parts of Scotland.

The cock capercaillie has an unfortunate habit of stuffing itself with pine needles, and Major Hugh Pollard recommends steeping the bird in new milk for an hour after it is plucked 'to abate too strong a turpentine flavour', but an old cock caper is best dealt with in the manner recommended by Nazaroff in *Halcyon Days in the Urals*:

Draw and clean it and rub the inside thoroughly all over with salt, pepper and mustard; stuff it with onions, sew it up and bury it in the ground for twenty-four hours. Then wash it well and let it soak in milk for twelve hours and for ten in vinegar. After that, skin it, lard it well and roast over a slow fire for half an hour. Then steam it for three hours, butter it well all over and give it to the dog, if he will eat it, for nobody else could.

The young birds are quite acceptable from September to November, although officially in season from August to December. The crop and ducts of the bird should be removed as soon as possible after it is shot, and it should be kept at least a week—two weeks would be better during the cold weather. Cover the breast with rashers of fat bacon and roast in a moderately hot oven, basting frequently. A rich chestnut and pigmeat stuffing is recommended.

COOT (COMMON COOT)

Fulica atra

A European water-bird which is more like a small wild duck, in shape and plumage, than other rails. It is called in French *foulque morelle*, *macroube* and *judelle*. It abounds in marshy lands and open inland waters. It is about 18 in. in length and weighs up to 2 lb. A slow and particularly stupid bird, the coot owes its safety to the fact that it is hardly worth killing for food. But it is edible and it is eaten, under some other name, in some of the less reputable of London's Soho Restaurants, in salmis or pies. It should be skinned, not plucked, as soon as killed, like a rook. There are regular coot shoots on the Norfolk Broads and elsewhere in England, but there is only one part of Europe where the coot is killed for food on a commercial scale: it is in Herzegovina, where coots are smoked and kept as a highly valued winter food.

G

CORNCRAKE OR LANDRAIL

Crex crex

A small migratory bird of real gastronomic merit. The plumage is of various shades of brown above and yellowish-white below, rendering it quite inconspicuous. It haunts the open country and agricultural land, and it has a way of running along the hedgerows or in the corn, instead of rising before the gun, which makes its life safer than that of other birds. 'Even when he (the landrail) does rise, he often escapes, for his apparently slow, cumbersome flight is disconcertingly hard to judge.'—M.H.P. The corncrake usually makes its nest in some long grass, on the ground, and lays from nine to eleven eggs, cream coloured and blotched with red and grey.

The corncrake arrives back in Europe, from its winter quarters in Africa, towards the second half of May, and its peculiar 'crake-crake' pairing call is unmistakable. Full-fledged birds are but 10 in. in length, and they are not fit to eat until September, or after the harvest, when at their fattest and ready to embark upon their southward voyage to their African winter quarters.

In culinary French the corncrake is known as *roi des cailles*, although it is not a quail; but probably because it used to be said—maybe believed as well—that there was always a corncrake acting as leader when the quail returned to Europe in the spring. (It is also called *re de quaglie, rey de las codornices* and *Wachtelkönig*, in Italian, Spanish and German.) The corncrake used to be considered a great delicacy but it is now too scarce to shoot.

CRANE

Grus grus

A wading bird, resembling the heron, which is no longer considered fit for human consumption. But it had its ad-

mirers in the past among princes and kings and their cour-
tiers. In 1519 and 1520, when crane was served to the Lords
of the Star Chamber, its cost was 4s.; in 1534 and 1535,
when a capon cost 2s., a crane cost 6s. On 6th June, 1543,
the purchase of 'a young pyper crane' from Hickling is
mentioned in the accounts of the City Chamberlain of Norwich, which leads one to believe that cranes must have been
bred near Norwich at the time. (*Trans. N. and N. Nat. Soc.*,
VII, ppl 160 *et seq.*) In a MS. dated 1605 and published in
Vol. XIII of *Archaeologia* (p. 315), entitled *A Breviate touch-
ing the Order and Government of a Nobleman's House*, there is a
'Dietarie' for each month of the year, and the crane appears
from November to March only, when birds cost from 3s. 4d.
to 5s. each. Further evidence that cranes were plentiful in
Norfolk during the sixteenth century is supplied by the list
of presents sent to William Moore, of Losely, on the occasion
of the marriage of his daughter, on 3rd November, 1567,
including nine cranes 'out of the marshland in Norfolk'.
(*Archaeologia*, XXXV, p. 36.)

Crane is hard of digestion, and maketh yll juice, but
beyng hanged up longe in the ayre, he is the lesse
unholsome.

(Elyot's *Castle of Health*. London. 1539, f. 31.)

CURLEW

Numenius arquata

A migrant bird of the plover kind, about 24 in. in length,
drab coloured above, mottled with dark brown and white
beneath. It has a remarkable sickle-shaped beak, 5 to 7 in.
long, a slender and graceful body and long legs. Its chief
breeding grounds are the northern lands of Asia and Europe.
It is also called whaup in Scotland. The eggs are usually four
in number and brownish-green, with cinnamon markings.
The curlew feeds on berries, grubs and insects on the moors,

where it breeds, and on small crustaceans and molluscs when it reaches the sea. This duality of diet is responsible for the apparently conflicting statements about the Curlew's gastronomic merit. Young curlew, 'stewed in milk and served with a plain run butter and lemon sauce, are excellent', is the verdict of no mean judge, Major Hugh Pollard, who adds:

> Curlews are very good if they are inland birds fresh from their breeding-places on the moors, but after a short spell at the sea they get decidedly fishy.

Molly Castle writes:

> I have eaten curlew freshly shot from feeding on the black ooze of Belfast Lough and found them excellent, plainly grilled, while they have been very good in salmi when purchased for 1s. 6d. from game-hawkers in Dublin.

Curlews were served to the Lords of the Star Chamber in 1519 and 1520, when they cost 1s. each; in 1567, when they cost 1s. 6d.; in 1590, when the incredible amount of 8s. was paid for one curlew; and in 1605, when three cost 15s.

The curlew is still shot and sold for food in England, but the demand is no longer what it was: thus whilst the average price of curlew in London, in 1807, was 3s. per bird, it had fallen to 9d. or 1s. in 1941.

There is an old Lincolnshire saying:

> 'Be she white or be she black,
> The Curlew has tenpence on her back.'

Another version runs thus:

> 'A Curlew lean or a Curlew fat
> Carries twelve pence on her back.'

DOTTEREL OR DOTTREL

Eudromias morinellus

A bird of the plover family, which occurs in many parts of Northern Europe and Western Asia. It is chiefly known in

England as a summer visitor, appearing in small flocks of eight or ten towards the end of April and staying during May and part of June, when they are fat and much esteemed for their delicate flavour. Hence Drayton's reference to it in *Song xxv:*

> 'The Dotterel, which we think a very dainty dish,
> Whose taking makes such sport, as no man more
> would wish.'

They were retailed in London, in 1807, at 3s. per bird, and it is on record that seventeen couple were counted in one London poulterer's shop in 1845. It is now protected by law.

FIELDFARE

Turdus pilaris

A little bird which resembles the missel-thrush and is a regular winter visitor to the British Isles, Southern Europe and North Africa, breeding in North Europe and West Siberia. It often takes the place of the lark in the steak-and-kidney-and-lark pie. It is a poor singer, compared with the Lark, but just as good in a pie.

GANNET OR SOLAN GOOSE

Sula bassana

A large white sea bird with black-tipped wings which breeds on a number of rocky islands round our coasts, on the Faroe Islands, and Gulf of St. Lawrence. From time immemorial the solan goose from the Bass Rock, near Edinburgh, has been esteemed as an article of food. Taylor, the Water Poet, writing in 1618, describes 'the soleand goose' as:

> most delicate fowle, which has very good flesh, but it is eaten standing at a sideboard, little before dinner, unsanctified without garlic; and after it is eaten it must be well liquered with two or three rowsers of sherrie or canarie sacke.

Up to about 1848 there was still a demand for young gannets from the Bass, and till at least 1885 they were sent to London, and many Midland towns, where they were eaten in the commoner eating-houses.

In London, gannets were sold as Scotch grouse, plucked and cooked, at 10d. each, but gradually the demand ceased and the flesh was considered to be rank and fishy. Sir William Jardine, writing in about 1845, says:

> We have once or twice eaten them boiled like ham and considered them by no means either strong, fishy or unpalatable.

The gannet is still eaten by the fishermen from Lewis in the Outer Hebrides, who annually raid Haskier for young birds, which they salt for winter use.

As late as 1856 eggs were sold in London at 6d. a dozen and, according to an old advertisement, were eaten at Buckingham Palace.

GODWIT

Limosa limosa (black-tailed Godwit)
Limosa lapponica (bar-tailed Godwit)

Godwits are found in the Old World and in the New. They are large wading birds, with long legs, a long bill, and a body like that of a large pigeon, resembling the curlew, to which they are greatly superior gastronomically. Black-tailed godwits formerly bred in considerable numbers in the eastern counties, from Yorkshire south, but owing to their nests being robbed and the birds netted and shot in the spring, they ceased to breed in England from about the year 1829. In London, the price of godwit, which was 3s. per bird in 1807, fluctuated from 1s. to 6s. in 1922. Godwits are cooked like woodcock.

The *bar-tailed godwit*, which is sometimes called the

sea-woodcock, breeds from the north of Norway eastwards and is a common winter visitor in the British Isles.

Sir Thomas Browne calls the godwit 'the daintiest dish in England', and Ben Jonson refers to the bird more than once:

> 'Your eating
> Pheasants and Godwits here in
> London, haunting
> The Globes and Mermaids;
> wedging in with lords
> Still at table.'
>
> (*The Devil is an ASS*, Act III, Sc. 3)

> 'I had a brace of does sent me, Gentlemen, and half a dozen pheasants, a dozen or two of godwits, and some other fowle, which I would have eaten whilst they are good, and in good company.'
>
> (*The Silent Woman*, Act I, Sc. 4)

GROUSE

Lagopus scoticus

In great Britain and Ireland the name *grouse*, when not otherwise qualified, applies exclusively to the *red grouse* or *Scotch grouse,* the best, in our opinion, of all game birds in the world, during two months, from mid-August to mid-October of the year when it was born. It is generally regarded as an insular form of the willow grouse, which has ceased to put on a white, protective plumage during the winter months. The grouse is a very clean feeder, living upon the young and tender shoots of heaths which abound where it is bred, in Scotland, Yorkshire, and the Pennines; also in Wales and in the West of Ireland. All attempts to introduce the grouse in France and elsewhere have failed, and there is no name for this bird in any other language. A young grouse, that is a bird from the 12th August to the end of December of the year when it was bred, has soft downy plumes on the breast and under the wings, pointed wings and rounded spurs.

The only other game bird which might dispute the claim of the grouse to be the best of all would be the grey partridge, an excellent bird indeed. But if we give precedence to the grouse over the partridge, it is because of its greater individuality and the greater intensity of its flavour. A partridge may be a little more or a little less plump, but it is otherwise exactly the same, whether shot in Norfolk or in Cornwall; and whether shot this year, last year or the year before. Not so the grouse. It always has the distinctive grouse flavour, as any and every first growth of the Côte d'Or is obviously a wine of Burgundy, but there is between the birds shot in Derbyshire and those shot in Perthshire, as well as between the birds shot in one season and those of the previous year, the same degree of variation that exists between the different growths of the Côte d'Or of different vintages. Major Hugh Pollard, who acknowledges the influence of seasonal changes and locality upon what he calls:

> that subtle alchemy of digestion which endows the bird with his special value,

yet places the grouse third in order of gastronomic merit, after the partridge and the pheasant. He considers the distinctive flavour of the grouse a disadvantage :

> for it is not easily abated by other subtleties, so that, however you dress your bird, whether as soup or braise or pie, the dominant flavour is always grouse, and short of violence with a clove of garlic or a curry that would make coke palatable, it is impossible to cover it.

But why cover it? All the subtleties of delicious sauces and garnishings are devised to help chicken, veal, cod and all food without any flavour or one that is not attractive, but not the flavour of a young grouse. What is true is that the flavour of grouse, good as it is, is somewhat too assertive to be enjoyed continuously, day after day, twice a day, like bread or potatoes. And there is yet another point in favour of the grouse: it is as good—some even say better—when eaten cold. Of course, an old grouse, that is a bird of the year before, is quite another thing, and a poor thing, and on no account should a young bird and an old one be cooked at the same time nor in the same way. Plainly and lightly roasted is the best way to deal with a young bird, whereas the most suitable funeral for an old bird is the soup pot or the game paste jar.

In 1757, the price of grouse on the London Market was 3s. 6d. per bird; in 1922 it fluctuated from 5s. 6d. to 8s.; and in 1941 from 4s. 6d. to 7s. 6d. In 1942, the Ministry of Food fixed the maximum retail price at 6s. per bird, irrespective of age and condition.

The late Professor George Saintsbury, whose authority as a critic ranked very high in the realm of gastronomy as well as in the world of letters, wrote:

> While nearly all the game birds are good, and some eminently good, grouse seems to me to be the best, to possess the fullest and at the same time the least violent flavour—to have the best consistency of flesh, and to present the greatest variety of attractions in different parts.

Grouse have *no* spurs.

GUINEA-FOWL

The guinea-fowl is a native of West Africa which has been domesticated in England since the fifteenth century, when it was known as a turkey, probably having been first introduced from Turkey. That was before the bird known today

G*

as a turkey had ever been seen in Europe. When Shakespeare speaks of a turkey, he means a guinea-fowl. There are various species of guinea-fowl, but they all have one characteristic in common, they never run to fat and their flesh is naturally dry. They are usually barded or larded and roasted on a spit or in a moderate oven or stewed in a cocotte, but they may be prepared for the table in any way suitable for a chicken.

Guinea-fowls' eggs are excellent when boiled seven or eight minutes, that is hard boiled; they may be described as a larger edition of the plover's egg, which they resemble in texture.

GULLS

Black-headed Gull (Larus ridibundus)
Common Gull (L. canus)
Herring Gull (L. argentatus)

These handsome sea birds are no longer eaten, but there was a time when, in England, gulls were netted and fattened during the winter months in the poultry yard, which may have been sufficient to make them lose their fishiness. They must have been highly valued since they cost the enormous price of 5s. each, in 1590, when bought for the Lords of the Star Chamber, at a time when beef cost but twenty pence per stone. In England today, since the sale of plovers' eggs has been prohibited, gulls' eggs have to a certain extent taken their place in the West End restaurants. The commonest species of gull in the British Isles is the herring gull.

During the seventeenth century young black-headed gulls, termed puets, were netted and held in high esteem as a delicacy after being fed on bullock's liver or with corn or curds from the dairy, which may have imparted a more pleasant flavour.

(*British Birds*, edited by H. F. Witherby)

HAZEL-HEN

Tetrastes bonasia

A game bird which inhabits chiefly the pine forests and birch woods of mountainous districts in many parts of Europe, from the Alps to Russia and eastwards to Siberia and even Japan. It feeds mostly on berries and its flesh is white, tender and of fine flavour. It has never been appreciated to any great extent in England, although large quantities used to be sent to the London Market from Scandinavia and Russia, either frozen or chilled. Where the hazel-hen is shot, it is best plainly roasted or prepared in any way suitable for grouse. It is very good when cooked with fresh cream, in the French way, or sour cream, in the Russian way. Older birds and cold storage birds are best potted or in soups.

The French name of the hazel-hen is *gélinotte*.

JAY

Garrulus glandarius

A destructive, screeching but rather beautiful bird which is common in most European countries, including the British Isles. It is capable of doing great damage in the kitchen garden and has a passion for green peas. It must be shot in self-defence and it may be eaten, in austerity times: cats will not eat jays. Its French name is *geai*.

KNOT OR KNOTT

Calidris canutus

A European sandpiper, breeding in arctic regions and migrating south, frequenting the shores of the British Isles in very large companies at certain times of the year. It is rather larger than the snipe, having a shorter bill and shorter legs. They were taken in large numbers on the coasts of Lincolnshire in nets such as were used for catching ruffs, and, when fattened, they were preferred to ruffs by some people. They were provided for the Lords of the Star Chamber in 1605. They are also called *robin sandpiper* and *robin snipe*. They may be served in any way suitable for snipe (q.v.). Their loss of popularity is evidenced by the slump in their market value: in 1807, they fetched from 3s. to 4s. each, in London; in 1922, they cost 3d. and in 1941, from 2d. to 3d. each.

LAPWING, PEEWIT OR GREEN PLOVER

Vanellus vanellus

Also called *lappinch*, in Cheshire, and *vanneau huppé* or *dix-huit*, in France. It is the 'common' plover in England, where it is a resident, its numbers being augmented by a great influx from the Continent in the autumn. It used to be shot and netted in large quantities and supplies were also imported from Holland. It is now protected in most English counties. Its eggs, which may no longer be offered for sale in England, are excellent, whilst the bird itself is not generally considered as good as the golden plover; yet its price on the London Market, rose from 9d. and 1s. in 1807, to 1s. 4d. and 1s. 6d. in 1922, and from 2s. 6d. to 2s. 9d. in one of the large London Stores, in 1942.

> 'The lapwing, by some called the greene plover, is by some likewise in high esteeme, and yet it is inferiour to the plover.'
>
> (Hart's *Diet of the Diseased*, London, 1633, p. 81)

It is probable that the 'plover' which Dr. Hart had then in mind was the golden plover, the best of the plover family from the gastronome's point of view. In French, whenever the name of *pluvier* is used without any qualification, it means the *golden plover*, whilst the lapwing is always referred to as *vanneau*, a bird which appears to have enjoyed a greater measure of gastronomic reputation in the past than it does now. Thus, according to an old French proverb :

'Qui n'a mangé grive ni vanneau
N'a jamais mangé bon morceau.'

And a Provençal proverb places the lapwing on par with the woodcock and the golden plover:

Se vuos mangea de buoi mousseu
Mangea bécassin, pluvié e vaneu.

LARK

Alauda arvensis

Larks, by which skylarks are usually meant, in England, are widely distributed in Europe and Asia. In France, the commonest species is the crested lark (*galerida cristata*), known as *alouette*, in the spring, when they are not killed for food, and *mauviette*, after harvest and vintage, when they are fat and fit for the spit. Formerly skylarks were caught in England on migration by birdcatchers, in nets and snares, and from 20,000 to 30,000 were often sent yearly to the London Market. (Yarrell.)

Larks are still occasionally eaten, in England, in the traditional steak, oyster, kidney and lark pie, but there was a time when considerable numbers of these little birds were also eaten roast. Larks were sent to the London Market, chiefly from Dunstable, during over 200 years; also, but not quite to the same extent, from Cambridgeshire. Yarrell states that 1,255,500 larks were taken during the winter of 1867–68.

Larks were provided for the Lords of the Star Chamber

on many occasions: they cost but 6d. per dozen, in 1519 and 1520, rising to 8d., in 1534, 1s. in 1605 and 3s. 4d. in 1635. Their price, on the London Market, was 4s. per dozen in 1807; 3s. in 1922, and 4s. in 1941.

> What! Is the jay more precious than the lark
> Because his feathers are more beautiful?
> > *(Taming of the Shrew,* Act IV, Sc. 3)

> Let his grace go forward
> And dare us with his cap like larks.
> > *(Henry VIII,* Act III, Sc. 2)

This is an allusion to the method of catching larks in Shakespeare's days, after attracting them and dazing them with small mirrors and a red cloth: in this case the 'cap' referred to is Cardinal Wolsey's red hat.

> Larks are of a delicate taste in eating, light of digestion, and of good nourishment.
> > (Venner's *Via recta ad vitam longam,* London, 1628, p. 61)

> Larks are not fit for the spit that do not weigh over 13 oz. to the doz.
> > (Dr. Lister. Queen Anne's physician, 1703)

MOORHEN.　MOAT-HEN,　WATER-HEN.
GALLINULE

Gallinula chloropus

The names of a small water bird very common in this country. It is about the size of a bantam hen, dark olive-brown above, iron-grey below, with white tail coverts, which are conspicuous as it swims, and a scarlet frontlet in both sexes. It lays from seven to eleven eggs, dull buff in colour, with reddish spots. In country districts moorhens haunt ponds, lakes and streams in safety as they are too poor fare to tempt poachers. Their price on the London Market was 1s. per dozen in 1807; from 4d. to 9d. each in 1922;

and from 4d. to 6d. each in 1941. Major Hugh Pollard, no mean authority, has stated that

> waterhen skinned and then fried in hot fat makes an excellent salmi or braise.

The moorhen never appears to stop eating: it is a great devourer but a poor converter. Where it is plentiful the mallard and other wild ducks do not come on account of the food shortage. To grow or scatter food to tempt wild duck is a waste of time, money and labour, unless moorhens have been first of all destroyed or scared away.

ORTOLAN
Emberiza hortulana

The French name, which is used in English also, of a European bunting about 6 in. long, enjoying a high degree of reputation among gastronomes. There was a time when they were plentiful but they have now become quite rare; they used to be netted, fattened and prepared for the table in any way suitable for quail (q.v.). They migrate southwards in the autumn and return to breed in most countries of Continental Europe and western Asia towards the end of April. They feed on insects and seeds, when free, but, unlike most other wild birds, they do not sulk when in captivity and very quickly get fat on oats and millet.

PARTRIDGE
Perdix perdix

The common or 'grey' partridge, also called paitrich, in Scotland, is the best partridge, gastronomically; it is a finer bird than the red-legged partridge (*alectoris rufa*), or French partridge, called *bartravelle* or *perdrix* rouge, in France, which was first introduced in England by Charles II, in 1660, but not with any great measure of success.

In the British Isles the partridge generally mates in March and its eggs are hatched out in a normal season during the first two weeks of June. Shooting is not allowed before 1st September and the young birds are at their plumpest and best in October. A young partridge—*un perdreau*—should not hang more than three or four days, in a cool, airy place, after being shot. It possesses such a delicate and exquisite flavour of its own that it should not be 'high', nor should it be served with any strong sauce, such as onion sauce or sauce madère. It is best served with just a little gravy, plainly roasted, baked or grilled, some straw potatoes and a little cress, if liked, but no Brussels sprouts or any other bulky vegetable, least of all members of the cabbage tribe.

Young birds, that is birds of the year, are easily distinguished from their parents: their first flight feather is pointed at the tip instead of rounded until the autumn moult, and it is a sure birth certificate. The colour of the feet is not quite so sure a guide: in the earlier part of the season, the feet of the young partridge are yellowish-brown, but as soon as the cold weather sets in they become pale bluish-grey, like those of the older generation.

Old birds, that is birds over fifteen months old, are an entirely different proposition and they are best stewed, braised and served with a variety of vegetables, not excepting cabbage.

Partridges have been highly prized in England for many centuries past, but it is somewhat disconcerting to our modern notions to find that game was eaten at all times of the year, quite irrespective of mating seasons, as we eat chicken all the year round. Partridges were served to the Lords of the Star Chamber at most of their sittings from 1519 to 1639, the cost of the birds rising from 6d., 7d. and 8d. each in the earlier accounts to 2s., 3s., and as much as 3s. 8d. on one occasion, in the seventeenth century.

'The painted partrich lyes in every field
And for thy messe is willing to be killed.'
(Ben Jonson. *The Forrest. II*)

'Killed' was the right word to use at a time when the poor
little birds were set upon by trained hawks. Thus Dr.
Richard Layton, writing to the Lord Privy Seal, Thomas
Cromwell, from Harrow-on-the-Hill, on 25th September,
1537:

I send by the bringer perisse [pears] of Harrow . . .
and partridges my own hawk kills.

The previous year (27 Hen. VIII) a Proclamation
had been made 'to preserve the partridges, pheasants
and herons from the King's Palace at Westminster to
St. Giles in the Fields, and from thence to Islington,
Hampstead, Highgate and Hornsey Park.

(W. E. Glegg)

'If the partridge had the woodcock's thigh
It would be the best bird that ever did fly.'

On the London Market the price of partridges has remained very much the same in recent years. In 1757, a
partridge cost 2s. 6d. in London; in 1807 the price varied
from 4s. to 5s. per bird; in 1922 it was from 4s. 6d. to
5s. 6d.; and in 1941 from 3s. 6d. to 6s. 6d.—the higher
price being paid for young birds and the lower for old ones.
In 1942 the Ministry of Food fixed the maximum retail
price of partridges at 5s. per bird, young or old.

PEACOCK

Lat. *pavo cristatus*. Fr. *paon*. This bird, a cousin of the
turkey, is never eaten now, but it used to have pride of
place upon the tables of the noblest in the land in former
times, in spite of the fact that its flesh was surely as tough and
tasteless then as it is now. In 1470 the then Archbishop
of York set before his guests one hundred peacocks, a

wonderful sight if the birds were brought into the banqueting chamber, as they most likely were, in all the splendour of their stiffly displayed tails. It was customary at the time, and long after, for the peacock 'course' to be heralded and brought into the hall in a procession of dishes headed by a stuffed peacock in full feather, its tail sweeping over the bearer's shoulders and its head filled with soaked wool which was set ablaze, a practice which has survived in an altered form, when the Christmas pudding is set alight.

Among the delicacies of this splendid table one sees the peacock, that noble bird, the food of lovers, and the meat of lords. Few dishes were in higher fashion in the thirteenth century, and there was scarce any noble or royal feast without it. They stuffed it with spices and sweet herbs, and covered the head with a cloth, which was constantly wetted to preserve the crown. They roasted it and served it up whole, covered after dressing with the skin and feathers on, the comb entire, and the tail spread. Some persons covered it with leaf gold, instead of its feathers, and put a piece of cotton, dipped in spirits, into its beak, to which they set fire as they put it on the table. The honour of serving it up was reserved for the ladies most distinguished for birth, rank, or beauty, one of whom, followed by the others, and attended by music, brought it up in the gold or silver dish, and set it before the master of the house, or the guest most distinguished for his courtesy and valour; or after a tournament, before the victorious knight, who was to display his skill in carving the favourite fowl, and take an oath of enterprise and valour on its head. The *Romance of Lancelot*, adopting the manner of the age in which it was written, represents King Arthur doing this office to the satisfaction of five hundred guests.

(*Antiquitates Culinariae; or curious tracts relating to the culinary affairs of the Old English, by the Rev. Richard Warner, of Sway, near Lymington, Hants.* London. Privately printed. 1791)

PHEASANT (COMMON PHEASANT)

Phasianus colchicus

The pheasant is the most beautiful game bird in the British Isles. It is a native of the East, but it was introduced into Europe at an early date: it has never been domesticated, but it is largely hand-reared and almost hand-fed as well, or was in pre-war times. The cock-bird is much more beautiful than the hen, but the hen is more tender and as a rule fatter. Pheasants which manage to elude the sportsman's gun and the many snares and dangers threatening their existence from the day they are hatched—and even earlier—may live for fifteen years or more, but long before they reach such an honourable old age they cease to be of interest to the gastronome. Young birds are best. It is easy to tell a young cock pheasant by his spurs: they are rounded and pointless for the first year, short but pointed up to the second year, very sharp and quite long in older birds. A young hen has soft feet and light plumage: an old one has hard and rough feet and a darker plumage. In the British Isles pheasants are in season from October to February and at their best from November to January. The flesh of the pheasant is dry and rather tasteless: that of the breast and wings is white, whilst the legs are dark and are more highly flavoured. To correct the natural dryness of the pheasant, it is supplied with a tightly-fitting waistcoat of bacon fat before cooking, and, if roasted, it must be basted abundantly. To correct its tastelessness, it must 'hang', not too long, of course, but long enough for the first signs of incipient mortification to be detected by sensitive nostrils. It is impossible to say how long a pheasant should 'hang' before it is cooked, as it depends upon the manner in which it was shot, the time that passes between the shooting and hanging, the weather conditions at the time and the place where it is kept. It should be a cool place, with lots of fresh air, and fresh cold air for choice. In warm weather, three days may be the limit of safety, whilst in the winter twelve days may not be excessive, provided the bird has not been badly 'shot' and has not suffered in the packing and transit from the shoot to the hook in the larder. Of all game birds the pheasant is the one that not only can be kept longest but must be kept. A pheasant cooked the day after it is shot, young and plump as it may be, will be tough and insipid: the same bird, a week later, will be tender and succulent.

We know from the Privy Purse Expenses of Henry VIII, that this monarch reared pheasants in large quantities at his palace at Eltham, and there is no lack of evidence of the high esteem in which the pheasant has been held by all gastronomes past and present, in spite of which the cost of pheasants in England has never been excessive. Thus, in the Star Chamber accounts, pheasants served in 1519 and 1520 cost 16d., 18d., and 2s. each; in 1567, their cost had risen to 6s. 8d. per brace; in 1590, to 10s. per brace; in 1602 it was 8s. 4d., and in 1605, 8s. 4d., 13s. 4d. and 16s. 4d. per brace, on different occasions; in 1635, their cost was 8s. 6d. and 8s. 9d. per bird. By 1757, their cost had risen on the London Market to 6s., and in 1807, to 7s. and 8s. 6d. per bird. In 1922 the cost of pheasants in London was 6s. 6d. for a hen and 8s. for the cock, and in 1941, these prices had risen to 12s. and 15s. 6d. In 1942, the Ministry of Food fixed the maximum retail prices for pheasants sold in England at 8s. for the hen and 9s. for the cock, irrespective of age and condition.

> 'Fesaunt exceedeth all foules in sweetnesse and wholesomenesse, and is equal to a capon in nourishing. . . . It is meate for Princes and great estates, and for poore Schollers when they can get it.'
>
> (Cogan's *Haven of Health*, London, 1612. p. 132)

' Fertile of wood, Ashore, and Sydney's copp's,
To crowne thy open table, doth provide
The purple phesant, with the speckled side.'

(Ben Jonson. The Forrest. II)

PIGEONS

In the British Isles the three principal species of pigeons are
the wood pigeon or ring dove (*columba palumbus*), the
stock dove (*c. oenas*), a smaller species wanting the white
on wings and neck, and the rock dove (*c. livia*), breeding
round the coasts, wherever there are cliffs, but now mixed
with tame birds and only found in a pure state in parts of
Scotland; the turtle dove (*streptopelia turtur*) is a summer
visitor, principally south of the border.

A large number of different kinds of pigeons are found
throughout the world, some of large size, resembling the
wood pigeon, others dressed in gorgeous colours, in which
the green predominates. The green fruit pigeons found in
the East and Africa, feed principally on wild fruits and nearly
all are good to eat, but they should be skinned, not plucked,
as the skins are very tough.

Tame pigeons should be starved twenty-four hours before
being killed and, if possible, all feathers should be removed
while the bird is still warm. It is advisable to hang the pigeon
head downwards as soon as it has been killed so that it may
bleed freely, failing which the flesh will be very dark. It is
most inadvisable to scald pigeons in order to remove
feathers, as this toughens the skin and outer layer of flesh.

PLOVER

All members of the family *charadriidae* are entitled to the
name of plover, but there are three members of that large

family which deserve more than any of the others the attention and gratitude of gastronomes: they are, in order of gastronomic merit, the golden plover, the grey plover, and
the green plover or lapwing. The golden plover and the
grey plover are highly prized for food, in England, where
they are still fairly common during the winter; the green
plover, better known under the names of lapwing, peewit or
peweet, is still abundant in many parts of the British Isles
and it is protected by law in some of the English counties.
During the seventeenth and eighteenth centuries the name
green plover was applied to the golden plover, but it was
transferred to the lapwing during the nineteenth century.

Another plover, which is not protected and needs no protection, as it is unfit for human food, is the black-headed
plover or crocodile bird: it is said to enter the gaping jaws
of crocodiles basking in the sun, on mud banks, after they
have enjoyed a square meal, and to feed upon the 'bits and
pieces' which they find among the great reptiles' fangs or
adhering to their jaws.

Plovers were served to the Lords of the Star Chamber on
many occasions, sometimes under the name of green plover
but usually merely under that of plover. They cost but 2d.
each, in 1519, 3d. in 1520, 3d. and 4d. in 1534. In 1567,
10 plover cost 4s. 4d.; in 1568, 3 green plover cost 15d.,
on one occasion, and 6d., 7d., and 8d. each on three other
occasions. In 1590 and 1605, they cost either 6d., 8d. or
10d. each.

> Plover is of some reputed a dainty meat, and very
> wholesome; but they who so judge are much deceived;
> for it is of slow digestion, increaseth melancholy, and
> yeeldeth little good nourishment to the body.
>
> (Venner's *Via recta ad vitam longam*. London, 1628.
> p. 63)

Plovers' Eggs

Hard-boiled plovers' eggs are—or were once upon a time—a joy to which gastronomes looked forward in April. Well-meaning but ill-informed law-makers, in England, made the sale of plovers' eggs an offence in order to protect the birds. As a matter of fact the plover invariably sits upon a four-egg clutch and no more; the eggs are pear-shaped and the pointed ends converge towards the centre of the saucer-shaped nest. Before Parliamentary interference with the plovers' eggs trade, expert collectors used to rob the plover's nest of two eggs out of the four and no more, which meant that the bird laid another two a little later on, and these were also taken away; the bird laid another two and was then left in peace, eventually hatching four birds, a couple of weeks later than she would have done had there been no tampering with her first clutch: this was all to the good, as the chicks had a much, better chance to live after, rather than before the last bad frosts of the early spring. Plovers' eggs are olive-brown thickly blotched with black and they harmonize perfectly with the dull meadow lands in which they are laid rather stupidly, since many thousands must be turned over every year by the plough.

If you live in the country, you may still 'find' plovers' eggs and enjoy them, although you may neither sell them nor buy them. They need barely five minutes simmering in all-but boiling water to be sufficiently hard boiled. The yolk is of a rich orange colour, the white being of a translucid mauvy shade of mother-of-pearl appearance.

If you have no facility for gathering plovers' eggs yourself, you must needs be content with gulls' eggs, similar in shape but a little larger than the plover's, and also slightly greener or bluer in colour.

PTARMIGAN (WILLOW-PTARMIGAN OR WILLOW GROUSE)

Lagopus lagopus

PTARMIGAN (COMMON PTARMIGAN)

Lagopus mutus

ROCK PTARMIGAN

Lagopus rupestris and *L. leucurus*

Member of the grouse family, of which there are two main sorts, the willow ptarmigan and the rock ptarmigan, also known as white partridge and rock partridge (*perdrix blanche* in French), although their feathered legs show they belong to the grouse and not to the partridges. It inhabits chiefly northern Europe and Siberia, but it occurs on the mountains of Scotland, not below 2,000 ft. altitude, from Perthshire and Argyllshire northwards. It is the only bird in the British Isles to put on a white coat in winter. In the U.S.A. the ptarmigan is represented by an almost identical species, known as the white-tailed ptarmigan: it is found in the Rockies. The ptarmigan may be prepared for the table in any way suitable for grouse (q.v.) to which it is distinctly inferior gastronomically.

In 1922, ptarmigan sold on the London Market at from 2s. 6d. to 4s. 6d. per bird according to quality, but in August 1942, the Ministry of Food fixed the maximum retail price of ptarmigan, 'in feather', at 3s. 6d. each irrespective of condition.

PUFFIN

Fratercula arctica

Puffin is the name of several species of sea birds of the auk family.

Their flesh is excessively rank, as they feed on sea-weed and fish, especially sprats; but when pickled and preserved with spices, they are admired by those who love high eating. Dr. Caius tells us that in his day the Church allowed them in Lent, instead of fish; he also acquaints us that they were taken by means of ferrets, as we do rabbits.

The puffin is a rather ridiculous-looking bird, about one foot long, with a short neck and a deep-grooved, parti-coloured, laterally compressed bill: it has white cheeks, a blackish upper part and foreneck and white underparts. It lays but one egg a year. The puffin provides the staple food of the Faroe Islanders and its flesh is dried and exported.

PURR

An Old English name, now obsolete, for the common dunlin, a regular visitor to the British Isles, and a bird which nobody would think to kill, even if not protected by law, as it is in England. Yet they figure in the accounts of the dinners served to the Lords of the Star Chamber, in 1602, when purrs cost 1s. 8d. each on one occasion, and 2s. on another.

QUAIL

Coturnix coturnix

The common quail is a migratory game bird wintering in tropical Africa and India, and breeding throughout the greater part of Europe, and eastwards as far as N.W. India. Considerable numbers formerly nested in the British Isles. The majority of birds exposed for sale in England were caught in Egypt on migration and imported alive in this country, where they were fattened and then killed. South of the Zambesi River, there is a resident African form, and in

China and Japan another variety, the *Japanese quail*. This bird has for long been kept in captivity by the Japanese for the sake of its eggs—one hen may lay as many as 200 eggs in a year. The black-breasted or rain quail (*c. coromandelica*) is very similar to the common species but it is not such a fine table bird; it is confined to India. A handsome African species is the harlequin quail (*c. delegorguei*). In Australia, there is the stubble quail (*c. pectoralis*), which is considered the best game bird in the country. The swamp quail (*synoicus ypsilophorus*), also known as the silver or Tasmanian quail, belongs to a different group: it is also found in Australia. Small quails of the genus *excalfactoria* inhabit S.E. Asia, Australia and Africa. The blue-breasted quail (*excalfactoria chinensis*) ranges from India and South China to Australia, where it is known as the king quail. The African species (*e. adansonii*) occurs throughout the greater part of the Black Continent. In India, there are also two scrub-haunting forms, the rock bush quail and the jungle bush quail (*perdicula asiatica*).

Quail should be eaten the day after they have been killed or as soon after as possible. They are plucked, singed and drawn from the neck; the head and neck should be removed, and the tips of the wings cut off: they can then be trussed like a small pigeon, or flattened out like *Squabs à la Crapaudine*.

On the London Market, quail fetched 2s. 2d. each in 1757; from 3s. to 4s. in 1807; from 2s. to 4s. 6d. each in 1922; and from 3d. to 1s. 9d. each in 1941, at a time when prices had gone up generally. The explanation of this apparent anomaly is that the pre-war quails, in England, were fattened and imported birds, far better than the hungry and lean home-killed visitors of wartime days.

In the U.S.A. the names of quail and partridge appear to be interchangeable, one or the other being used for the same bird in different parts of the country. As a rule, however, quail is qualified as in bob-white quail, California quail, Massena quail, mountain quail.

RAIL

There are a number of small, wading birds known by the name of rail in the Old as well as in the New World. They all haunt bogs and marshlands, feeding upon the creeping, crawling life of swamps and they are very poor fare, not to be compared with their cousin, the landrail which lives on the land and feeds on seeds and berries. In Europe, Western Asia and North Africa, the commonest rail is the water-rail (*rallus aquaticus*): it abounds in the British Isles. The plumage is darker than that of the landrail and the bill is partly red. It glides with ease and speed through reeds and is a good swimmer. It is excellent eating, cooked and served like snipe (q.v.). According to a letter of Sir Thomas Browne, M.D., written in the second half of the seventeenth century, and published in *Notes and Letters on the Natural History of Norfolk*, 1902, 'the ralla or rayle we have counted a dayntie dish' (p. 25).

In the U.S.A. there are a number of different species of rails, the smallest being the sora rail or Carolina rail (*porzana carolina*), the largest the king-rail (*rallus elegans*) found on the Atlantic seaboard wherever there are salt marshes, whilst the only one fit to eat is the Virginian rail (*rallus limicola*), which prefers fresh water to salt.

All over the southern portion of the Australian Continent, as well as in Polynesia proper and the Philippine Islands, the commonest rail is known as banded-rail or landrail (*rallus philippensis*). It is a bird of semi-nocturnal habits, feeding on insects, seeds and the succulent parts of various native grasses.

REDSHANK

Tringa totanus

A common European shore bird, allied to the sandpiper. It is brownish above and white below, with bright orange-coloured legs and feet. When served to the Lords of the Star Chamber, in 1519, redshanks cost 6d. for ten, and their price had not appreciably altered by 1922, when it fluctuated, on the London Market, between 4d. and 9d. apiece; in 1941, in spite of war conditions and rationing, they were offered in London at from 4d. to 6d. each.

ROOK

Corvus frugilegus

Opinions are divided as to whether the rook is the farmer's friend or his foe, but there is far greater evidence in favour of the rook than there is against. The rook devours an immense quantity of grubs and wireworms and other pests, of which there does not appear to be any shortage at any time, whereas there is very little evidence that rooks eat much if any grain. Rooks are both sociable and quarrelsome: they build their nests in large colonies, known as rookeries, not for defence but for company. The Wild Birds Act of 1880 protects rooks in the nesting season, a protection which is a hollow mockery since a proviso of the said Act specifies that:

> any person who owns or occupies land may kill rooks in the nesting season.

In 1940, an Order was issued that:

> Whenever a rookery becomes so populated that the birds are likely to damage crops, the occupier can be told by the local War Agricultural Executive Committee to reduce the numbers. Failure to do so will be a punishable offence.

Adult rooks being unfit to eat and difficult to kill, the 'reduction of numbers' of rooks usually takes the form of the most unsporting shooting of the fledglings still in the nests, and these are eaten in rook pies in many parts of rural England.

RUFF AND REEVE

Philomachus pugnax

These visitors to the British Isles used to appear in the Fens early in the spring and disappear about Michaelmas. The reeves laid four eggs in a tuft of grass the first week in May and sat about a month. Fowlers avoided shooting the reeves (hens), not only because they were smaller than the ruffs (cocks), but that they might be left to breed. They used to be caught by clap nets, sometimes with decoy, in Lincolnshire, the Island of Ely, and the East Riding of Yorkshire, where they were fattened on bread and milk, hemp seeds and sometimes boiled wheat. When sugar was added to the diet, the birds became 'a lump of fat' in a fortnight and fetched 2s. and 2s. 6d. apiece.

In olden times, ruffs and reeves were highly prized as food for the rich, more particularly when game was out of season, and they were among the most expensive of the dainties served to the Lords of the Star Chamber, costing 6s. and 6s. 8d. each, in 1602 and 1605.

They should be cooked soon after being killed, being trussed and treated in any way suitable for woodcock.

Ruffs and reeves (which are particularly found in Lincolnshire and the Isle of Ely) are very delicate birds and must be trussed like the woodcock, but not dressed with the guts. When done, serve them up with gravy and bread sauce, and garnish the dish with crisp crumbs of bread.

(W. A. Henderson)

At the beginning of the nineteenth century, ruffs and reeves were sold in London under two classes, 'fatted' or 'shot', the first costing on an average 5s. each, whilst the 'shot' birds rarely fetched 3s. and often sold for 1s. 3d. The last time when these birds appeared in the London Market quotations was in 1922, when they cost from 8d. to 1s. 3d. each, all, apparently, 'shot' birds. (In Picardy, the ruff is called *paon* and the reeve *sotte*.)

SHOVELER. SHOVELAR

Spatula clypeata

A widely distributed wild duck in most temperate parts of the northern hemisphere. It is also called river duck and spoonbill. Its French name is *souchet*. It breeds in the British Isles and North America, wintering farther south, reaching India and Central America. Shovelers keep aloof from other ducks, but appear to be almost indifferent to the presence of man: this may be due to the fact that they are surface-feeding birds and scavengers delighting in decaying matter and filth, so that they are not considered as fit for human consumption. But their meat, like that of the least particular scavenger of the sea, the lobster, is of excellent flavour and very tender. In olden days, when the spoonbill was called shoveler, it was highly valued for food. In 1590, for instance, 5s. per bird was the price paid for some shovelers served to the Lords of the Star Chamber, a much higher price than that paid for any other bird, wild or domesticated. In 1941, the price of shovelers on the London Market varied from 1s. to 2s. per bird.

> Shovelars feed most commonly upon the sea-coast upon cockles and shell-fish; being taken home, and dieted with new garbage and good meat, they are nothing inferior to farred gulls.

> (Muffet, p. 109)

There are related species of shovelers inhabiting the southern hemisphere and known respectively as South African shoveler, Australian shoveler, and South American shoveler or red shoveler.

I know of no surface-feeding duck about the value of whose flesh there is more divergence of opinion. I once knew an old epicure from Baltimore, who considered himself an absolute authority on food and drink. At a certain shooting club, he used to pick out for himself as a breakfast dish, a young shoveler still with pin feathers in its plumage. Most American sportsmen consider this a fairly good bird for the table, although not equal to mallard or teal. Audubon almost goes into raptures in speaking of it, but he does the same for almost every other duck. Nevertheless there is plenty of evidence to the contrary, and it certainly never fetched a high price in the markets. The truth is that the shoveler averages thinner than any of its relatives, and is seldom in really prime condition. The flesh, when poor, is not fishy in flavour but rather muddy.

Among European sportsmen there is the same difference of opinion. Some consider it very good, others think it rather mediocre. But in India it seems to be universally despised, due no doubt to the very filthy nature of some of the village ponds on which it feeds. Both Hume and Marshall (1879) and Baker (1908) consider it one of the worst ducks. Undoubtedly it is strongly flavoured there, due to the abundance of animal food provided by the warm winter climate. On the other hand there may be a large element of prejudice involved in the stigma cast upon it.

(J. C. Phillips)

SNIPE (COMMON SNIPE)

Capella gallinago

GREAT SNIPE

Capella media

WILSON'S OR AMERICAN SNIPE

Capella delicata

JACKSNIPE

Lymnocryptes minimus

PIN-TAILED SNIPE

Capella stenura

RED-BREASTED SNIPE

Limnodromus griseus. (See *Dowitcher*)

The name, when not otherwise qualified, refers to the common snipe, a larger bird than the jacksnipe or half-snipe, but smaller than the great snipe or solitary snipe. The common snipe (Fr. *bécassine*) is common in the sense that it is widely distributed from Ireland to Japan and from Siberia to the Cape of Good Hope. But it is one of the finest of all game birds, both for the sportsman and the gastronome. Its upper plumage is mottled with black and chestnut-brown, some of the feathers edged with straw-colour; the chin and throat are reddish-white; the lower parts white without spots; the flanks are barred transversely with white and dusky; its tail has fourteen feathers. It is normally $11\frac{1}{2}$ in. in length. It lays four eggs per clutch; they are olive in colour, spotted with brown and ash. It breeds in marshes and feeds upon worms and all sorts of creeping forms of life that it finds in mud, which it probes with its long bill, the tip of which is flexible and very sensitive. When disturbed, the snipe rises suddenly, with a curious and most disconcerting twisting flight, and a sharp cry, and then settles down to very fast and quite straight-line flying. In September and

October, large numbers of snipe arrive in marshy districts of England, and after a short rest they distribute themselves among other and sometimes much farther suitable feeding grounds so that they are never long together. In the British Isles, snipe are in season from October to February, but at their best in October and November.

In the U.S.A. the snipe which is called Wilson's snipe or American snipe (*capella delicata*) is the same as the common snipe except that it has sixteen instead of fourteen tail feathers.

In Africa, from Abyssinia to the Cape, the Ethiopian snipe (*capella nigripennis*) is very abundant and highly esteemed for food. It is just as good as the European snipe. In India and some parts of Africa there is also the painted snipe (*rostratula bengalensis*), which has the appearance of a snipe, but a slow rail-like flight and is of poor value for eating.

> The snite or snipe is worse than the wood-cocke, being more unpleasant to the taste, harder of concoction and nourisheth lesse; and is very apt to engender melancholy.
>
> (Hart's *Diet of the Diseased*. London. 1633. p. 80)

In spite of such uncomplimentary remarks, the snipe has been—and still is—very highly prized as a table delicacy. During the period 1519–1639 covered by our accounts of the dinners provided for the Lords of the Star Chamber, snipe were invariably served for their lordships' delectation during the winter months, the price of the birds rising from 2d. apiece in 1519, to 20s. for eighteen in 1639. In 1757, snipe cost a shilling each in London; and their price fluctuated from 2s. to 3s. 6d. in 1807, and from 1s. 6d. to 2s. 6d. each in 1922, and again in 1941. In 1942, the maximum retail price of snipe was fixed by the Ministry of Food, at 2s. per bird.

H

SWAN

Cygnus olor

A fine bird to watch on the water or in flight, but a poor one to eat. The male bird is called the cob, the female the pen, and the young, cygnets. Cygnets used to be served on festive occasions in England.

At the banquet given by the Bishop of Durham for King Richard II, in 1387, fifty swans graced the board. On Christmas Day, 1512, five swans were provided for the Duke of Northumberland's table; on the following New Year's Day, four more, and on Twelfth Day of the same year, another four swans.

In London, cygnets are still eaten once a year, in the ceremonial and traditional manner, at the Vintners' Hall, in the City. The Thames swans are 'Royal' birds and are marked by the swan warden of the Vintners' Company, and his acolytes, with two 'nicks' in the shape of a V, on behalf of the sovereign. It is one of the privileges of the Vintners to enjoy a 'feast of cygnets' once a year. The birds are brought into the Hall according to ancient usage, heralded by six musicians garbed in the old style of swan herds, playing an ancient lilt, 'All in a garden green', on wood-wind instruments: they are followed by six swan uppers, in their striped jerseys and white ducks; then by two swan markers, in their blue and red old-time watermen's coats, and each carrying his quaint swan crook. Next come the cooks, bearing on high the great pewter dishes of smoking hot cygnets. The procession advances to below The Salt and opens outwards to admit of Mr. Swan Warden, in his flowing sable gown, his Stuart cap, gaily embellished with a great white swan's feather: he is escorted by the barge master, resplendent in blue coat and silver lace and the silver badge of his office (of barge master) upon his right upper arm. Also in attendance the bedel and stavesman, in flowing gowns and armed with their silver-topped quarter-staffs; Mr. Swan's silk standard is borne aloft behind him. The music stops; Mr. Swan approaches The Salt, doffs his cap with flourish and reverence and proclaims in voice 'that all may hear': 'Master, I crave your acceptance of these roast cygnets for the delectation of your guests.' The Master replies: 'Let them be served, Mr. Swan,' whereupon the procession withdraws with music as it came and soon after the cygnets are served according to the ritual which has not altered in any material point since the 'Presentation of Cygnets' was enacted on the same spot, if not actually under the same roof, for the first time, a great many years ago. (*From information supplied by Commander Harold B. Tuffill, when Clerk of the Vintners' Company.*)

TEAL (EUROPEAN TEAL)

Anas crecca

One of the smaller wild ducks, which is excellent for the table. In the fen country it is also called half-duck, a name which is given in other parts of England to wild ducks other than the mallard. In France it is called *sarcelle*, and is one of the water-fowls allowed to be eaten on abstinence days. It is also differentiated as *sarcelle d'été* and *sarcelle d'hiver*, the first being the resident bird and the other the visitor. The teal is indigenous to the British Isles and breeds in many parts of Great Britain and Ireland, especially in the eastern counties and in Welsh bogs and Scottish moors with swampy tracts. There are 'summer teals', that is all-the-year-round birds, in England, but they are few compared to the considerable numbers arriving in September or October to spend the winter where food is not frozen or snowed under. They feed on water insects, worms, grubs as well as seeds and decaying vegetable matter. In England, they are in season from October to February, but at their best before Christmas.

On the London Market, the retail price of teal appears to have remained fairly constant: thus, in 1757, it was 1s. 6d. per bird; in 1807, from 2s. to 3s. 6d.; in 1922, from 1s. 9d. to 3s.; and, in 1941, from 2s. to 2s. 6d. The maximum retail price of teal was fixed at 2s. in 1942.

> Teal, for pleasantnesse and wholesomenesse of meat excelleth all other water-fowle.
> (Venner's *Via recta ad vitam longam.* London. 1628.
> p. 62)

The price of teal provided for the Lords of the Star Chamber rose from 2½d. per bird in 1519 to 8d. in 1605.

THRUSH

Turdus ericetorum (Song-Thrush)
Turdus viscivorus (Mistle-Thrush)

The name of a number of small song birds very widely distributed in all temperate parts of the world; in the British Isles, the song-thrush and the missel thrush or mistle-thrush, a larger bird and not so good a singer, are the more common species. They feed on insects and grubs, seeds and chiefly berries, when there is no ripe fruit in season, but their love of all the fruits which man loves best has brought large numbers of them to an untimely and brutal death. The wise gardener, however, finds means of protecting his fruit without shooting or trapping thrushes, as they are of the utmost usefulness in the lifelong war which all gardeners have to wage against insects and their grubs. No true gastronome would countenance the killing of a thrush for food, even if ready to admit that it was quite as good as a lark, on occasions when a thrush found its way by accident into the classical steak-kidney-oyster-and-lark pie. On the Continent, thrushes are killed and eaten without any qualms of conscience, like many other small songsters, but it is rather unexpected to find a recipe given by gentle Mrs. Beeton for roasting one.

TURKEY

Meleagris gallopavo

The usual 'short' or abbreviated form for turkey-cock (Fr. *dindon*), turkey-hen (Fr. *dinde*) or turkey-poult (Fr. *dindonneau*), a large and excellent American game bird, domesticated for nearly four hundred years, and one of the most valuable domestic fowls.

The name was first of all given, in England, to the guinea-fowl, which was originally introduced from West Africa before any of the birds now called turkeys had been seen in Europe; they were quite erroneously given the name already given to the guinea-fowl, a name which has stuck to them ever since.

The first to be introduced into Europe was the Mexican turkey; it had been domesticated in Mexico before the advent of the Spaniards, who brought specimens to Spain in 1530; some of them reached England round about the year 1540, before any specimens of the North American turkey, and English colonists, soon after, introduced the Mexican turkey to New England. In England, farmers breed chiefly the black Norfolks and the Cambridge bronze, the latter being the larger as well as nearer the original Mexican breed than the first, which is preferred by those who place flavour before size. In the U.S.A. the bronze turkey is the largest and most popular: the average standard weight of the adult cock is 36 lb. The white Holland turkey, which is known in Europe as the white Austrian, comes next in

popular favour: its average weight is 28 lb. for an adult
cock. It is a pure white bird, whereas the plumage of the
bronze is distinguished by a rich, brilliant, bronze sheen,
with white barring of the wings and edging of tail feathers.
Another popular turkey, in the U.S.A., is known as the
Bourbon red; the general colour of its plumage is a rich
brownish red, with the primary and secondary feathers of the
wing and the main tail feathers pure white. Its standard
weight is 30 lb. for an adult cock. In England the tendency
is to breed rather smaller birds. Turkeys have been domesticated so long that there are many sub-species, some better
than others, but not even the best of them is likely to compare
in flavour with the wild turkey, which still inhabits the high
table-lands of Northern Mexico and neighbouring States,
up to an altitude of some 10,000 ft. above sea-level. During
the eighteenth century several attempts were made to introduce some wild North American turkeys into England,
chiefly in Windsor Great Park and other royal forests.
According to Jesse's *Country Life*:

> in the reigns of George I and George II, Richmond
> Park could boast a flock of two thousand wild turkeys
> .   .   .   Turkeys are kept wild at Holkham Hall,
> Norfolk, by the Earl of Leicester, to whom they afford
> the same sport as any other bird in cover.

The turkey provides the exception to the rule that it takes
a long time to break down the prejudice of English people
against anything new in the matter of food or drink. The
turkey was enthusiastically hailed and made welcome as
soon as it appeared on the tables of the well-to-do people in
England, and it displaced in a very short space of time the
peacock, curlew, bittern, whimbrel and other fowls of the
air and the sea, which figured on most bills of fare up to the
beginning of the seventeenth century. One must bear in
mind, however, that the name turkey was first of all given to

the guinea-fowl, so that when we read in the first part of
King Henry IV (Act II, Sc. 1, v. 19):

> 'Odsbody, the turkeys in my pannier are quite
> starved.'

one forgives Shakespeare for introducing a name that would
have been quite unknown in the days of Henry IV, but one
must not forget that he was referring to birds which we
know as guinea-fowls, two or more of which could be cooped
in a pannier.

Even later, in the 1633 edition of Dr. Hart's *Diet of the
Diseased* (p. 78), when we read:

> Turkies of a middle age and reasonably fat, are a
> good, wholesome, nourishing food, and little inferior
> to the best capon.

it is obvious that the reference was to guinea-fowls.

By the time of Queen Anne's reign, a turkey was a turkey as
we know it, and people had probably already forgotten that
the name had ever been that of the guinea-fowl: it was
already then the bird that was expected to grace every board
on Christmas Day:

> Sometimes with oysters we combine,
> Sometimes assist the sav'ry chine,
> From the low peasant to the lord
> The turkey smokes on every board.
>
> (John Gay)

Poultry breeders recognize two quite distinct breeds of domestic turkey in this country—the black-plumed Norfolk
breed, and the more variegated Cambridge breed—and it is
believed that the former is descended from the North
American bird, and the latter from the more southern
form. . . . The turkey is ready for the table in about
nine months, when a large cock may weigh as much as 20 lb.
In the olden days, when big flocks were 'walked' into

London—a journey often taking a week or more—the birds were protected from 'cold feet' by being shod, their feet being tied up in sacking and provided with leather boots. Geese do not allow themselves to be shod, and the feet of these birds, when similarly driven, were protected by a coat of tar covered with grit. As a result the phrase to 'shoe a goose' was once a cant simile for attempting a hopeless task.

The turkey cock is larger than the hen and less economical, as its bones are heavier; as a rule the hen is also more tender than the cock. A large turkey cock with sharp spurs is best stuffed by a taxidermist: it is an old bird to be avoided by all cooks. The best turkey is a hen from seven to nine months old which has been reared in semi-liberty, and given plenty of food, but made to scratch for at least some of it. Its legs should be black, the neck short, the breast broad and plump, and the flesh snow-white.

WIDGEON. WIGEON

Mareca penelope

Widgeon was the name of the male bird, in Old English, and whewer, the name of the female, but widgeon is now used for both duck and drake: Latham says that the young males used to be sold in London under the name of Easterlings and the females under that of lady fowl; in Northumberland, they use the name *Whew* for both. In culinary French the bird is usually (and quite wrongly) called *sarcelle:* its real French name is *canard garrot* or *canard siffleur*. It is a wild duck, a little larger than the teal but smaller than the mallard. It breeds in the British Isles, Sweden, Russia, Siberia and North America, migrating as far south as California and India. The widgeon is one of the clean-feeding wild duck and one of the least shy. It usually keeps away from the sea and salt waters, feeding for choice upon the short, sweet grass which geese also love. Hence its

name grass duck, in Lapland. In the U.S.A. a closely
related species (*anas americana*) is also called baldpate.
There is also a related South American species (*anas
sibilatrix*). In the British Isles, the widgeon is in season from
1st August to 15th March, but it is at its best in October and
November only. Widgeons may be prepared for the table in
any way suitable for teal (q.v.) or wild duck.

On the London Market, the price of widgeon has never
varied very much: it was 1s. 6d. per bird in 1757; it fluctuated from 2s. to 3s. in 1807; from 2s. 6d. to 3s. 6d. in
1922; from 3s. to 4s. 6d. in 1941, and it was fixed at 3s. 6d.
(maximum retail price) in 1942, for birds 'in feather', no
game bird being allowed to be sold otherwise than in the
feather.

In India, they are considered as inferior to many other
species (Hume and Marshall, 1879; Baker, 1908). On the
Chinese coasts also there seems to be great variation in the
quality of the flesh. According to La Touche, the Foochow
widgeon are very good, whilst those from Swatow are very
bad. I see no reason why widgeon feeding on *zostera* alone
are not just as good as our most delicious North American
brant from the east coast.   (C. J. Phillips.)

In the Argentine and Chile, the Chilian widgeon (*anas
sibilatrix*) is highly valued as an article of food.

WOODCOCK

Scolopax rusticola

A greatly-prized bird which is widely distributed from the
British Isles to Japan and Java. In the U.S.A. there is a
somewhat smaller bird, the American woodcock (*philohela
minor*).

Woodcocks were provided on many 'meat' days to the
Lords of the Star Chamber and at a cost which rose from 1s.
per bird in 1534, 1535, 1567 and 1590, to 1s. 6d. and 2s.

H*

each in 1605. The price of woodcock in the London Market was 2s. 6d. in 1757; from 3s. 6d. to 7s. 6d. in 1807; from 4s. 6d. to 6s. in 1922; from 3s. to 6s. in 1941; and its maximum retail price was fixed at 4s. in 1942.

'They (woodcocks) come into England at the fall of the leafe, and depart again at the spring, but whence they come and whither they goe, it would trouble a good doctor to define. When the woodcock goeth, the swallow cometh.'
(Cogan's *Haven of Health*, London. 1612. p. 133)

'. . . four woodcocks in a dish'
(*Love's Labour's Lost*, Act IV, Sc. 3)

The woodcock is not a marshland bird like its small cousin, the snipe, and its diet is a mixed one of heather shoots, worms, insects and all forms of life hiding in mud, moss or foliage. As a result of its omnivorous habits, the woodcock carries much meat in proportion to its size, a 12-oz. bird being fully sufficient for one person of normal appetite.

In the British Isles woodcocks are in season from 1st August to 15th March, and at their best in October and November.

Both in France and in England the woodcock has long enjoyed a high reputation for gastronomic excellence, whilst its name has been used when referring to brainless people. It is in that sense that Claudio uses it when he asks:

'Shall I not find a woodcock too?'
(*Much Ado About Nothing*, Act V, Sc. 1)

Also, in Beaumont and Fletcher's *Loyal Subject* (Act IV, Sc. 4):

'Go, like the woodcock,
And thrust your head into the noose.'

But in Ben Jonson's *Every Man out of his Humour* (Act II,

Sc. 3), when Savolina says: 'I love not the breath of a wood-cock's head', she is not referring to any *fumet* but to the *fumée*, the tobacco smoke from a pipe which was known as a 'woodcock's head' owing to its supposed resemblance to the bird's head and beak.

In French, a *bécasse* is still commonly used in the vernacular for a 'simpleton', and the antiquity of its gastronomic reputation is evidenced by this very ancient quatrain:

> 'Le bécasseau est de fort bon manger,
> Duquel la chair resueille l'appetet,
> Il est oyseau passager et petit,
> Et par son goust fait des vins bien juger.'

EGGS

In China, it appears, there are connoisseurs of vintage eggs, but vintage eggs are a closed book to us, and we prefer new-laid eggs.

The fresher the egg the fuller it is, and there are two ways of finding out how full an egg is, hence how fresh it is. One way is to place the egg between one's eye and a strong light, holding the egg vertically, when it is possible to see whether there is a void at the top end, and how great it is. The other way is the trial by water, laying the egg horizontally in sufficient cold water to cover it; if it lies flat, it is full and fresh; if it shows a slight tilt, it is probably good enough to fry or to scramble; if it sits up, it is not fit to eat.

The shell of an egg is porous, particularly so after it has been washed to look nice and clean, a process which removes the fine film covering all eggs when they leave the hen. If an egg is left on top of a piece of cheese or in too close quarters with smoked fish, or anything else that is strong-smelling, the egg will acquire through its porous shell the next-door smell, and such a smell may be most acceptable 'next door', where it belongs, but most objectionable when it taints the egg.

If your eggs are your own, or your own hens', they are best kept *unwashed* and in a cool, airy place, not in a refrigerator. If they are from a shop, they are best used immediately: there is every likelihood that their waiting has already lasted quite long enough.

If you must use eggs which have been stored in a refrigerator, it is advisable to run a little warm water over them before attempting to do anything else with them: if you put them straight into boiling water, they will crack, and if you try to whip them for an omelette they will sulk. When the whites are beaten for cakes and adding to all sorts of pastry, they will be lighter and make lighter work as well as lighter paste if beaten warm instead of cold. One must also bear in mind that whipped white of egg may be of fine or not so fine texture, looser or stiffer, according to the beater used. For meringues and soufflés, for instance, it is best to use a rotary beater or an egg-beater with small wires; it will produce a smaller volume of fine texture than a whisk with heavy wires; this sort of beater will produce a larger volume of looser texture, more suitable for angel cake, for instance; and the number of strokes will have to be double or more.

As a matter of general rule all eggs ought to be cooked rather slowly, whether cooked in hot water, butter, olive oil or any other kind of fat. One should also bear in mind that eggs must never be boiled, except in their shell. Boiling curdles eggs, so that it is important not to let any preparation containing an egg or some egg to boil. To make sure, it is best to cook up all dishes containing egg in a double-boiler, or in a saucepan which fits into another one filled with boiling water. Even then, if the smaller or inside saucepan be thin and the water in the larger pan boiling fast, the egg may curdle.

CARVING A DUCK

'We all look on with anxious eyes
When father carves the duck,
And mother almost always sighs
When father carves the duck.
Then all of us prepare to rise
And hold our bibs before our eyes
And be prepared for some surprise
When father carves the duck.

'He braces up and grabs a fork
Whene'er he carves a duck,
And won't allow a soul to talk
Until he's carved the duck.
The fork is jabbed into the sides,
Across the breast the knife he slides,
And every careful person hides
From flying chips of duck.

'The platter always seems to slip
When father carves a duck,
And how it makes the dishes skip,
Potatoes fly amuck—
The squash and cabbage leap in space,
We get some gravy on our face,
And father mutters Hindu grace
Whene'er he carves a duck.

'We thus have learnt to walk around
The dining-room, and pluck
From off the window-sills and walls
Our share of father's duck;
Whilst father growls, and blows, and jaws,
And swears the knife was full of flaws,
And mother jaws at him because
He couldn't carve a duck.'
(George H. Ellwanger. *The pleasures of the table.*
London. 1903 edition. pp. 87–88)

VIII

VEGETABLES

SCIENCE HAS placed beyond doubt the fact that our physical and mental fitness depends to a great extent upon the presence in our daily diet of infinitesimal quantities of various mineral salts, and a whole alphabet of vitamins. We also know for certain that fresh vegetables are the richest—and incidentally the cheapest—source of supply of most such precious minerals and vitamins. We all know that vegetables are good for us. It does not mean that we all love vegetables, any more than the average school-boy loves soap because soap is good for him. It is true that vegetables, like many other good things and good people, are often dull; but it is our fault nearly always. There is neither sense nor excuse for being content, as so many people are content, with the same half-a-dozen 'usual' vegetables, mostly boiled to death in 'plenty of fast boiling water'. There are ever so many different vegetables for us to enjoy at different times of the year, and there are countless ways of preparing them for the table, cooked or uncooked. The four fundamental rules, practically without exceptions, which should be remembered whenever one buys or cooks vegetables are the following:

1. The freshest are always the best; young and small ones are better than the larger and older; wilted and bruised vegetables may cost less but are worthless.

2. Vegetables should be cooked in a minimum of time and water.

3. Add salt to the water in which vegetables are cooked, but never bicarbonate of soda.

4. The water in which most vegetables are cooked must not be thrown away, but saved for soups and gravies.

VEGETABLE ADVENTURES

Conservatism is fairly-rooted for all time in the kitchen garden. 'What little Bauer don't know, little Bauer won't eat', says the German proverb. It took a few hundred years to persuade peasant Europe to grow the potato, and then only under stress of famine. And so today we ring the changes from cabbage to cauliflower, broccoli to beans, with scant thought for novelty. In the flower garden another spirit reigns. One might almost suppose the motto there to be 'Omne ignotum pro magnifico est'.

Let me here present the fruits of a few years' adventuring among strange vegetables, chequered years with more blanks than prizes, like the rest of life.

To start the alphabet—artichokes, and, of these, those called 'Jerusalem'.

The tale that hereby hangs is that these, belonging to the sunflower family, were supposed to turn their flowers to the sun, and hence in Italy, Girasole, and in England, Jerusalem. The sunflower (parenthetically) does not turn with the sun, but that's another story.

The Jerusalem artichoke is usually held in little esteem in England, but it has its time and season, and best of all I think when it replaces fried potatoes with a pheasant. As an ingredient of a salad, too, it should be tried, as it responds admirably to oil and vinegar. Turned into soup it has a washing-day flavour and appearance; workhouse 'skilly', I fancy, must look like this.

In the bean family I have this warm year succeeded with the American lima bean, an excellent addition to September and October vegetables. A climber with short fat pod in the broad bean manner, the beans are shelled and cooked as broad beans are. No beany flavour survives their cooking, but a nutty flavoured cream of admirable texture. Coming from Central America, a warm year is necessary to bring them to perfection, but where tomatoes ripen out of doors there lima beans should always be grown as a likely gamble.

Among the cabbages the Quintal d'Alsace merits a trial, odourless in the cooking, eatable uncooked in a salad, best of all when baked with a little butter, it will convert many who are lukewarm about cabbage into fervent followers.

Celeriac, a celery which runs to root instead of leaf-stalk, is not new, but neglected in England. Nothing better can be found to go with boiled meats.

Peas are England's particular pride, and, unless one happens to be born in France, no infantile *petit pois* can rival a good marrowfat. There should be a corner, however, for a few mangetout peas, of which the pod is eaten with its contents. Coming in when the other peas begin to fail, they make a welcome change.

In the potato world I am a heretic. Not for me are those bursting globes of well-cooked starch, but the firm yellow soap texture of the Dutch or Austrian kipfler, which retain their 'new potato' character throughout the winter, and are the only ones to fry. So rare were they in England that my trial varieties had to be imported from the Continent. The two above and the French Belle de Juillet will be passed with honours by those who share my heresy.

The squash or pumpkin, which all who have visited the southern United States will know, is little used in English cookery. No more plastic material can be sent to the kitchen. As a diluent for over-sweet jam, a crust for meat pudding, a less watery vegetable marrow; these are obvious uses, and a hundred other variations will suggest themselves to an imaginative cook. In an airy shed they keep for a month or two.

Tomatoes are now always with us, and none better than home grown have I yet discovered. The yellow varieties are worthy of a trial. One called primrose gage is extremely delicate in flavour and might well deceive those who find the tomato flavour uncongenial.

Such are a few of the prizes; of the blanks silence is perhaps best, but it may be helpful to the adventurer to record a few.

China and Japan have developed several distinct vegetables. There is the Komatsuma from Japan, a mustard used as a spinach. The Santi Sa, a lettuce with Chard-like ribs of a toughness which seemed unsurpassable until the burdock known as Tokyo Long was attempted. Life was too short to persevere long with this most adamant of roots.

The Chinese Pte Sai cabbage, where the ribs are thickened in the manner of the chard beet, proved edible but disappointing. Perhaps a dry season does not provide its favoured conditions.

A word in conclusion may perhaps be whispered in the cook's ear. Most vegetables have juice enough of their own to be cooked without water. Peas on a cabbage leaf, cabbage with a little butter, turnips baked in the oven, give a hint that I hope will be followed up.

Lastly, a counsel of perfection to many, but to country dwellers a maxim which should never be departed from. All green vegetables should be cooked while alive. Peas gathered and cooked at once will be a revelation to town dwellers, and asparagus no less. To gather vegetables for the next day's supply, or peas before breakfast is to discard one of the greatest privileges of country life.

(Edward A. Bunyard)

TURNIPS

Indeed cookery has an influence upon men's actions even in the highest stations of human life. The great philosopher Pythagoras, in his *Golden Verses* shews himself to be extremely nice in eating, when he makes it one of his chief principles of morality to abstain from beans. The noblest foundations of honour, justice and integrity were found to lye hid in turnips, as appears in that great Dictator, Cincinnatus, who went from the plough to the command of the Roman army; and having brought home victory, retir'd to his cottage: for when the Samnite ambassadors came thither to him, with a large bribe, and found him dressing turnips for his repast, they immediately return'd with this sentence, 'That it was impossible to prevail upon him that could be contented with such a supper'.

(*The Art of Cookery in imitation of Horace's Art of Poetry.* 1709)

EDIBLE FUNGI

The first man who dared eat an oyster must have been a brave man: unless some Eve-like woman made the poor fellow swallow it to please her. And there are many foods that are excellent, both as to taste and goodness, yet far less attractive to look at than a freshly opened oyster. A newly-skinned hare or a split calf's head are horrible sights, but there is no need to think of that when enjoying a *Civet de lièvre à la Royale* or a *Tête de veau en tortue.* There are many fungi in all parts of England which are allowed to grow unplucked and to die unmourned simply because they do not look tempting, although they are excellent when properly cooked. There is also at the back of many people's minds the fear of being poisoned by a 'bad' mushroom. As a matter of fact there are but few fungi that are unwholesome, and only one that is really dangerous. Unfortunately, this poisonous fungus, the black sheep of the flock, the *Amanita phalloides*, is one of the most harmless to look at; it is not unlike the 'field' mushroom in appearance and size, but with the difference that the gills are white instead of pink and the stem has no ring, two very easily detected characteristics which should suffice to place it out of court at first sight.

The one mushroom which everybody knows and practically everybody enjoys is the common field mushroom, with the pink gills that turn brown-black with age and air. It is the sort that is cultivated on a large scale, commercially and artificially, and sold in shops. We all know that the shop specimen is not to be compared as regards flavour with the naturally grown field specimens, but few of us ever have the chance to wander early in the morning in dewy meadows in search of field mushrooms for breakfast, and so we have to be content with the shop specimens, however long they may have been on their way to town and in the market.

Those of us who have—maybe occasionally only, during a short holiday—the chance to look for mushrooms and other fungi in meadows and woods, ought to have a more open mind, as well as hand, when out on gathering expeditions. We must not be shy, in green pastures, of the horse mushroom: it does not look like a horse, but like a half-sucked ostrich egg, or a large edition of the ordinary field mushroom: its gills are white but its stem has a ring. That is before it opens out; when it does, the gills turn to brown, and the parasol-like cap is five and six inches across, and even more. It is quite safe and quite useful for making mushroom soups or sauces, but not nearly so good as the smaller variety for grilling or tossing in butter.

In the fields, in early summer, one of the commonest of fungi and one of the most neglected is the puffball. Its skin is pure white, silky, often cracked, and its flesh is milk-white, firm and it can be sliced like a thick curd: such slices, fried in bacon fat, are delicious with bacon, eggs or kidneys for breakfast, and if there are no eggs, nor any bacon and still less kidneys, try puffball fried slices with sliced, *sautés*, potatoes; their teamwork is very good. Of course, when the puffball gets old, its flesh turns brown and then, like us all, only much quicker, it returneth to dust: needless to say old puffballs are not fit to eat.

A fungus which is not so particular as regards its home is the parasol mushroom. It bears an egg-like cap, at first, on a stem about a foot in height, and it is found in fields, hedges, clearings of woods and almost anywhere. When the cap opens out, it stretches to six, seven or eight inches across, and is covered with rough, dark-brown scales, showing patches of lighter brown skin between the scales. It has short, white gills, running to a collar which stops them from reaching the stalk. They are later than the ordinary field mushrooms, rarely appearing before late summer or early autumn.

Another fungus which is plentiful in woods and spinneys at the same time of the year is the *bolet* or *cèpe*, the ugly toadstool, olive-brown outside and dirty yellow below. It does not look at all appetizing in the 'raw', but do not be deceived by looks. Do not kick it stupidly but pick it and clean it and cook it *à la Bordelaise*, with just a little garlic, and you will enjoy it very much indeed. It has very little flavour of its own, so that your conscience may be quite at rest as regards garlic: it will not kill the mushroom flavour, which never was there. The best of the *cèpe* is its consistency, and the fact that it will absorb, make its own and offer to you in a pleasant form any appetizing flavour given to it in the cooking. It is not nutritious and it is not easily digested by everybody, but it makes a change, and after all it is so cheap, just waiting to be picked.

In the same woods where the *cèpe* flourishes, and at about the same time of the year, it is not rare to find a very different sort of fungus, the chantarelle, which is called in French *girolle*. It looks like a tiny, bright orange umbrella turned inside out by the wind, from two to three inches across and its stem from two to four inches high. Its gills are branching ridges on the outside, fading off into the stem. They are solid rather than tender, sometimes somewhat rubbery, and of poor flavour, but quite safe and useful to garnish a stew or with well-seasoned scrambled eggs.

There are all sorts of other absolutely safe fungi growing in plenty, such as the shaggy cap, the fairy ring, the cauliflower fungus, the forky cap, the blewit, the oyster mushroom, the honey agaric, the beefsteak fungus, and others, all safe but none of them comparable as regards flavour to the morel or morille, one of the earliest sorts and, to my mind, the finest of them all. There are different kinds of morels, some growing best in sandy soil and others on clay, some found in pine woods and others at the foot of elm and ash, but all of them have the same distinctive and delicious perfume, not only when freshly picked, but even when dried. They are small and have a shrivelled look which is not prepossessing; this is quite immaterial; they are the best of all edible fungi, even if they do give some trouble to prepare; the cause of this is that their very fine gills often hold fine sand or grit and they need cleaning with much care. Although I have no hesitation in giving the morille pride of place, I am anxious to be fair to the puffball, which Lady Sysonby so much admires, and here is what she wrote to *The Times* about it:

Sir,—I notice that the Keeper of Botany at the Natural History Museum will give advice on edible fungi, and would like to add my mite by warmly recommending the ordinary puffball.

'My cook, after washing her hands of all responsibility and frankly expecting to see me writhing in agony on the floor if not dead, cooked them beautifully cut in thin slices and fired in butter. They taste exactly like ordinary mushrooms but with a very delicate flavour. The puffballs must be in perfect condition, creamy white all through.

(Yours faithfully, Ria Sysonby. Bath)

ONIONS

The crescendo character of the fragrance for which various 'Lilies of the Kitchen' are famous—or infamous—has been wittily described by the author of *The Philosopher's Banquet*:

If Leekes you like, but do their smelle dis-leeke,
Eat Onyons, and you shall not smelle the Leeke;
If you of Onyons would the scente expelle,
Eat Garlicke, that shall drowne the Onyons' smelle.

I START WITH ONIONS

A. But I have sought this tranquil solitude,
To ponder deeply on this wondrous book.
B. I pray you, what's the nature of its treasures?
A. 'Sauce for the million', by Philoxenus.
B. Oh, let me taste this wisdom.
A. Listen then;
'I start with onions, and with tunnies end'.
B. With tunnies? Surely, then, he keeps the best
And choicest of his dishes for the last.
A. Listen. In ashes first your onions roast
Till they are brown as toast,
Then with sauce and gravy cover;
Eat them, you'll be strong all over.

(The Banquet of Philoxenus the Leucadian. In
Athenaeus, I. 8)

THE PEA ACROSS THE AGES

The English climate has many detractors, but among
them will not be found gourmets, golfers or gardeners.
For sunbathing we must indeed voyage afar, but for
peas at their finest, home is the only place. And so it
has turned out that England has played a dominant part
in turning the small, rather bitter pea, material for
soups and stews, into the luscious marrowfat which
proudly demands a course of its own on the menu. Not
so, we fancy, can it have been in the days of the *Iliad*.
Peas, sure enough, have been found in the remains of
old Troy, but Homeric heroes would surely have
scorned them, save as a seasoning. Probably they were
not very well-flavoured in early days, or the Roman

rustic writers, Palladius, Cato and the rest, would hardly have preferred the chick pea and lupin, to us merely food for cows and chickens.

The pea in early days was, no doubt, valued as a winter vegetable, one of the few that could be dried and kept, and thus the Salic Law stretched a protective arm on their behalf.

The 'Pitance' given at the convent door was a soup of dried peas and must have been a welcomed change to the eternal salt meat of the medieval winter. Even in those days cooks had thought out a few culinary variations: 'Pois conraes', 'civotées', and 'Pois au Lart', figure in the old records. Taillevant, whose famous *Viander* throws so much light on the fourteenth-century table, went a step beyond, in fact, a 'Cretonne' of fresh peas illustrates well the over complication of the medieval cookery. The peas were cooked to a purée, almonds, eggs, ginger and saffron added, which must have extinguished any flavour of peas. For 'Pois au Lart' the peas were cooked in the pod and a few 'belles lesches et loppins de Lart' joined them with verjuice, heated wine, cinnamon and sugar! For the simple life at table we must go forward, not back, it seems!

Even in the thirteenth century the pea was sold in Paris streets ready cooked, and as a soup, and it was not till the time of Louis XIV that it moved from such humble surroundings into royal circles. The reason was that somewhere in Europe gardeners had begun to raise new varieties of better flavour, and we get a hint from our Elizabethan writer, Fuller, who tells us that peas were imported from Holland, 'Fit dainties for ladies'. At Versailles they had an even greater success, and Mme de Maintenon, writing in May 1696, says: 'The chapter of peas still goes on. The impatience to eat them, the pleasure of having eaten them, and the joy of eating them again are the three points of private gossip. There are also ladies who, having supped with the King (and supped well) take a dish in their rooms, at the grave risk of indigestion. It is the mode, it is the rage.'

With such patronage, the pea could not stand still, and soon we read of many varieties. In England in the early seventeenth century we find the Hastings pea (? Hâtive), and we meet this again in one of Wheatley's 'Cries of London.'

The first great forward stride, however, was made in England in the early nineteenth century, and to that fine old English gentleman, Thomas Andrew Knight, must the greatest credit be given. A Hereford Squire, a man of culture and a great gardener, Knight was one of the first in England to raise plants by cross-fertilization, and to him belongs the honour of introducing the first wrinkled pea. The round pea is round because its starch is firm and unchanged. At germination the starch changes to sugar, and so becomes less in volume. The wrinkled pea has begun in the pod to dissolve some of its starch, and is thus sweeter, and when it dries takes on the wrinkled form known to all gardeners. From its unusual tenderness the new variety was called marrow pea, and from this we obtain our name of marrowfat pea.

The other great step forward was the production of early and later varieties which so valuably extended the season, and so today we can have peas from mid-June to mid-October from out-of-doors.

Following this lead, many other gardeners took a hand in the development of the pea. Goss and Harrison were leaders, and then, in 1850, a Dr. Mclean, of Colchester, began his work which put the English pea ahead of all competitors, and his strains are probably in the ancestry of all modern varieties.

Other raisers followed, Laxton, Culverwell, and the famous houses of Sutton, Veitch, etc., set a standard which has been maintained and surpassed by them or their successors today. The very perfection of the English pea has produced an unfortunate culinary schism between England and France. In France it is

Petit Pois aut nullus. Even our distinguished visitor, Mr. Boulestin, in writing for English households, recommends Petit Pois, and I have made endeavours, I fear unsuccessfully, to convince him that no Englishman would choose these delicious adolescents in preference to those perfect marrowfats who look back at their childhood and forward to their age, but belong to neither. Fortunately we are agreed on both sides of the Channel that the pea should sing its own song with as little accompaniment as possible. *A l'Anglaise* always strikes me as having a slight sardonic twist when applied in a French restaurant to potatoes, but for peas we take it in the best of faith.

A touch of bacon, a few onions, parsley and cerfeuil is the mode of the 'Bonne femme'. *A la Française* demands onions, butter, lettuce and sugar.

If we pass to the Haute Cuisine here is 'Alibab' on peas; *Languedocienne*. Take Bayonne ham, asparagus, carrots, and the fat of ortolans! The reward, we read, is a *'parfum inoubliable'*. It seems a little extreme—but let us preserve an open mind. The blending of peas and young carrots is, however, well known abroad, and should be more adopted here: by some curious chemistry they both enhance each other.

I must now turn to the garden, and here the secret of success is plenty of water. Deep digging so that roots can push into the moister soil, plenty of rotted vegetable matter, a sponge to catch and to retain it, frequent cultivation to keep a dust mulch all the season, are *sine qua non*, the plural of which I do not know.

As to the varieties, all reputable firms have their favourites, and as peas are raised from seed, there is such a thing as a good strain and a bad one. A good firm will not have a bad strain.

Peter Pan, appropriately, does not grow up, and with little marvel, also dwarf, we can start the season. Gradus and Ne Plus Ultra and Gladstone, though old as peas go, are still unsurpassed for flavour.

Finally, one must again insist that the master secret

of pea flavour is freshness. Those who have their own
gardens can have them gathered as they should be,
immediately before cooking. A few hours even will
rob the pea of some of its delicious freshness—'immediately' should be underlined by all good cooks, and
the gardener, on pain of dismissal, brought into line.
Not without some culinary wisdom was the gentle
Elia, who rejoiced in his new dwelling in Convent
Garden as bringing him as near as possible to fresh peas
and strawberries!

(Edward A. Bunyard)

POTATOES

A few years ago I found myself the guest of my good
friend E. A. Bunyard, at a dinner of a Society to the
members of which, he told me, he was giving a post-
prandial lecture. When he had got me fairly in the
room, and had softened my natural asperity with good
wine and good food, he casually mentioned that he
was going to talk about the potato, as though this were
a complete explanation of his eccentric choice of a
guest. What he said I have long since forgotten; by
way of extenuation I have also forgotten what I said in
the subsequent debate, if anything, though I probably
did say something, for such is my habit. But I retain a
vague impression that he was very rude about the
potato. Poor Sassenach, of course he was. How does the
song go?

Fried fish and chips are absolutely ripping;
But you couldn't have the chips, if you didn't have the
    dripping
Of the Roast Beef of Old England, which makes us
    what we are today.

(If I have misquoted, I apologize to the Co-Op-
timists.) But there you have the Englishman's idea of
a potato: chips! Personally, I think 'Good-bye, Mr.

Chips' is a great book; and I read it in its allegorical sense.

Slay me the savage who cooks a potato with fat. Butter, yes; the better the butter, the more appropriate. I suppose fat contains nitrogen, and there will not lack Smellfunguses to make a ' scientific' defence of its use with potatoes. And they will, doubtless, remark, irrelevantly, that you eat potatoes with meat, the gravy of which permeates them (forgetting that the average cook prefers to make gravy according to the advice given in the advertisement pages of cheap periodicals, and relies on corn-flour and so-called meat-extract to take the place of the natural juices that are so rarely served.) But the real answer to this kind of argument was given by a colleague of mine many years ago. 'Bacon and cabbage is a very good dish', he said, 'and a bottle of stout is a very good thing. But that's no reason why you should pour the stout over the bacon and cabbage and eat the mess out of a soup-plate.'

Except for the baked potato, the only good potato is the boiled potato. You may serve your boiled potatoes in a great many ways, but boiling must be the foundation of the cooking. How the Englishman has survived his daily choice of 'roast or boiled', of which he usually takes the roast, it is difficult to explain, outside a belief in miracles, and the patience of God. These filthy, greasy lumps of half-heated starch, with a surrounding integument that entangles the teeth and delays mastication, are more deadly than grape-shot, for their effect is moral as well as physical. Of course, the alternative boiled potato has been misboiled. It has been peeled first, and it probably has not been 'sized' so that the little ones have cooked as long as the big ones; and, when removed from the pot, it has not been dried, but has been left to soak in its own moisture until thoroughly soggy. In my notable military career (of which the true story has not yet been written) I gave severe punishment to any cook I found peeling a raw potato.

But nothing could restrain them. They went to detention or field punishment with the exaltation of martyrs, conscious that they were right and I was a bloody persecutor (and they did not use the adjective in its literary sense, either). And why blame them? They were following the tradition of every English kitchen, a tradition which owes its origin to the fact that it is easier to peel a cold, raw potato than to peel a hot, cooked one. So they cheerfully threw away all the valuable flavouring and hoped I might some day get sense.

Boil your potatoes; steam them if you prefer that process, which certainly has produced agreeable effects in my experience. In any case, dry them afterwards; then by all means peel them, and serve them in a napkin laid in a dish. Or leave them their jackets until the last moment; lay skin-plates on the table, and let each man peel for himself. A plain, boiled potato, so served, is the best of all accompaniments to a roast or grill; for myself, I go further, and like it best with any dish of meat or fowl, or even game. But the potatoes must be floury; a waxy potato is no use for anything, except potato salad, in which form, for some reason, it can be very agreeable. I am told you should boil and peel the potatoes, and put them hot into the mayonnaise or oil and vinegar, as the case may be. They soak up the condiment while cooling. But don't serve them tepid.

New potatoes are a dish apart. There is only one person in the whole world that knows how to cook new potatoes, and that is my aunt's maid. The mystery is enshrined in very obvious outward processes; just the boiling, having scrubbed them well, then dishing them up just coated, and no more, with melted butter, with a dusting of powdered mint and parsley (the latter a loathsome weed, which in this one setting justifies itself). But nobody else can do this in exactly this way; and the magician comes, not from Ireland, but from Cambridgeshire. However, the new potato is not an Irish dish; I fancy most of the Irish new potatoes used to be exported to a more luxurious market. We eat them later, and I think they taste best when they are still rather precocious; Channel Islanders and such-like. That is why I always associate new potatoes at their best with a flat in Drayton Gardens one early Easter—1910, I think. Yes, it was 1910; the year of King Edward's death, of Halley's comet, of pitiless mildew in Bordeaux (sparing to some extent Château Haut-Brion). Good Friday fell on the Feast of the Annunciation, and a fierce Anglophobe of my acquaintance chanted, 'When Our Lord falls into Our Lady's lap To England shall follow a great mishap.' She afterwards said that it betokened the death of the King; but she did not discover that until May. I think that this year has given us the earliest Easter since then; I trust that no runes are current, foretelling further misfortune.

Mash if you will your boiled potatoes with plenty of butter and a little milk, or even cream. A little baking gives mashed potatoes a pleasant crust, and various concomitants may be added—mushrooms, crisp celery, or various kinds of nuts, for those who like that sort of nonsense. Once you have boiled him you can hardly spoil your potato, so long as you keep him clear of greasy fat. Sole à la Belle Otéro shows him up very well; most cookery books will contain recipes worth trying. Potato cakes are delicious. Kail Cannon (or however it spells itself) might be served more often. The cabbage is redeemed.

But let there be no more chips or straws or wafers or other filthy prostitutions of the good honest creature that is itself the best exemplar of the old Irish proverb: 'Be natural, and you'll never be awkward.'

(Maurice Healy)